These Are My

PEOPLE

The Merle Kilgore Story

Mark Rickert

Virginia

Published in the United States by WriteLife Publishing
(An imprint of Boutique of Quality Books Publishing Company)
www.writelife.com

978-1-60808-172-1 (p)
978-1-60808-173-8 (e)

Library of Congress Control Number: 2016947894

Book design by Robin Krauss, bookformatters.com
Cover design by Ellis Dixon, ellisdixon.com

dedication

This book is dedicated to Hank Williams, Jr.,
who told me to "Saddle up, and go for it."

Table of contents

Let's say there had not been a Merle Kilgore. There would have been a big empty spot in [the Country Music] business. He contributed songs; he contributed his knowledge and his friendship in bringing people together. This business is pretty big, but his footprint is over a considerable part of it. His association with Hank Williams, and Hank Williams, Jr., and Johnny Cash—he helped those people. They owed a lot to Merle, and they knew it.

Ralph Emery

Merle was more to me than a manager. He was a father figure, he was a mentor, he was my business advisor; but most of all, Merle Kilgore was my best friend[1].

Hank Williams, Jr.

Author's Note

As a disclaimer, I know there are more stories out there and more books that will probably never see the light of day. Country Music singer Bill Anderson, the long-ago Country Music Association Entertainer of the Year, suggested to my agent, Stan Cooper, that a single book could never contain all the stories about Merle, and I think he's right about that. It seems that everyone in the Nashville music business—especially the old-timers—has a Merle Kilgore story. That's what made him legendary. If you hung around Merle long enough, you'd eventually have your own story to tell.

But you won't find all those stories here. For that reason, I don't claim that my version is the definitive Merle Kilgore story. All I can hope to do is give my own telling of it, a secondhand account through the eyes of his grandson. I should also point out that most of the stories in this book are Merle's stories; I merely brought them all together.

On that note, allow me to quote the title of an Elton John album: *Don't shoot me; I'm only the piano player.*

Merle Kilgore

Merle Kilgore died a Country Music legend.

His funeral spoke volumes about his life. The memorial service looked like a Sunday night television special on the Nashville Network. It was February 15, 2005, and the Country Music industry came en masse to the Ryman Auditorium to say goodbye to him, a great man with the highest accolades; a man so popular in Nashville that his guests were mostly Country Music stars and big business executives. Everyone wanted to sing and share their memories from the Ryman's stage. People in the industry truly loved him, and they made that abundantly clear. Merle *inspired* them; he made them laugh, and he kept a good tempo. They were going to miss him.

His wife, Judy—along with publicist Kirt Webster, Co-Head of William Morris Endeavor Entertainment's country division Greg Oswald, and Hank Williams, Jr.'s, road manager Bob Smith—made sure to send Merle off with a flash-bang farewell. They lined up the Ryman Auditorium for the rally spot.

It was a significant location; a country music patron couldn't ask for a better place. Once housing the Grand Ole Opry, today it's a major venue for hundreds of performing artists. It's still referred to as the Mother Church of Country Music because in 1892 it was built as a place for worship and named the Union Gospel Tabernacle. Even today it looks like a church, with the severe pitch of its roof, its soaring redbrick walls, and rows of arched windows framed in white limestone.

Inside there are oak pews, creaky wooden floors, and stained-glass windows that cast colorful auras in the morning hours. Sure, it looks a little stiff, but it's been a pretty rocking place ever since it became friends with Country Music.

According to local lore—and this is something that would have interested Merle—the Ryman is an active hotspot for ghostly activity, home to a parade of haunts, it seems. Its first apparition is a riverboat captain, Thomas G. Ryman, the man who commissioned the construction of the Union Gospel Tabernacle after visiting a Nashville evangelical tent revival and finding Jesus. His ghost has been showing up ever since his church became a music hall. There are other ghostly visitors, too, like the Confederate soldier whose body is supposedly buried somewhere beneath the auditorium's limestone and ashlar foundation. Then there's the star of the midnight hour, the legendary Hank Williams, Sr., who makes an occasional surprise showing, appearing as a mist and assuming the shape of a tall man wearing a white cowboy hat and Western suit like those worn by classic cowboy movie heroes.

Do I believe the Ryman's haunted? Maybe so, in an unconventional sense. Let's just say, I believe history has a way of becoming a ghost, a living memory of the past, and one that influences the present. Maybe ghosts and memories share a significant something in common: they both rely on the living to help them exist.

I thought about those ghosts on that crisp February morning as I stood looking down at my grandfather. We were all gathered in the Ryman's historic auditorium, and Merle's coffin was resting on a bier in front of that very famous stage. The coffin and the stage made for an unsettling image, a juxtaposition of life and death, entertainment and stone-cold reality.

But in a strange way, I also felt glad for Merle. He was my grandfather and I'd always cared deeply for him. I'd been waiting a long time to see this, the day when Merle Kilgore finally nabbed top billing for a major Nashville show.

In a way, Music City, U.S.A., owed him that; it knew it, too.

Here's the down-and-dirty of his resume. He was, by and large, a singer/songwriter with a list of major credits. His biggest claim to fame was "Ring of Fire," which he co-wrote with June Carter, a song that *Rolling Stone* later hailed as number 87 in its "500 Greatest Songs of All Time" (2004)[2]. And Merle had other million-selling titles, too; under his creative thumb were hits like "More and More," "Johnny Reb," and "Wolverton Mountain," just to name a few. Later in life, he became the personal manager and executive vice president of Hank Williams, Jr., Enterprises.

His songs are familiar to popular culture, but his name is mostly forgotten among the general public. This is mainly because Merle's time as an entertainer came and went long ago. Nonetheless, he had his moments in the spotlight, moments when he shared the stage with Country Music giants. Less known are his shining moments behind the curtains, managing the career of a Country Music superstar. Through it all, he helped shape the face of Country Music.

Nashville made sure to celebrate his passing. His death rattled the bones of the industry, and for that reason, many important people came to the memorial service.

The stage had several things going on up there that day. There were flower wreaths and potted plants, microphones and vacant stools for the guest musicians, and there were amplifiers and cables snaking across the floor. And there was also a staged setting. It was Merle's Nashville office, or at least, everything from that office—his desk, heaped with his papers, his green sofa, his magazine-scattered coffee table. Photographs of Country Music heroes decorated the walls, from Hank Williams, Sr., to Colonel Tom Parker and Elvis Presley. A fiery red phoenix—the Ruger symbol shared by Hank Jr.—unfurled its wings above the door like a holy relic. The setup reminded me of a scene from a play, maybe an intermission, with a built-in element of anticipation. It was as if at any moment the stage lights would come on to find Merle—that great bulk of a man with black-and-silver hair and mustache—hunching over his desk, brooding over a contract. In his deep, baritone voice, he'd bellow out his signature phrase, "Are you *shitting* me?" The audience would then laugh and some would stand up and applaud, and the play would end, and everyone would go home happy.

But not today.

Today was not an intermission, but the closing of the curtain, and Merle Kilgore was *gone*.

As if this wasn't all impressive enough, Country Music stars Marty Stuart and Travis Tritt had signed on to host the service. Standing at the podium, they looked big and flashy in their black suits and great shocks of hair, and they smiled and did their best to turn the service into a celebration.

"Friends and guests, welcome to the Merle Kilgore Show," Marty announced and then made a motion with his hands—*Yes, Amen!*—to encourage applause from his audience, because that's obviously what Merle would have wanted, and everybody knew it.

The place filled with laughter, a sound that teetered desperately close to a sob, and with it came an understanding. We all knew what Marty was getting at: A Merle Kilgore tribute show was long overdue, considering all the contributions he'd made to the industry. Willie Nelson apparently once told him, "Merle, you should get your own show. Every time I turn on the TV, it's you on some talk show talking about somebody else." At least, that's what Merle told me.

Everyone knew Merle deserved his own show. Among those turning out for Merle's final curtain were Kenny Chesney, Big & Rich, Wynonna Judd, George Jones, Kix Brooks, and even Kid Rock (a few

of these artists treated us to a song, performed in Merle's memory).
Hank Williams, Jr., was there, too—of course he was.

I'd seen Hank Jr. just the day before at the funeral home. Some
people had doubted that he would come to the visitation. This
was a hard time for him, they said. Too many people crowding and
suffocating him might make him uneasy. But Hank Jr. surprised us
all. Not only had he visited the wake at Hendersonville's Memorial
Garden Funeral Home, but he also parked himself in a chair next to
Merle's coffin and greeted everyone who came to say goodbye. I recall
seeing a long line of folks wanting to shake his hand. We were all
shocked. Hank is a private man, and he was suffering a private grief.
But on that day, he honored Merle by greeting *Merle's* people. I'm sure
Hank knew how much that would have meant to him.

It was like that in those final days. People went out of their
way to say goodbye. The industry gave an impressive farewell party,
recognizing Merle Kilgore as a Nashville man-of-business, a Country
Music Association board member, a singer/songwriter and entertainer,
and a lifelong member of the club who brought the industry countless
contributions. It was a collective agreement: Merle had played a
significant role in the Country Music business. More importantly, he
touched many hearts, from the indelibly famous to the everyday "Joe,"
and he brought smiles and encouragement to the world.

I don't know if it's my place to weigh and measure his fame
(besides, how do you measure an idea like "fame" anyhow?), but I'll
make a fair assessment. Let's say he was just famous enough, and his
early fame directed the entire course of his life, enabling him to grow
into a recognized businessman, someone sought out by newcomers to
the Country Music business hoping to hear his stories. I think there
are different types of fame, and there are different periods of fame, and
Merle enjoyed them all. Most of all, he had true fame because he had
fans, and most of those fans were more famous than he was. That's

why, I feel, his personal history is unique. His personal narrative and the stories he told were usually about other people. *His* people.

There was always a book in him. I think he wanted to write it himself, but he never got around to it. He was a great storyteller, and he had plenty to talk about. Having worked in the entertainment business since his early teens, he'd witnessed some impressive moments in the evolution of Country Music. Somewhere along the way, he became a credible source of historical knowledge. After all, he lived this particular time in history and witnessed remarkable happenings. For that reason, people in the business—even celebrities like Marty Stuart and Travis Tritt—visited Merle at his home in Paris, Tennessee, just to "sit at his feet" like students in class. Merle's personal history was like a memoir of Country Music history, supported by a cast of famous friends. Merle spun a good yarn, and everyone knew it. He had impeccable timing and a sharp wit, and his stories always ended with a punch line or an occasional insight.

In turn, those who told the story of Country Music—radio personalities, talk-show hosts, magazine writers—often painted Merle into the canvas of the Country Music landscape. Ralph Emery, an acclaimed disc jockey and Nashville television personality, was maybe Merle's biggest fan. Ralph practically wrote the book on Country Music history, and he loved to bring in "Big Merle" on his show, portraying Merle as a true voice of Country Music. In this way, he added credibility to Merle's stories.

As a result, those stories were published a hundred times over. Fortunately, Merle had the foresight to keep copies of it all.

Not long after we buried Merle, Judy Kilgore, his widow and my step-grandmother, came to me about writing a book. Judy wanted me to capture Merle's stories and preserve his memory. Besides, a book just made sense—not just because he was beloved by the industry or because he wrote famous songs—but because a story about his life would also tell a story about Country Music.

She'd made a good point, and then a better one: I owed it to myself to discover Merle's story.

But at this time—around 2008—I was reluctant to get involved with such a big project. I had another year or so to go before I finished my master's degree, and my job at the university writing lab gobbled up most of my free time. And then one night I had a dream. It was a dark night under a purple sky dusted with stars, and I found myself sitting on a grassy hilltop with a young Merle Kilgore—a man in his mid-twenties, slim and tall, wearing an open-collared shirt and blue jeans and boots. He drank whiskey straight from a bottle. He didn't know me, or that I was his grandson, and we talked like old friends. All the while, I sat with quiet amusement, thrilled with having entered into my grandfather's early life.

I woke from the dream feeling it had been significant. I called Judy and told her I wanted to write the book.

So I got started.

I didn't have to look far to learn Merle's story. A legendary self-promoter, Merle never stopped publicizing himself. Over the course of his career, he sat for thousands of interviews with television and radio shows. As a young man, he'd begun stockpiling his interviews in trash bags—newspaper clippings and printed announcements, photographs, and videotapes and radio interviews. He managed to keep these things through several divorces, endless moves, and even an angry wife who nearly succeeded in burning everything he owned. These annals captured the bulk of his stories; fragments, revealed in interviews from the *Talk of the Town* or *Nashville Now* with Ralph

Emery, newspaper clippings from the *Tennessean*, and guest talks on WSM Radio. In his later years, Judy helped Merle organize it all into a manageable library.

While this library became the core of my research, I had more to use than old newspaper clippings to write about my grandfather. I spent a lot of time with him. We were a close family once upon a time. When I was a kid, my brothers—Matthew and Andrew—and I paid many visits to my grandfather's home, visiting him and his wife, Judy, and their kids, Duane and Shane. In the early Eighties, we spent several long and important summers at his Cullman, Alabama, home. We got to know him even better when, in the mid-Eighties, he moved to Paris, Tennessee, following Hank Williams, Jr., and his entire operation.

I have fond memories of Merle's lake house on the Tennessee River. The "Boogie Shack" was a place of friends and family, and many celebrities knew it. Marty Stuart often talked about it with fondness; and Hank Jr. knew the place very well, since he lived just up the river from Merle.

The Boogie Shack sat on a hill facing the water. It had a nice big deck out back that looked on down and across the river. The house had a woodsy cabin feel, with stained wooden walls and floorboards. It was furnished with comfortable furniture and nothing too fancy. A pathway led to the bottom of the hill and then became a boat dock that wrapped around a little boathouse. Merle had two boats there: the "Boogie King," complete with an "Elvis Room" in the hull, covered in white fur carpet and gold trim, and the "Paradise Cove," a nifty pontoon boat that he adored.

At the Boogie Shack, Country Music was everywhere. Music was always on the radio, and gold records were on the walls. Country Music history books were on the bookshelves; CDs, videotapes, and DVDs were stacked in the TV cabinets. Infused in all of this was the feel of history, like the 1950s Coca-Cola machine in the sunroom—a gift from Dottie West and a reminder of the distant past, when Merle was young, and so was Country Music.

Merle threw lots of parties there; he'd bought the place for that very reason. Every summer, he'd have his people over, including his children, Pam, Steve, and Kim, and their families. Summer weekends, we'd all eat barbeque on the back deck and listen to music and laugh at Merle's stories. Then he'd take us out on his pontoon boat, and we'd drift until the sun started to set.

You never knew who'd come over to the Shack. Sometimes famous people visited; most times a hopeful Country Music singer tagged along, toting a guitar and a promise of entertaining us later when we found a cove to anchor down in. You could tell those young entertainers wanted to shadow Merle and learn something from him. But like everyone, they just enjoyed his company and they wanted to hear his stories.

That included me and my brothers. Whenever Merle started down memory lane, we all listened with incredulous smiles, knowing that no one back home would ever believe us. It was those stories that needed a home.

Before starting the project, Judy and I went on several road trips in hopes of capturing Merle's spirit. We toured the Shreveport Municipal Auditorium, home of the Louisiana Hayride, and explored its back dressing rooms and its creaky stage where Merle sang long ago. We found his childhood home in Shreveport, where the homeowner invited us inside and let us poke around for a while. We visited Billie Jean Jones, ex-wife to both Hank Williams, Sr., and Johnny Horton, and listened to her early memories of Merle. We even went to the homes of Tillman Franks and Claude King, who reminisced with distant eyes and bittersweet smiles. Then on a balmy summer afternoon, we drove to Wolverton Mountain and met with the Clowers clan, where stories of Merle's adolescence are still kicked around, since clearly his song put the mountain on the map.

These visits brought Merle to life for me. By the end of our pilgrimage, I couldn't wait to tell his story. To me, it was just too damned interesting to let fade away.

It also seemed important to sketch a character portrait of Merle, something by which to remember his bigger-than-life personality. He had a legendary charisma, so much that it burned in his eyes and turned heads when he walked into a room. He looked like a star—*Yes, Amen*. Sure, his appearance changed over the years—from the tall singer of the Fifties and Sixties with smoldering eyes and a pleasant grin to the heavyset, leather-clad *Boogie King* of the Seventies. Merle never lost his gusto, not even after he left the stage. It stayed with him until the end.

By the last decade of his life, I think he tapped into his most endearing qualities. Six foot five and maybe 250 pounds, Merle was big and important looking, with thick, silver-black hair and mustache. He wore black suits and big slugs of diamond-studded gold on his fingers that he referred to as his *bling*. He swaggered when he walked and laughed louder than anyone around him. He spoke with a baritone voice and tossed around catchy colloquialisms. His persona had flashes of Southern Black gospel—inspired by his favorite evangelist, the exuberant C.L. Franklin—and so everything was, Yes, Amen! or Hey, brother! or Hey, all right! My man!

He was funny and animated, quick with a joke and a barking laugh. A laugh always seemed to lurk in his deep-set eyes—eyes that glowed like the bright headlights of a semi-truck. You could say he had a *knowing* gaze. *Yes, Amen.* Once on a cruise ship, he told a joke and made a man laugh so hard that he dropped over dead (the man's widow) later told Merle that she wasn't angry; dying with a laugh was just the way her husband would have wanted to go).

Merle bolstered an impressive energy. He beamed; he radiated. *Yes, Amen.* That's why he succeeded as Hank Jr.'s opening act for twenty-plus years. It was this frenetic energy that got the crowds roaring, drunk with excitement. Back when he performed, he'd take the stage and pump his fists and shout, "Get on the whiskey!" And his shows ended with him spreading his arms wide and shouting, "Yes-*sah*! These are my people!"

Toward the end, he became a sage in the business. Gretchen Wilson, Grammy Award-winning Country Music artist, told me an interesting story in 2009 when I crossed paths with her at the Ryman Auditorium. According to her, she reached out to Merle for advice one time when she was in Australia and became an instant fan. She'd spent a bad day at the recording studio that day and was faced with something big. She recalled she was a nervous wreck. Someone at the studio said to her, "Gretchen, you look down on your luck. I think you need to talk to someone—someone who understands what you're going through." And then, they gave her a name.

She'd heard of this *someone* before: Merle Kilgore. Country Music Association's Manager of the Year of 1986.

Gretchen called Merle from the studio. She told him everything—how she felt nervous, scared, whatever the case. He talked to her for a long time, discussed the trials of show business, said some funny things. Then Merle said, "Gretchen, I want to teach you something."

"Okay," she had said, smirking as she told me the story. "I'm listening."

"Whenever someone asks you, 'How are you doing today?' . . ."

"I'll say . . . ?"

"You'll say: 'Are you *shitting* me?'"

She loved it. She had a good laugh, and apparently, it brightened her day.

I suppose his tagline empowered her. It was as if to say, "Am I doing okay? Well, just take a look at me. Do you even have to *ask*? I am doing just *fine*."

That brief interlude must have left a lasting impression. During the 2005 Grammy Awards, which aired on the night of Merle's funeral visitation, Gretchen performed before a live audience and wore a black T-shirt with the words "Remember Kilgore" written across the chest.

It took a special kind of personality to inspire people the way Merle did, and incidentally, he traced the origins of his charisma to a single moment in time, to a long-ago chance encounter with a magnetic force of nature. It was then that Merle received perhaps the greatest lesson of his life: the secret of *lower and slower.*

Hank Williams, Sr.

Merle Kilgore's story may have ended in Nashville, but it began in Shreveport, at the Louisiana Hayride.

This was a special place—a convergence of powerful cultural currents in the early twentieth century, where black musicians brought about their own style of blues and soul, and where white musicians borrowed and transformed it. The result: a music that was sort of dangerous.

Wyatt Merle Kilgore inadvertently became a part of this Country Music event horizon. Although he was born in Chickasha, Oklahoma, in 1934 by some act of providence, his father—Wyatt Kilgore, an Internal Revenue Service taxman—moved his family to Shreveport to investigate the dubious business of a certain politician who will remain nameless here. (As it turned out, Mr. Kilgore never uncovered a scandal, but that's no real concern to our story.) What is important is that the Kilgores became rooted in Shreveport, a city destined to become a vortex for great movements in culture and music, and my grandfather had the good fortune to get swept up into it.

Merle's story begins in 1948, just three years after World War II, the same year that station KWKH kicked off its barn dance radio program, the Louisiana Hayride, broadcasted live from the Shreveport Municipal Auditorium. The auditorium still stands there today, a hulking block of brick and limestone reaching two-and-a-half stories high. If you didn't know any better, you might think it's a courthouse or a prison. But in the early Forties, the auditorium was anything but institutional, especially once KWKH, one of the region's few clear-channel 50,000-watt radio stations, began broadcasting the show all across northeast Texas, northwest Louisiana, and southwest Arkansas[3].

From the start, the Hayride's management wanted to take on the Grand Ole Opry, but they had a different approach in mind than the path the Opry had taken. Whereas the Opry held to strict guidelines concerning its artists and acceptable musical styles—all in the name of preserving its wholesome family image—the Hayride loosened its belt and gave its artists more room to experiment. Essentially, the Hayride was free to take greater risks, and so it welcomed new artists and encouraged innovative sounds.

Even though the Hayride and the Opry were competitors, they benefited from one another. If unknown hillbilly singers came to the Opry with musical styles that challenged their conventions, the management would send them to the Hayride. This suited the Hayride just fine, because lots of promising acts didn't fit the Opry's narrow parameters. The problem was what happened once the artists got popular; they immediately packed their bags and left for the Opry. It never failed. The Hayride just couldn't keep them. All the prestige belonged to the Opry, after all.

In the twenty-first century, the Hayride's name has been nearly forgotten. But let's be perfectly clear about this: the Hayride produced a roster of artists who forever changed popular music.

In many ways, the Hayride changed the *world*.

In 1948, the year the Louisiana Hayride started up, Merle was fourteen, tall for his age, with a boyish face and disarming grin. He was a precocious teen who dressed in sports jackets and concerned himself with business. Already he'd started a makeshift lawn-mowing company and discovered how to turn a profit without mowing a single yard (his father shut down his business after finding Merle dozing on the porch swing, insisting it was unethical that Merle made all the money while his friends did all the work).

But this was short-term stuff anyway. Merle had his heart set on hillbilly music, the Louisiana Hayride, and the excitement it generated. Convinced that he had the right stuff for the job, he probably assumed the music business was his natural birthright, given his close proximity to the Municipal Auditorium.

Then came his big break. His friend, Ed Knighton, invited him to his father's party. As Ed explained to him, his dad was a renowned physician, and he often orchestrated the hospital's charity balls showcasing Hayride singers to entice large donations. As a result, Dr. Knighton had befriended a handful of artists over the years, and Ed expected those same friends to come to the party.

Merle accepted the invitation and arrived later that night at Dr. Knighton's mansion to find an impressive party buzzing with important people wearing fancy clothes. Right away he spotted several country singers, most importantly the Bailes Brothers—Kyle, Johnnie, Walter, and Homer. The four brothers were handsome and tall, and they wore easy smiles. With them were a few members of the band, including a bass player named Leon. For a while, they all chatted about the Hayride, and when Leon broke away from the group, Merle followed after him.

"Ah, Leon?" he asked the bass player, gently pulling him aside. "Can I ask you a question? How do you make it in the music business?"

Leon drew from his cigarette, then blew smoke in Merle's face. His answer was short and to the point. "You wanna be a star? Hang around somebody famous, kid."

Still this advice begged another question. How could a fourteen-year-old high school freshman befriend a celebrity? Oddly enough, the answer to that question arrived on the coattails of the first. Again, it was the Bailes Brothers who lit the fuse. They were talking about the Hayride's newest singer, a pass-off from the Grand Ole Opry, a known drunk and a potential wild cannon. The Opry was "scared of him." They didn't want a drunk messing up their squeaky-clean reputation. Instead, they let the Hayride have him for a while, just to see how things worked out. If the guy could handle the Hayride and keep his nose clean, then the Opry would reconsider.

"What's his name?" Ed piped in.

"His name's Hank," Johnnie offered. "Hank Williams."

The story of Hank Williams, Sr., is a sad one. If you don't already know, Hank is arguably the greatest legend of Country Music. He was truly iconic as the tall and lanky cowboy, dressed all in white—from hat to boots. Then throw in a guitar and a radiant smile.

But his music resonated with darker themes; he sang in a high, lonesome voice, projecting a character with an eternally-broken heart, lost and haunted. Nor was he faking it. He died at twenty-nine years old. But take a look at his pictures. He didn't look twenty-nine. He looked older. He was old in the eyes.

Unlike today's polished personalities, Hank was a raw, powerful talent—tragically flawed, a poet, and a self-defeating alcoholic. Then there was his sudden death. He died too young, never even hit his thirties. This came as a complete shock to the nation.

All that made him a legend. He was the original Country Music superstar. No doubt, that's why he's in the Country Music Hall of Fame *and* the Rock and Roll Hall of Fame.

If there's any question of Hank's genius, I think a live recording of Elvis Presley says it all. It was at the 1973 Aloha From Hawaii Rehearsal Concert. Elvis was dressed in his gaudy white jumpsuit and bellbottoms, a pink lei draped around his neck. He tells his audience that he'd "like to do the saddest song" he has ever heard, and then asks his audience to bear with him while he composes himself. He launches into the Hank Williams classic, "I'm So Lonesome I Could Cry," and you can see a tear in his eye the moment he starts. Midway through the first line, he smiles to himself, then quietly shakes his head, knowing he'll never make it to the end of this song without crying. By the second verse, his face is streaming with tears. It's an incredibly heartfelt performance, and I'm relating it here because it illustrates the gravity of Hank's music. Elvis recognized it and it moved him to tears.

But all this came later. Back in 1949, Hank Williams was just a man, a singularity, infinitely dense, and only moments from exploding into stardom.

Like the Bailes Brothers said, Hank already had the interest of the Opry when he came to Shreveport. Just the past year, he'd lived in Nashville, working closely with Fred Rose of Acuff-Rose Publications and establishing himself as a songwriter. Fred helped Hank polish his work, and within that year's time, Hank had a contract with MGM and a hit song on the radio.[4]

But Fred worried about Hank's obvious struggle with alcohol. He tried to get Hank to stop drinking, and when that didn't work, he let the Hayride deal with it.

"You stay sober for a year," Fred allegedly told Hank, "and I'll bring you back to the Opry."

Hank Williams went to Shreveport with all the potential in the world, and Merle had a plan to meet him. There were several pieces of information that helped him triangulate his efforts. First, according to Horace Logan, KWKH studios started broadcasting at five a.m., Monday through Saturday, and at six a.m. on Sundays, and most performers gathered at the studios before sunup.[5] Second—and Ed supplied him with this little gem—the elevators at the station followed a strict time schedule and remained powered off until seven a.m., forcing early-comers to use the stairs. Since Merle finished his morning paper route before most folks got out of bed, he'd have no problem getting to the station before Hank did.

He arrived at Murrell's Bantam Grill before sunup that morning. Peeking into its plate-glass windows, he searched for anyone who would fit the description of hillbilly singer but saw only a few stuffed-shirt types at the counter, their heads hanging over cups of steaming coffee.

Cruising around to the front lot, Merle hit the brakes, surprised. Ed Knighton was waiting there, balanced on his bike, his eyes wide with alarm. Merle rode up next to him, and Ed offered a thin smile that suggested he'd had the same idea, a discouraging situation for Merle given they couldn't *both* carry Hank's guitar.

There was a sputter, a cough of car exhaust. The boys waited and listened. Moments later, a wheezing Chrysler sedan with peeling wood panels nosed into the radio station's parking lot. The car stopped and, with a great shudder, coughed a final cloud of black smoke and died.

"That can't be him," Merle told Ed. "He's supposed to be a star."

Suddenly Ed started running. It took Merle a moment to realize what had happened. Ed had gotten the jump on him. Not bothering with his bike, Merle lurched into a sprint. The two boys raced to the car. Luckily, Merle was quicker and gained on Ed in no time. Then he was in the lead.

The driver's door swung open on rusted hinges, and a man unfolded himself from the car's dark interior.

"Oh, wow!" Merle whispered as whatever doubts he'd harbored vanished like a fog in a fierce sunrise. "That *is* him! That's Hank Williams!"

Merle had never seen anything like him.

He was tall and wore a white Western suit that glistened with rhinestones. A white cowboy hat sat on his head, glowing like a halo. In that gray parking lot, Hank shined like an angel. He was Hollywood squeezed into a cowboy suit.

The boys surprised Hank. He heard the scuffle of shoes and spun around. "Boys, boys!" he shouted. "What's going on?"

The boys panted for air. Merle wheezed out, "Listen, Hank. The elevators don't work 'til seven o'clock, and you'll have to carry your stuff all the way up."

Hank frowned. More intriguing than handsome, he was tall, with a slender build and a slight stoop. He had a narrow chin and prominent ears, and his face was composed of hard, straight angles, and his mouth formed a thin line. His eyes were perhaps his most striking feature. Beneath slim eyebrows, they burned with a strong fire, dark and bottomless. They didn't seem like eyes belonging to a man in his late twenties.

Hank rubbed his chin and muttered, "You mean I gotta walk all the way up there?"

At that moment, Ed surfaced like a drowning man thrusting up from the watery depths, nearly gasping for air. "My dad's Dr. Knighton!" he cried in a desperate attempt to gain some leverage over the situation. "And my daddy knows the Bailes Brothers."

Merle spoke up. "We were fighting over who gets to carry the guitar."

They all fell silent as Hank shifted his eyes between the two boys. Finally, his gaze settled on Merle. Then he pointed a finger and said, "Grab it, hoss."

That Saturday evening Merle showed up to the Hayride to carry Hank's guitar. It must have felt incredibly important to him. A lot of hype already surrounded Hank, mostly because the radio station had been playing his recordings as preparation for his arrival, and Merle got to share in that, even gaining access to the backstage area. By default, he'd become part of Hank's entourage.

The Municipal Auditorium was big enough to hold about 3,500 people, although in its early days, the crowd might number only a few hundred. The auditorium had a basic layout, like an open gymnasium, with bleachers and balconies that ran along the walls and a sprawling hardwood floor that was packed with foldout chairs on concert nights. Red curtains framed the stage, while the canvas backdrop was painted with a red barn and a metal silo in a field of wheat.

The Hayride followed a set schedule. Horace Logan, the Hayride's manager, would most often kick off the show by appearing in a black cowboy suit with holstered Rugers hanging on his hips. He would then explain the rules like this: Every band got two songs. After that, it was up to the audience. If the crowd demanded an encore, the band could come back and sing another song. This went on until the crowd stopped demanding encores. In this way, the audience dictated who stayed and who left.

"Now listen, boy," Hank told Merle. "They're getting ready to start this here show, and I want your help. What I need you to do is tell me who my competition is—who's good and who's not. I want to know everything about them."

Merle agreed to help; Hank couldn't have picked a better informant. Merle rarely missed a Saturday show at the Municipal. He knew all the performers, the crowd pleasers and the gimmicks, the bands that never encored, and the bands on the brink of national success. So when the performers marched out onto the stage, Merle rattled off all he knew about them.

Hank listened and didn't say much. But every so often, he nodded and muttered something like, "He's perty good. Perty good."

Toward the end of the evening, the Bailes Brothers marched onto the stage. By far the Hayride's hottest act, the brothers were former Opry stars with several chart toppers under their belts, including the hit "Dust on the Bible." They'd moved to Shreveport to co-found the

Louisiana Hayride. That night the Brothers encored several times. Hank, however, didn't look impressed.

Eventually, Merle asked, "Well, Hank? What do you think?"

Hank bent over, gathered his guitar from his case, and then rose to his full height as he slipped the guitar's strap over his neck. He started for the stage but stopped to look over his shoulder at Merle with his dark, cold eyes. "I'll eat 'em alive," he said, then disappeared beyond the curtains.

This surprised Merle. After all, the Bailes Brothers had been instrumental in convincing the Hayride's management to bring Hank to Shreveport after the Opry turned him away. From Merle's perspective, the Bailes Brothers were Hank's best friends at the Hayride, and so it didn't make sense for Hank to be so callous.

Curious, Merle got up and edged to the curtains, watching breathlessly as Hank took his place before the microphone. In just a few moments, Hank's performance changed everything. His opening fast-paced number "Move It on Over" had a contagious energy, but it was Hank's fierce stage presence that drove the audience wild. Something about Hank mesmerized them. His appearance and the way he carried himself in a cowboy posture like men in Western movies hit a nerve with the crowd. He wore a sparkling white Western suit and a cowboy hat and a mischievous grin. He didn't move much, but there was a lot of enthusiasm in the way he wagged his knees, swayed his hips, and bopped his head. The women craved it; the men respected it.

I'll eat 'em alive had not been a hollow boast but a simple statement of fact. That night, from the launching pad of the Hayride, Hank exploded like a rocket, rising with the unharnessed force of raw talent, fueled from a magic drawn from the deepest wells of creativity. Hank knew it. The audience knew it, too.

"This guy," Merle said to himself, "is something special."

Hank became an overnight sensation, drawing huge crowds to the auditorium every Saturday night, often selling out its 3,500 available seats. While radio stations all across the nation played his hits, Hank and his Drifting Cowboys endlessly toured the region, playing honkytonks and high school auditoriums all across Ark-La-Tex area, only to hurry back to Shreveport to make the morning Johnny Fair Syrup Program at KWKH studios.

But all this was just quiet thunder, the kind that rumbles off in the horizon. The lightning didn't strike until Hank's live Hayride performance of "Lovesick Blues," and after that, Hank Williams became a star[6].

"It was the yodel," Merle once said in an interview with BBC Four. "When he hit that yodel, that's when [the girls] came out of their chairs." Then, with his signature irreverence, he added: "They threw babies at him."

It was this song, a lonely man's anthem with a catchy yodel that drove the kids crazy. At the Hayride, they cried, "Encore!" over and over, forcing Hank to repeat himself a handful of times before the management stopped the show. February the following year, MGM released the song, and it went to the top of the Billboard charts. Hank reaped all the rewards of a major celebrity. He bought a new home in Bossier City and traded in his beat-up town car for a 1948 Packard sedan with whitewall tires, round headlamps, and a sloping rear end. Hank was finally living like a star.

Merle made carrying Hank's guitar his chief concern. For those hanging around the Hayride, Merle's face was all too familiar; he'd become somewhat of a groupie, but a useful one at that. Eventually he started getting odd jobs here and there, helping Hank's Drifting Cowboys haul equipment, set up stage, and even sell songbooks in the lobby of the Municipal on the nights when Hank performed. These side-jobs didn't pay well, but Merle didn't mind much. After all, he was hanging out with somebody famous.

There's no way of knowing how Hank felt about Merle. But from Merle's perspective, Hank Williams took interest in him, entrusting him with insights that would one day lead to Merle's own artistic endeavors. It seemed that every moment spent with Hank yielded another lesson about art, like the time he showed Merle how to play a D chord on his own wrist. But no matter what he taught, Hank's teachings were unforgettable, and they transformed Merle's life. At least, Merle believed they changed him, and isn't that enough?

One day, Merle spotted Hank backstage at the auditorium stretched out on a couple of folding chairs, his face buried in a thin booklet. Hank had taken off his cowboy hat, and for the first time Merle noticed the bald spot on his head, but this shocked him less than the title of Hank's reading material.

A *Young Romance* comic. The pink cover showed a young couple kissing.

"Hank!" Merle called out in surprise. "What ya reading a sissy book for?"

Hank drew his shoulders in as if Merle had dumped a bucket of cold water on his head. "Sissy book?" he growled, his cheeks turning red, either with anger or embarrassment, or maybe both.

Merle checked himself. The last thing he wanted to do was to upset Hank. "Well, my sister reads that stuff," he explained, referring to the stack of *Young Romance* comic books on his sister Charlotte's bookshelf.

"Boy," said Hank, waving the comic book at him, "where do you think I get the ideas for my songs?"

Merle's jaw dropped. Could it be possible that the secret of Hank's genius lay within the floppy covers of a girly comic book? To Merle, it was nearly overwhelming. "Wow," he gasped, keeping his voice down, lest others heard their secret. "So that's how you do it?"

The anger left Hank's face like air hissing from a balloon, and he relaxed his shoulders and fell back into his chair. "Well, it's a start," he told him and once again flipped through his comic book. "I get ideas from everywhere I look—comic books, television, even from what people say. If I hear something I like, I write it down in this here book." He showed him a tiny notebook that he kept in his jacket pocket.

Merle caught his breath as if Hank had shown him a treasure map.

"But you also gotta be honest to write a heart-song," Hank added.

Merle frowned. "A heart-song?"

"You got to be in love first. You got to be in love and have your heart broken in a million pieces. You can't fake it—you gotta live it. Then you tell it to somebody in a song, real simple, so when they hear it, it reminds them of a time when someone broke their heart and it tears them up all over again."

"Oh," said Merle. He'd never been in love. He didn't even know what that meant—not really.

"People love sympathy," Hank went on. "They love to be sad. They'll rush out and buy that record so they can feel sorry for themselves. But it's got to come from the heart or it's just going to be another song."

Merle quietly sank into his seat as he wrestled with this idea. Hank's advice was considerably more complex than the tip that Johnnie Bailes had given him, and Merle already knew what he had to do next. Not only did he have to fall in love, but he had to get his heart broken, too.

Hayride performers had some play with their schedules. While they all had obligations to KWKH—from morning radio programs to weeknight and Saturday performances at the Hayride—there were often gaps in their schedules that allowed them to perform elsewhere within the tri-state area. It was during one of these outings that Merle was asked to come along and help. The gig was in central Texas, only a few hours from Shreveport, and Merle tagged along to help. It's not clear why the band brought him (I can't imagine Hank bringing Merle all the way from Shreveport just to carry his guitar), but it's probable that he was there to help out with setting up the stage equipment and selling merchandise out in the lobby. Either way, Merle had a big job on his hands.

Once the convoy rolled into town and parked on the square near the courthouse, everyone got out and stretched their legs. Merle assumed they would all grab a bite to eat at the diner, but Hank had something else in mind. He went over to Merle, placed a hand on his shoulder, and said, "Boy, I need you to do me a favor."

Merle was eager to please. "Sure, Hank. Whatever you say."

Hank led him over to the driver's side door of his sedan. "Listen. The boys and me are going to get some coffee. While we're gone, I need you to do something." He jingled a set of keys before Merle's eyes. "Take these. I want you drive the car around the square a few times and ballyhoo the show for us."

Merle's eyes flew open wider. "You want me to do *what?*"

"You know, talk about the show. Say something like, 'Hank Williams live tonight at Center, Texas. Showtime eight o'clock.' You know. Something like that. Do a good job."

With his mouth still hanging open, Merle looked with quivering eyes over at the Packard limousine's sleek hood, then to the dual bullhorns mounted on the roof that were wired to the CB microphone clipped to the dashboard inside.

The idea of ballyhooing for Hank was almost crippling—mostly because Merle didn't know how to drive. He certainly didn't own a license, and to make matters worse, there was a big trailer hitched to the back of the Packard. Wouldn't that make it even more difficult to maneuver?

"Oh, uh, Hank," said Merle, aware that his voice was shaking, "I don't know how to shift the car too good, and, well . . ."

With his arm still draped over Merle's shoulder, Hank guided him over to the driver's side door and jerked it open. "Boy, now listen to me. This has got an electronic clutch on it. You don't have to shift it under thirty miles an hour."

Beads of sweat gathered along Merle's forehead. He could see that there was no way out of this one. He said nervously, "Is that right?" He gazed warily into the Packard's interior, where the dashboard looked as alien as a control panel on an airliner.

"Now, there's nothing to worry about," Hank prodded. "Just drive her around the square a few times." He reached inside and unhooked the microphone from the dash, then he waved it in front of Merle's face. "Here's the mike. Just push the button and start talking."

Merle touched the microphone and tugged its rubbery cord. It didn't seem like too much to ask. Besides, if he could pull this off, he'd earn Hank's respect, and that was worth taking a chance. "Yeah, okay," he said, nodding. "I'll do it."

"Thanks, boy." Hank grinned, clapped him on the shoulder, and then hurried off with the others toward the diner.

Carefully, Merle slid in behind the wheel and turned the key. The engine started, purring smoothly. He put the car into drive and then pressed his foot to the gas pedal. The Packard lurched forward, maybe a little too fast, but the car was on the road. So far so good. Smiling big, Merle and the Packard drifted around the town square while other cars passed him on the right. He sat back, glowing with pride, and then his eyes slid to the microphone clipped to the dashboard. With a heavy sigh, he rolled his shoulders back, brought the mike to his lips, and mashed the button.

"Hank-Williams-live-at-Center-Auditorium!" he shrieked. All that nervous tension caused Merle's voice to rise until he sounded almost womanly. He cleared his throat and tried again. Through the open windows, he heard his own shrill voice echoing across the town square. "Showtime-tonight-at-eight! Hank-Williams-in-person!"

Everything came out as one long word.

He made a single loop around the square and had started around again when Hank darted into the road, waving both arms like a ground crewman directing a cargo jet. A brick formed in Merle's stomach as he brought the Packard to a sudden stop. Hank rushed over and stuck his head into the window.

"Boy," Hank growled, "you, sound like a screeching woman. Speak lower and slower. You got that? Lower and slower."

Hank disappeared from the window. Merle's shoulders rose and fell as he drew a heavy breath and expelled it. Gripping the steering wheel, he waited for his nerves to untangle. This didn't seem fair. He wanted to hang around the others, not embarrass himself as he circled the town square.

He put the Packard back on the road. Clutching the microphone in one sweaty hand, he brought it to his lips, but hesitated. Hank's words echoed in his ears, and he muttered to himself, "Lower and slower; lower and slower." This became a kind of chant, and I think those words must have evoked some kind of magic for him, because a change took hold of him, a light ignited in his mind, chasing away his doubts and worries. The idea made him bigger somehow. Lower and slower. He drew his shoulders up, pressed the mike to his lips, and when he spoke, he hardly recognized the smooth, velvety purr that came echoing back through the window. It was the voice of a showman.

"Hank Williams live at Center Auditorium. Showtime tonight at eight! Hank Williams live!"

On the surface, it doesn't seem like much. But I think for Merle, even the tiniest lesson coming from Hank amounted to something of monumental importance to his self evolution. This was largely due to Hank's incredibly magnetic personality, matched with Merle's impressionable state of mind and willingness to learn. The result was a bolt of lightning, straight between Merle's eyes, and by the fourth or fifth time around the square, he'd become transformed. He was no longer hunching over the wheel, but sitting back, cool and confident, with stars in his eyes.

Lower and slower meant be sure of yourself. It meant be comfortable in your own skin. Even more importantly, it meant find your own voice.

On June 3, 1949, (less than a month after the birth of his son), Hank Williams made his farewell performance on the Hayride. Just as everyone had feared and expected, the Honkytonk Shakespeare had became too big for Shreveport, and the Opry had come for its star.

Merle faced the next three years with fierce determination. He developed professionally by taking guitar lessons from local talent manager and upright bassist Tillman Franks, and in his free time he toted guitars for Hayride artists, always mindful of making connections. His sophomore year saw him working for a local radio station and performing on the weekends with his band, Merle and Ed and their Moonlight Valley Boys.

Then came perhaps the greatest agent in his artistic evolution— he fell in love. Her name was Ginger, a fellow student, with red curls and an irresistible smile. By his senior year, he'd grown tall and handsome, and he beamed with an unbridled charisma that earned him recognition as "Senior Personality" from his senior class at C. E. Byrd High.

In the fall of 1952, he attended Louisiana Tech in Ruston, Louisiana. It was his parents' idea—not his. Moving away from Shreveport only interfered with his plans for Hayride stardom. But college wasn't so bad; he found plenty of ways to keep active in the music business. During his first semester, he nabbed a job as a disc jockey at KRUS Radio. On air, he called himself The Tall Texan, an obvious misnomer, since he was born in Oklahoma. Nonetheless, the name caught on in Ruston, and his reputation flourished. He even put a band together and started performing at high school parties and on fast-food restaurant rooftops. By the time he performed during halftime at a Louisiana Tech basketball game, The Tall Texan had become something of a local celebrity.

When he went home for the holidays a semester later, Merle—then eighteen—had stars in his eyes. He was a seasoned radio personality and a sought-after entertainer. His road-worn '46 Packard, stenciled with the name "Ole Bessie," was a rolling self-promoting billboard, with its sides reading: "The Tall Texan, Merle Kilgore, playing your favorite western and hillbilly music, Radio Station KRUS—1490." On the back it read: "Here goes The Tall Texan. Honk when you pass by, neighbor!" He must have felt pretty big, cruising back into his hometown.

With a week to kick around in Shreveport, he spent the first few days visiting with his family and friends. His mom doted on him, and Ginger threw him a welcome home party and he serenaded her with his guitar out on the porch swing. Everything seemed fine and familiar until he dropped by the Bantam Grill one evening, hoping to run into some old pals.

The sun was setting when he arrived at the café. He spotted a shadowy figure standing by the front door, his back against the wall, hands in his pockets, one foot kicked up behind him. He wore a black Western suit with black boots. A cowboy hat sat on his head, its brim tipped low to hide his eyes. As Merle moved closer to the figure, he smelled sour whiskey and cigarette smoke.

Dropping his gaze, he hurried for the door, hoping to sidestep any social graces, when a voice stopped him cold.

"Ain't you gonna speak to me, Merle?"

Stunned, Merle stopped and looked up, meeting the eyes of Hank Williams.

The last three years had not been kind to Hank. He looked worn and dangerously thin, with a hollowed-out face and dark, sunken eyes. He looked haggard beyond his years, in need of a shave, a bath, and maybe ten years' worth of sleep.

For a moment, Merle groped for the right thing to say. It never came. "Hank!" he finally managed, but his voice sounded too loud, too overjoyed. "I didn't see you standing there!"

Dropping his eyes to the blacktop, Hank dragged on his cigarette and said in a low, somber voice, "I'm back, boy."

"Man, that's terrific." Merle forced a smile, but it felt wrong, as if the very act of smiling was deceitful. In truth, all he wanted to do was throw his hands in the air and shout for help.

Hank's current situation wasn't exactly news to Merle. He'd kept a close eye on Hank's career over the years, from Hank's incredible debut at the Opry when he'd sung a record seven encores of "Lovesick Blues," to his rise in Country Music fame. But recent news had taken a turn for the worse. Hank had hit hard times—mostly because of his drinking—and earlier that year, the Opry had booted him off the show after catching him onstage with a pint of whiskey tucked into his boot. They'd had enough of his drinking. Not long after that, Audrey filed for divorce. Then he'd gotten arrested in Alabama for carrying a gun.

Three years. That's how long it'd been since Hank's farewell performance on the Hayride. Only, his eyes didn't show three years. More like fifty years.

Of course, Merle knew about Hank's return to the Hayride. Everyone knew about it. After the Opry, he'd come back to Shreveport and married Billie Jean Jones—the daughter of the Bossier City sheriff and possibly the prettiest girl in Shreveport—taking their vows onstage during a show. It sounded like Hank had it together, but looking at him at that moment, Merle knew differently. Hank looked like a walking dead man.

"I'm playin' this Saturday night," said Hank. He flicked the glowing cinder of his cigarette across the parking lot; for a brief moment, it traveled in an arc like a falling star before disappearing. "You gonna be there?"

"You bet, Hank," said Merle. "I'll be there Saturday night, and I'm gonna carry that guitar, if that's all right with you."

Hank smiled and fixed his jaundiced eyes on Merle, where a trace of their old intensity still lingered, if only for a moment. "You know what, boy? I've been expecting you."

At that moment, a black Cadillac lumbered alongside the curb. When the backdoor opened, Hank tipped the brim of his hat back from his brow and shuffled over to the car. Before climbing inside, he threw Merle a halfhearted smile and disappeared into the dark interior.

Saturday night came and brought with it an angry thunderstorm, flooding Market Street and washing over the parade of cars milling toward the Municipal Auditorium. The rain got so bad that it forced Tommy Smith, Hank's guitarist and acting chauffer that evening, to sit forward and hunch over the steering wheel, his sight limited to just a few feet in front of the Cadillac's grill. Luckily, he had Don Helms sitting in the passenger seat acting as his second set of eyes. Alone in the backseat sat Hank, not saying much.

Disgusted with the rain, Tommy glided the car into the auditorium's crowded parking lot, aiming for the building's backdoors. They were going to get drenched, especially once they started unpacking the trunk.

"Well, now, you be sure to watch for Merle," Hank spoke up from the backseat. "He's supposed to be waiting for me."

This obviously took both Tommy and Don by surprise, and they cast skeptical glances at each other before meeting Hank's eyes in the review mirror.

"I don't think so, Hank," said Tommy, shaking his head. "That boy of yours ain't gonna show. Just look outside."

Hank wasn't put off. "Tell you what. Ten dollars says ol' Merle will be here, waiting in the rain for us to pull up so's he can grab this guitar."

Don chuckled, his brow arched in doubt. "Ain't nobody standing out here in this rain," he said quietly.

Tommy shrugged. "I got ten dollars says the boy's a no-show."

"I'll get in on this, too," said Don. "Even if the boy did show, the rain woulda washed him into the gutter by now."

Eager to win his bet, Tommy gassed the Cadillac, pulling up closer to the building, bringing the car as close as possible to the backdoors. The headlights swept across a lone figure standing in the rain, his shoulders bunched, hands in his pocket. Tommy mashed the brakes, and all three men looked at Merle grimacing in the cold rain, his suit dripping wet, his hair plastered to his head.

"Hot dog!" Hank shouted and slapped his knee. He was leaning forward in his seat, his eyes flashing. "I knew that boy would show."

Tommy and Don shared a cursory glance as they dug their wallets from their pockets and stuffed cash into Hank's outstretched hand.

If this part of the tale seems farfetched, then I'm going to have a job selling you its conclusion. But I'll tell it anyway. According to Merle, he carried Hank's guitar, following in the wake of the Drifting Cowboys as they trudged into the building's back corridors that echoed with music from the stage. When they rounded a corner near the dressing rooms, Merle spotted Billie Jean, who flung herself at Hank and showered him with kisses. She said something to Hank about how worried she'd been about his drinking.

Just then, applause exploded from the auditorium as the last performer exited the stage and stormed into the back corridors, his band in tow. It was Johnny Horton, a newer Hayride artist. He was dressed like Hank, in a white Western suit, only his was stitched with cactus cutouts, and he had a red scarf around his neck and his guitar slung over his shoulder. He looked flushed and sweaty, having just finished his act, but he glowed with an easy smile.

Hank called him over, and Horton obeyed, his face beaming a bright red. Hank said, "Hoss, I like your music. You got a lot of potential. You're gonna hit it big one day, I just know it."

"Well, I appreciate that," said Horton, loud enough so that everyone could hear. "That sure means a lot to me, coming from you, Hank."

"I want to introduce you to my wife, Billie Jean," Hank said. "Billie Jean, this is Johnny Horton."

A bashful grin spread across Horton's face as he took the woman's hand and gave it a light shake. "Nice to meet ya, Billie Jean."

"We gotta go, Hank!" someone warned.

Horton said goodbye and then hurried off to his dressing room. Once he was out of earshot, Hank leaned in close to Billie Jean and whispered something. Merle only caught a few words.

"You know what I think, Billie Jean?" Hank told her. "I think you're gonna marry that man one day."

(Incidentally, Billie Jean *would* later marry Johnny Horton. Find it hard to believe? That's the thing about my grandfather's stories: in his mind, all the old Country Music stars were psychic or had premonitions, or had powers of true insight and observation. These guys—at least in Merle's eyes—were spectacular vessels of divine inspiration and creativity.)

Hank went out and performed, and if he had looked like the walking dead a few moments earlier, he was reborn on that stage. A white light glowed all around him like a halo. That was how Merle saw him.

I'd like to tell you Hank Sr. underwent a personal transformation that night. I'd like to say he went on to recover from his drinking problem and got help, that he later returned to the Opry and won back his dignity. I'd like to say he wrote another dozen songs that the world will never forget. But that's not Hank Sr.'s story. Not even close.

Merle returned to finish his semester at Louisiana Tech, and he watched Hank's career from a distance. He heard the stories of Hank's downward spiral. But nothing could have prepared Merle for the news on New Year's morning.

Hank Sr. had died in the middle of the night.

Hank's death is still something of a mystery—a mystery explored in depth by BBC Four in a 2010 televised documentary entitled "Hank Williams: Honky Tonk Blues" (which included an interview with Merle). In the days following Christmas of 1952, the singer's booking agent sent him on a tour that would end in Canton, Ohio. Taking the wheel of Hank's powder-blue 1952 Cadillac, Charles Carr, a young college student, drove northeast toward West Virginia, taking on a nasty snowstorm that rolled in across the region that covered the roads in ice. While Carr white-knuckled the wheel, Hank relaxed in the backseat, easing into the holiday spirit with a bottle.

When they reached Knoxville, Carr stopped at a hotel, no longer willing to fight the bad weather; by the time they checked in, Hank looked absolutely smashed, and worse, he looked ill. A doctor came and checked his vitals. He gave Hank two shots of morphine mixed with Vitamin B-12 and gave Carr the okay to keep going.[7]

The next morning, Carr and a few guys helped carry Hank to the Cadillac, stretching him out on the backseat. Carr drove on, determined to get Hank to his show in Canton. But sometime in the early morning hours, an uneasy feeling washed over him. He glanced into the rearview mirror, saw Hank lying on his back, hands crossed over his chest, stiff as a board. Unable to shake his dread, Carr found a small gas station in Oak Hill, West Virginia. It was five-thirty a.m.

and two service men in jumpers shambled out to the Cadillac. One of the men caught Carr's eyes.

"Say, pal, mind taking a look at the guy in the backseat, see if anything looks wrong with him?" Carr asked in a high, strained voice.

The gas attendant frowned curiously, glanced into the rear window, and then returned to Carr with eyes the size of dinner plates.

"You mean the guy in the backseat? Oh, that guy's dead."

No one knows for sure what really happened. The coroner determined the cause of death as a heart attack. But the consensus is that narcotics and alcohol played a role.

Only one thing remains certain: Hank Sr. burned too bright for a body made of flesh and bone. Maybe a guy like that was never meant to last long. Whatever the case, he achieved a rare kind of fame and his music changed the world.

Twenty-nine years old, incredibly famous, and dead in the backseat of a Cadillac on the first day of the New Year—that was how Hank Williams left this world.

Hank's funeral was held on January 4, 1953, at the Montgomery City Auditorium in Montgomery, Alabama. The streets quaked with more than 25,000 mourners while guitar pickers sang their hearts out on every corner. It seemed like everyone in the world had come to say goodbye to Hank.

Merle couldn't make it to the service, but that night he held his own memorial at KRUS Radio where he worked the graveyard shift. Sitting alone at the control board with his feet propped up on a counter, he played a string of Hank Williams records, all the while listening closely to Hank's high-lonesome voice, searching his lyrics for hidden meanings and dark premonitions.

In his later years, Merle became a subject-matter expert and a go-to source on all things Hank Williams. He told countless stories about the singer and referred to him as a kind of supernatural phenomenon.

Clearly, Merle was more than a fan. He often attributed his own success to Hank. The legendary singer sparked Merle's imagination like no one else would ever do, offering insights that became forever seared into Merle's imagination. Just a few lessons from Hank Sr.—a few incidental tips—and Merle had the tools necessary to become an important songwriter. Only a year after Hank's death, Merle wrote "More and More," his first hit, and I can't help but wonder: if Merle had never met Hank Sr., would he have written that song?

I honestly don't think so.

webb pierce

In the 2006 remake of Wes Craven's horror schlock classic *The Hills Have Eyes*, the film opens with footage of an actual atomic blast, a mushroom cloud rising into the sky, while down below, powerful shockwaves raise the earth, then scatter it. The horror is contrasted by the sliding note of a steel guitar, an antiquated sound, and then Webb Pierce's nasal voice as he keens "More and More," a song recorded half a century earlier and written by an eighteen-year-old Merle Kilgore. My grandfather didn't live to see the remake of *The Hills Have Eyes*, but I think he would have gotten a kick out of it. This was his baby, after all, and it exploded into a mushroom cloud that changed the course of his life and launched him into the ranks of respectable Country Music songwriters.

How the song fell into Webb's hands was an incredible stroke of luck.

Webb Pierce was the newest honkytonk hero of the Hayride, achieving an unlikely superstardom in the wake of Hank's move to the Opry and the Hayride's uncertainty.

Webb's beginnings were somewhat ironic. Horace Logan, in his *Louisiana Hayride Years*, tells how Webb moved to Shreveport in the early 1940s and worked as a manager at Sears, Roebuck and Co. In his free time, he pursued a music career with his wife, Betty Jane, singing on morning radio stations and in dance halls and nightclubs. But Horace blocked any of Webb's attempts of getting on the Hayride;

the Hayride manager didn't think Webb had what it took. Five years is what it took for Webb to convince Horace. By then, it was 1949, and Hank Williams had just left for Nashville, leaving the Hayride to fend for itself. Maybe Horace was more open to new artists by then. Anyway, Webb pleaded with him, and this time Horace gave in, saying, "I'm gonna put you on with all those professional entertainers just so you can see how bad you are." [8]

Webb may not have looked like much—he was a shoe salesman, after all—but he quickly proved he had what it took. Handsome and dressed in Gene Autry-esque Nudie suits—flashy Western suits all the rage in singing cowboy movies—he brought a particular brand of honkytonk to the table. He had a high, nasally tenor, like he sang with his nose pinched shut, but this sounded just fine over a steel guitar and a wailing piano, especially when he sang about heartache and hard drinking. In his time, Webb became the *biggest* country artist, out-producing his contemporaries in terms of hits. Country Music Hall of Fame online points out that Webb had thirteen singles to top Billboard charts in the 1950s, and he became a Country Music icon and cornerstone of honkytonk[9].

Webb was sort of a show-off. Once the serious money started rolling in, he used it to promote himself, while at the same time indulging in an eccentric lifestyle. From Shreveport, he moved to Nashville, where he bought himself a big house and built a $30,000 guitar-shaped swimming pool in the back. So that no one would miss him, he drove around in a convertible Pontiac Bonneville, fashioned by Nudie Cohn (of Nudie suit fame; more on him later), with its interior inlaid with silver dollars. Meanwhile, Webb's costumes got louder and more flamboyant with each passing year. You could say Webb Pierce had a real panache for showmanship.

By Christmastime of 1953, Webb had become a big star. It'd been only a year since he had his breakthrough with "Wondering," a chart topper in 1952, and then hitting again with "That Heart Belongs to Me" after running off to Nashville and joining the Opry. The hits didn't stop there. He released one after the other in just his first year, so it must have really irritated him when he went home to West Monroe for the holidays—the native son returning—only to find he had competition.

Webb loved visiting his hometown. He'd often go walking through town just to reconnect with his personal history and soak up the glory of his celebrity. This meant meeting folks. Brandishing smiles to the starstruck citizens. Signing a few autographs. This also meant visiting his old hangouts and listening to his friends talk about how famous he'd gotten. His first stop was his old barbershop on the corner. The barber, Bill, had owned the shop for decades, and he'd cut Webb's hair a thousand times or more. Webb could only imagine how happy Bill would be to see him.

So he went inside, and the bell over the door jingled and dusty sunrays slanted in through the picture-frame window, just like old times. The place was nearly empty; just two old men sitting in swivel chairs, reading crumpled newspapers. Another man swept the floor. They didn't even look up to see who'd just stepped inside. When the head barber, old and thin and gnarled as a root, saw Webb, he snapped to attention and laughed.

"Well, I'll be! If it ain't the little Pierce boy, all grown up, big and famous."

Webb smiled. That was more how he liked it. With a laugh, he nodded toward the chair and said, "Long time, Bill. How about a shave?"

"Yes, of course!" The old man's eyes widened behind his glasses. "Come on over and have a seat."

Webb slid out of his jacket, hung it near the mirror, and then settled into the swivel chair. Bill tipped Webb back and wrapped his face in a hot towel, coaxing the honkytonk star to relax, all warm and snug in Bill's familiar chair.

"The boys and I, we talk about you all the time," said Bill, and I'm sure his voice brought back lots of memories.

Webb loosened his shoulders, laced his fingers on his chest. "Is that right?"

"The whole town's sure proud of you," the old man went on. "Everyone here claims you as his own."

"Well, I don't plan to forget where I come from."

Bill stepped away and tinkered with something at his station, and when he drifted back, he hummed lightly beneath his breath. "I was just telling them boys the other day that you sing at the Opry now."

"Yep," said Webb. He felt foggy with sleep. He yawned. "That's right, Bill. You should see that place. Just beautiful."

"But if I were you," said Bill, speaking from somewhere beyond the cloud of sleep Webb was nearing, "I'd get on that Tall Texan show."

"The Tall Texan," said Webb sleepily. "That right?"

"Yup. You get on that show and you got it *made*."

Webb's eyes snapped open. He sat up in his chair and jerked the towel from his face. "Got it *made*? Hell, I'm the number one artist in the world!"

Wide-eyed, Bill looked to his friends for help. They didn't offer any.

Webb didn't feel much like a shave anymore. He climbed out of the chair and tossed the towel aside, then put a few bucks on the counter.

"Didn't mean any disrespect by it, Webb," said Bill, who seemed genuinely distressed.

"Ah, forget it, Bill." Webb waved a hand as if swatting at a fly. "I gotta go."

He plucked his jacket from the hanger and then shouldered the door open, allowing a cool rush of air inside as the bell jittered over the door. Before leaving, Webb looked over at Bill and scowled. "I never even heard of The Tall Texan," he said and left.

Several hours later, Webb found a small pub a few blocks down the road. It was dark inside and small, with a few guys playing at the pool table, and a few more lonely souls sitting at the bar. As Web crossed the room, the men sitting at the bar all turned and looked at him, and then their eyes grew big as they suddenly recognized the honkytonk singer. Webb sauntered over to the bar and had a seat.

"Been a long time," said the John the bartender.

Webb took a stool and nodded at him. "Howdy, John. How's it been?"

"Good. Good. Not nearly as good as it must be for you. But good. What can I get you?"

"Whatever you got on tap will do."

With a nod, the bartender went away and came back with a frothy mug of beer. He set it down and propped himself on the bar with an elbow, narrowing his eyes. "Heard you was playin' the Opry."

"That's right." Webb sipped his beer and glanced at the gawking faces to his left and right. He felt that deep sense of satisfaction, and something else, since this was his home and these were his people. The recognition seemed somehow more significant here in Monroe. "I'm a regular there," he said so that everyone could hear him. "Going back shortly after Christmas."

The bartender lit a cigarette and squinted his eye against a thread of smoke. Then he shook the match out and pointed it at Webb. "Well, you'd better get on that Tall Texan show," he said all matter-of-fact. "Then you'll know you've made it."

Webb looked evenly at the man. He said nothing for a long time. *Everyone in this goddamned town is in on some sort of joke,* he thought. Finally, he drank deeply from his mug, wiped his mouth with his sleeve, and dug out a nickel for the beer. He started to walk away when he turned back to the bartender and said, "Who in hell is this Tall Texan I keep hearing about?"

John stood up straight. "He's got that television show. Comes on tonight. Channel Fourteen. Around five o'clock."

Webb's half-hooded eyes considered John's face for another moment, then he nodded goodbye and stormed out of the dark barroom.

Later that evening, Webb sat down in front of the television, wearing a bathrobe and nursing a drink, waiting for The Tall Texan show. His mind churned over the day's events. Everybody was talking about this Tall Texan character. He already didn't like the bastard. The only reason he wanted to see the show was so he could confirm what he already suspected—that half the town was full of idiots.

Following a Lucky Strike commercial, the show began. Its set was a Howdy Doody rip-off, with a general store from the Old West, complete with clapboard walls and a rough, wooden porch. Across the door, the words "TRADING POST" and "GEN. MDSE" were painted in clumsy, even backward, lettering. On the wall: "Zeke McGrew Justice of the Pease" (an intentional misspelling). In the hand-painted shop window was a merchandise display, a cowboy hat and Western boots.

"And now, ladies and gentlemen," an unseen announcer intoned, "please welcome the cowboy that everybody loves, The Tall Texan!"

Children were gathered along the sides of the set, and they let loose a barrage of wild cheers as a tall guy in a cowboy hat and Western bolo tie sauntered onto the porch with his guitar at the ready, backed by another guy on a steel guitar. The host was just a young guy, Webb realized, no more than seventeen or eighteen, and very familiar.

Webb leaned forward, squinting. He knew that face. He knew those eyes. Yes, there was definitely something familiar about the kid. Especially that grin—Webb was sure he'd seen it before.

"Where the hell do I know him from?" he muttered.

Following a jovial introduction, The Tall Texan launched into a country song, but Webb was thinking too hard to hear a single note. He knew the kid's face. But from where? It was driving him crazy. It was that grin. That damned grin. Webb knew it well. Then it struck him all at once, and he snapped his fingers and called out, "Well, hell, that's Merle Kilgore!"

He shook his head, laughing. He'd been led to believe that The Tall Texan was some sort of threat. But no, this was just Merle, the gofer boy from the Hayride who sometimes carried guitars for Hayride performers, including Webb.

Only now did The Tall Texan catch his ear. He listened, and slowly his smile dissolved into quiet admiration. When the song ended, The Tall Texan asked his viewers to "Stay put! More fun and music is on the way!"

But by then Webb was already reaching for the phone.

Several months earlier, while Merle was working at KRUS Radio, a visitor appeared, looking for The Tall Texan. The visitor—a short, heavy-set man in his late fifties—wore a smart suit and held an unlit cigar wedged between two chubby fingers. He introduced himself as J.O. "Red" Willett.

"Kid, I listen to you every time I drive through Ruston," he told Merle. "I like you. You got style. I'm building a TV station in Monroe, and I want you to host a show—your own show."

Merle could hardly mask his surprise. I think he'd been looking for a good reason to bail out of college. But he knew a little about business, and he stuck to one rule in particular: always keep your cards close to your chest. "Well, sir, I don't know," he told him. "See, I'm a student at Tech, and I'd have to drop classes. My folks wouldn't be too pleased to hear that." He waited a moment and then asked, "How much money are we talking?"

Red didn't even blink. "A hundred bucks a week, kid. And that's just the beginning."

Merle responded in kind. "When do I start?"

By the fall of 1953, The Tall Texan show aired once a week on KFAZ-TV, Channel 43, and later on KNOE-TV, and as Red promised, Merle had the show all to himself. His set was a charmed merchant's post from the Old West. You could almost smell the horse manure in the air. With KFAZ-TV being the first television station in Monroe, and one of only three in all of Louisiana, Merle quickly achieved notoriety in his town. Each night at five o'clock, KFAZ-TV broadcasted his show to about 16,000 televisions throughout Monroe. Most of those viewers probably thought Merle was a national celebrity. But the truth was that you really couldn't pick up KFAZ if you were outside a ten-mile radius from the station's transmitter. Still, you can't blame Monroe citizens for comparing Webb with The Tall Texan.

Hosting his own show meant having creative control. While each week a guest singer would come on and do a number, Merle also made sure to sing his own songs. This played right into his hands on the day he wrote "More and More."

He had met Ginger for breakfast in a small diner in Ruston when it happened. Over pancakes, she'd forced him to make a decision: a career in the music business, or Ginger. It'd been an unfair proposal and he'd told her so. In turn, she broke it off right then and there.

The breakup had left Merle brokenhearted. I'm sure it didn't occur to him until much later the immortal words of Hank Williams, who'd stressed the importance of this pain, naming it a necessary evil, an agent in the creation of a heart-song: *You got to be in love and have your heart broken in a million pieces.* I suppose, had Hank been alive, he would have pointed out the obvious: Ginger had done Merle a favor.

Shortly after that devastation, he'd been driving through town with Dot Salley, his hired photographer-turned-girlfriend, when the idea for the song fell into his lap. Dot was a rebound for him, no doubt, with Ginger far in the rearview mirror after calling it quits. He was still bitter about the breakup, but mending.

Maybe it was Merle's broken heart that had responded to Dot. With Ginger gone, it was now Dot sitting in his passenger seat. They had the windows rolled down that day, letting in the warm Monroe sun, and she mentioned her own ex-boyfriend and how she was getting over him more and more each day. She asked Merle about Ginger (he talked about her all the time), and he confessed that, more and more, he was forgetting about her, too. And then it had happened. He simply opened his mouth and sang. The song flowed out of him— lyrics, melody—the whole arrangement. It was as if he'd picked up a rogue signal transmitted from some divine radio station.

He went out on a limb by singing that song on his show later that evening. He hadn't really had much time to tweak it, but he felt good singing it. After the show, he went marching toward his dressing room, looking for Dot, when someone shouted at him to grab the phone. He had a call.

Merle picked up the phone in his dressing room.

"Merle Kilgore?" said a high, nasally voice. "This is Webb Pierce."

"Webb Pierce?" Merle stammered, eyes gaping. But his shock quickly abated, replaced with a wild excitement. Webb Pierce, the king of country, the biggest thing to hit the music scene since Hank Williams, was calling him direct. "How ya doing, Webb?"

"Doing good. I saw you on TV. I wondered whatever happened to you."

"You caught the show?"

"I did."

"Did you like it?"

"Sure I did," Webb said. "But listen, that's not why I called . . ."

With the receiver smashed against his ear, Merle twirled in a circle, searching the room, hoping to find someone standing there to witness this extraordinary moment. He thought maybe he'd poke his head out and flag somebody down outside the door. No one.

"I wanted to ask you about that song," Webb went on. "I love it. Who wrote it?"

Merle blinked. Had he sung a song tonight? "Oh!" he barked. Everything was coming back to him. "That one's mine. It's called 'More and More.' Just wrote it this week."

"Is that right?" There was a pause on the other end. "Well, I think you and I ought to talk. Maybe I can help you find a label. Then maybe see what we can do with that song."

"Sure, Webb. That'd be great!"

They exchanged numbers and Webb hung up. The air rushed from Merle's lungs, and he plopped down into one of the cushiony chairs, where he leaned his head back and laughed.

In the coming days, Webb introduced Merle to Lew Chudd, head of Commodore Publishing Company and Imperial Records, who signed Merle on with a five-year contract. It was under this label that Merle first recorded "More and More." But that contract went by the wayside once Webb entered the picture. He heard Merle's finished recording and decided the song had more potential than he'd at first realized. But it had to be done right. The sound, the timing—the thing had to be done just right.

Leaving nothing to chance, Webb made a decision that would forever change the course of Merle's career.

"I'm gonna make you some money, kid," he told Merle. "I'm gonna record that song."

Webb made good on his promise. He recorded "More and More" under his own label, Decca Records, and Webb's nasally, high-wailing whiskey voice gave the song a unique flavor. Once the record hit the radio waves, it immediately soared to the top of the Billboard charts, where it stayed for ten weeks. Of course, Webb took credit for his stylistic contributions by nabbing half the songwriting rights, but as Merle was fond of saying, "Half of something's better than a whole lot of nothing."

"More and More" became a million-seller, and Merle, at only nineteen years old, became a world-renowned songwriter.

Monroe town officials ordained June 5, 1954, as Webb Pierce Day and announced a parade, complete with floats, a marching band, tickertape—the works. Obviously, the town expected Webb to attend, and he agreed to conclude the parade with a sort of Santa Claus finale during the Macy's Thanksgiving Day Parade.

Merle—still a lanky teenager working at KNOE-TV where he had a five-piece band to back him—couldn't believe it when Webb called, asking him for a personal escort in the parade. This had already proven a good year for Merle, with his five-year contract with Imperial Records, a smash hit on the radio, and a slew of special appearances on major radio shows like the Hayride and even the Ernest Tubb Show in Nashville. But driving Webb through Monroe for a major publicity stunt would just about top it all.

Merle spent all week preparing for the event. The morning of the parade, Webb came by the TV station, and as a surprise, he brought with him Faron Young, presently home on leave from Army duty. After handshakes and laughter, Merle took them around back of the studio to show him the white Cadillac convertible, on loan from a friend.

"I figured we could ride with the top down," Merle suggested. "Webb, you can ride in the backseat and wave at the fans."

They soon loaded up and headed out, three Country Music artists, but only two of them looked like official stars. Webb and Faron shined in their expensive Nudie suits, and Webb himself looked like Gene Autry in the *Big Sombrero*, only covered in rhinestones. Nothing said, "I'm a goddamn star!" like a Nudie suit. Merle couldn't help but feel a little sour about that.

For a short while, they toured Monroe. Webb took them to the local park, where he relayed R-rated anecdotes concerning his adventures with girls from town. But when it was time to head toward the parade's rally point, the car started to shudder and hitch.

Merle's stomach rolled in dread. "Uh-oh . . ." he groaned while pumping the gas pedal with a frantic foot. It didn't help; the car gave another lurch and then died, forcing Merle to glide for the road's shoulder.

"What's the problem, Merle?" Webb called from the back, sounding alarmed.

"Man, I don't know what's wrong with this thing," Merle muttered. They came to a stop, and he hopped out, circled around to the front of the car, and popped the hood. He knew as much about a car engine as he did about rocket science, but looking under the hood felt appropriate. Nothing looked out of place. Letting the hood fall with a thud, he returned to the driver's seat and said, "Well, I just don't know. This thing's brand new."

"Aw hell, Merle," Faron sneered, shaking his head.

Webb gave a pensive look and then said, "What about the gas, Merle?"

Merle arched his brow. Yes—that made a lot of sense. His eyes went to the fuel gauge. It was stuck on E. "Uh-oh."

"For God's sake, Merle," Webb said with disgust. "Please tell me you put gas in the damn car!"

Merle cleared his throat. "I might have forgotten."

Both Faron and Webb groaned and slapped their hands to their foreheads.

"Hell, I should've driven myself," Webb drawled.

"Looks like we'll have to push her," said Merle, implying '*you* two will have to push.' He showed an apologetic grin, hoping his embarrassment didn't show, and said, "You push. I'll drive."

Grumbling and swearing, Faron and Webb hopped out, slamming doors in their wake, and removed their hand-tailored Nudie jackets before moving around to the back bumper. Hands planted against hot metal, with the sun blazing on their backs, they started to push.

Sitting in the cool comfort of the driver's seat, Merle whistled to himself, his face flushed with embarrassment, certain he'd never hear the end of this. Good news was that the nearest gas station was just over the hill.

Maybe a half-mile down the road they spotted a Texaco service station. Webb and Faron grunted as they threw themselves into their efforts, rolling the car even faster, but when they reached the station, Merle kept going.

Webb shouted, "Hey! You blind, Merle? There's your gas station. Pull in, for God's sake!"

Merle, sweating now but not from the June heat, glanced over his shoulder, shaking his head. "I can't!" he called back. "I owe that guy a dollar!"

"Oh, fer Christ's sake!" Webb howled.

The men kept pushing. They soon reached the next station, and Merle swung in alongside the pump. While Webb propped himself against the Cadillac, gasping for breath, Merle began fueling, his eyes glued to the meter. When it reached a dollar, he returned the pump and got back into the driver's seat.

Webb gave him a dull look. "Merle, what in hell are you doing? You only put in a dollar's worth!"

Merle shrugged. "That's all I got."

Webb's face flashed an angry red, and he said, "Well, hell, go on and fill it up, boy. I'll pay the damn thing." He shook his head reproachfully. "We don't want to break down on the side of the road again—especially during my own damn parade!"

Before we turn Webb loose from our story, I feel inclined to mention the $50,000 copyright infringement lawsuit that brought Webb and Merle to the courtroom. I'm sure this embarrassed both of them, especially Merle, who later worked in the capacity of various agencies that protected copyright law.

The lawsuit came about when the Commodore Music Company, operating as Imperial Music Corporation, attempted to sue Webb on claims that they owned the rights to "More and More." According to them, Merle was already under contract with the California recording company when he wrote it.

The court hearing took place later that year. But Webb had no intentions of paying out. The Opry star fought back, claiming he had a valid contract with Merle before Merle ever signed on with Commodore Music.

In a further attempt to convince the jury to throw out the case, Webb's defense team appealed to the court that "More and More" was just a rehash of "Slowly," written by Webb several years earlier. A guitarist was even invited into the court to perform both songs, allowing the jury to compare. The jury didn't buy it.

Even so, the court's decision ultimately favored Webb; Decca Records was found not to have violated copyright laws with "More and More," and execs with Commodore went home empty handed.

But they weren't the only ones unhappy with the trial. Merle left with broken spirits. In an attempt to dodge a lawsuit, Webb's attorney had constructed a defense that reduced Merle's song to an imitation. Merle was so bothered by it that later that night at work at KCIJ Radio, he shattered every one of Webb's records while on air.

But Merle didn't hold a grudge, and the two stayed friends for many years after.

While writing about the courtroom hearing of "More and More," I did some personal investigating. Was Merle signed on with Commodore when he wrote "More and More"? According to Dot Salley (my grandmother) in a conversation in 2008, she said: yes. In fact, as she recalls it, Merle had even told this to Webb, but Webb dismissed it, saying Commodore's contract wouldn't hold water in court because Merle had signed with the label before he was eighteen. I suppose neither of them imagined the song would become a smash hit. Had the song flopped, Commodore would never have known any better. But just the opposite happened. Webb recorded "More and More" under Decca Records, while also claiming half of the songwriter's rights, and it soared to the top of the Billboard charts and stayed there for ten weeks.

Horace Logan called Webb the unofficial talent scout of the Hayride,[10] and I suppose Webb felt personally driven to help young artists achieve success, to usher the worthy ones into the gates of stardom. I'd say he did as much for Merle's career as he did for anybody. Having a major celebrity record his song at such a young age was a major move for Merle. If anything, it affirmed his own gut feeling; he *could* do it—he could write a hit song. Without Webb in his corner, Merle's career may never have gotten off the ground.

But just like anything in life, the good comes with the bad, and Webb must have also felt obligated to share a final warning with his artists, the price of a ticket.

To this day, Dot remembers the warning clearly. She and Merle had just moved to Shreveport from Monroe, bringing them closer to the Hayride, and Webb had come over to visit. While Merle and

Webb relaxed in the living room, Dot hurried into the kitchen to fix them drinks, and when she returned with her tray, she paused at the doorway, alerted by the low voices from the other room.

"You can't have a family *and* a music career, Merle," she overheard Webb tell her husband. "It's one or the other. You can't have both; you'll have to decide."

To Dot's ears, it must have sounded like a gypsy curse, announced by the gatekeeper of the music business. *Ye may enter here. But ye may not enter with your family intact.*

The sting of those words sent my grandmother into a quiet rage, especially since she and Merle had just brought their first child, Pamela, into the world. Dot stormed into the room with her jittering glasses of iced tea. The men looked up at her in surprise; they were sitting across from each other and Webb looked especially relaxed with his feet up.

She set the tray down with a clatter and said, "Webb, you get your boots off my coffee table."

Webb quickly obeyed, and Dot rushed from the room.

My grandfather never told this story; it was Dot's alone. She never forgot it, partly because Webb may have been right or maybe because Merle simply took it to heart. Either way, their marriage seemed doomed from the start.

As for Webb, he had a long career in the music business. He lived long enough to become a caricature of himself, and after his death, his star faded some. It took a decade before the powers-that-be inducted him into the Country Music Hall of Fame in 2001. Some blame his late entry on his excessive lifestyle and his somewhat abrasive personality, especially toward the people running the Opry. But Webb did a lot of good, too. He certainly looked out for the little guys, while personally boosting the careers of a handful of artists, such as Faron Young and Floyd Cramer, both of whom became superstars in their own right.

But most importantly, at least to our story, he lit the fuse for

Merle's music career. While Hank Williams showed Merle *how* to be a songwriter, it was Webb Pierce who recognized the star-making quality of Merle and released his music to the world.

Faron Young

December 10, 1996, Country Music icon Faron Young shot himself in the head. The shot was heard by everyone in the industry. They recognized the enormity of this loss. But nobody—especially not Merle—saw it coming.

The sixty-four-year-old singer was discovered with a suicide note, requesting a cremation and a final wish: to be scattered across the waters of Tennessee's Old Hickory Lake.

Faron's son Robyn took it upon himself to give his father a proper goodbye. Not wanting to dump his father's ashes off a random boat dock, he located a fitting place for the ceremony: Johnny Cash's Hendersonville lake house, a place that had been familiar to Faron. But he needed help reaching a megastar like Cash.

When Merle got the call from Robyn, he didn't hesitate to help. He, like everyone in the Country Music community, was still in shock. Faron had been a lifelong friend, and they'd shared a lifetime of experiences together.

Merle called Cash, another longtime friend, and asked to conduct Faron's funeral service there at Cash's home. Cash responded with a resounding *Yes, absolutely*. Cash even made the arrangements. When family and guests gathered near the water, they found a quiet place, garnished with poinsettias and ribbons. It was there that friends took turns saying final words and telling their favorite stories about Faron.

Merle had plenty to say.

Country Music Hall of Famer Faron Young, the Singing Sheriff, was born and raised in Shreveport. He found success on the Hayride in 1951 shortly after Hank Williams left for Nashville, when everyone expected the Hayride to go belly-up. In fact, many attribute saving the Hayride from losing an audience to Faron and a handful of other performers.

The Hayride took a hard hit when Hank Williams left for the Opry. The inclusion of Webb Pierce to the Haryride roster had already done a respectable job in restoring much of its popularity by upping the status quo. Not only did he draw a new crowd to the Municipal Auditorium, but he also escorted in a new wave of country singers, many of whom he discovered himself. Faron Young was one of them.

Faron was just a local kid with a smooth voice and big dreams when he first met Webb, and many historians give Webb all the credit. Horace Logan, the Hayride manager, had something to do with Faron's fame, too. But what the history books always leave out is that Merle's mother Gladys Kilgore (my great-grandmother) also had a hand in the discovery of the Singing Sheriff.

In 1950, Gladys Kilgore was a substitute English teacher at Fair Park High School, where Faron was finishing his senior year. By this time, he'd developed himself as a singer with a voice good enough to grant him an occasional seat on the high school choir. Faron was a self-taught singer, shaping his early style after Hank Williams. Unlike Hank, who'd had his debut at age thirteen, Faron spent his early years practicing from the back porch of his farmhouse for an audience of cows and chickens. His handsome looks and stage presence— he famously winked when he sang, and his female fans went crazy with it—made him a crowd favorite. But young Faron's charm didn't impress Gladys Kilgore, his substitute English teacher. In fact, she found him unruly, disruptive, and an instigator, encouraging the other kids to misbehave. I'm sure all this acting out was in direct relation to a troubled home life, from a tragedy that resulted in the death of a sibling, to an abusive father. He often got in fights at school because the kids made a dangerous assumption that his short stature made him easy prey. But excuses or not, he'd single-handedly undermined Gladys' authority, and she couldn't have that.

A solution presented itself the day she heard Faron singing outside her classroom, surrounded by a few admiring girls. He had a smooth, charismatic voice, and he sang with an unabashed confidence. Gladys thought he had real potential, according to Robyn Young, who relayed a version of this story to me in July 2014.

Later that day, at the ringing of the bells, Gladys dismissed her class and asked Faron to stay behind. When the two of them had the classroom to themselves, she said, "Faron, I heard you singing in the hallway today. You've got a good voice. I think I can help you. My son Merle works some in the Country Music business. He's got friends who may be able to help you."

"All right," Faron said. "So what'll it cost me?"

"You have to do something for me. No more interruptions and smart-alecky comments. Can you agree to that?"

"Yeah," he said. His eyes searched her face. For once, she'd gotten his attention. "I can do that."

"And one more thing," Gladys went on. "I want you to tell the others to stop interrupting my classroom. Can you do that for me?"

Faron said he could.

The following day when Gladys started class, the chaos transpired as usual, with several students laughing and cutting up. This time Faron jumped onto his chair and shouted, "Listen up! Everyone best shut up and act right or I'll beat the shit out of you!"

Gladys was quietly mortified, and after the class bell, she held Faron back. "Faron Young! That was inappropriate!"

"Well, you told me to put 'em straight and I did," he told her.

"Yes, but I didn't tell you to do it like that!"

I don't know if Faron improved his grades or stopped smarting off in class, but I do know that Gladys introduced Faron to Merle, and Merle introduced him to several people who were instrumental in getting Faron into the Country Music business. Merle was especially helpful. The two became good friends, and Merle brought him around the Hayride.

But Faron didn't need much help beyond an initial introduction. Faron became a regular at the auditorium, shaking hands, promoting himself as a songwriter, and eventually Tillman Franks—who was then a manager at KWKH Radio—turned him over to Webb Pierce, the Hayride's unofficial talent scout. Webb took Faron under his wing and groomed him for the stage by finding him gigs at local dives.

It was 1950, and Merle, a junior in high school, opened for Faron at the Skyway Club, a wooden-framed dive near the banks of the Red River, across the street from Barksdale Air Force Base. The Skyway Club was no Hayride, but it was a good place to start. In fact, a lot of Hayride artists sang there, and the possibility of catching a surprise performance attracted big crowds each weekend.

This particular night was no exception, according to Judy Kilgore in a 2009 interview. Merle looked out on the crowded barroom as he peeked from the curtains. With a belly full of butterflies, he hurried to the back dressing rooms and then stopped at Faron's door. The room beyond was packed, noisy with laughter, fogged over with cigarette smoke. Merle didn't even try to get inside. Instead, he stood on tiptoes and searched for Faron.

He saw him sitting back in a wooden chair, flanked by two women, his arms around their slender waists. It was Faron's Western-cut Nudie suit—rhinestone-studded and canary yellow—that made him easy to find. He looked like a blazing sun; it was the kind of flash and flair that only a genuine Nudie suit could muster.

The Nudie suit was the work of Ukrainian-American fashion designer Nudie Cohn, who fashioned Hollywood Western costumes like those worn by classic movie star cowboys. The Nudie suit was often trimmed in rhinestones and fashioned from flamboyant colors such as peach, lavender, and gold. It was the hot item for many early Hayride and Opry stars, worn by everyone who could afford one, from Hank Williams to Porter Wagoner, from John Lennon to Elvis Presley (whose golden Nudie suit cost an estimated $10,000 to make).

In the early Fifties, the Nudie suit had accumulated only a whisper of its future popularity, but it still cost Faron a small fortune, not easy for someone with little money. Faron had been writing I.O.U.s since he started saving up. But the suit was beautiful and worth every penny.

"Hey, Faron!" Merle called, his voice cutting through the noise of the room. "It's a sellout crowd!"

Faron pinched an eye shut as smoke drifted from his cigarette. He offered Merle his half-cocked grin. "What can I say? They love me!"

Everyone laughed. Faron retrieved his arm from the waist of his lady friend (not without first patting her on the rear) and started to unfold himself from his chair when the unthinkable happened. A drizzle of gray ashes from his cigarette fluttered onto the breast of his yellow jacket.

Unleashing a sudden onslaught of curses, Faron jumped out of his chair, flapping his hands at his chest as if swatting off hornets. "Son of a bitch!" he shouted. "I jus' ruin't my goddamn suit!"

A hush fell over the room. No one dared say a word. Faron had a temper, and it was best to get out of his way when he was fuming. The silence lasted long enough to become awkward.

Merle drew his sleeve back, glanced at his watch, and said, "*Ooh.*

Look at the time. I better get ready!" Then he disappeared from the doorway.

After Merle performed a few songs, Faron Young charged out onto the stage with his guitar cradled in his arms, his yellow suit glowing like a light bulb. He launched into his first song without waiting for the crowd to quiet down, and soon his smooth, reedy voice filled the barroom. Whistles came in response to his megawatt grin and his secret little wink that every girl noticed but every guy missed. Tonight Faron seemed especially vibrant. At least, until the lights suddenly went out.

For one moment, the Skyway Club went completely dark. A tremendous boom followed from outside, forcing the band to stop. A few women screamed. Moving almost blindly onto the stage, Merle found Faron and said, "What happened, man?"

Faron shrugged. "Guess I was too much. I blew the damn power."

Someone opened a door at the far end of the bar and shouted: "There's been an accident! A plane just crashed in the field across the street!"

An excited gasp rippled all over the room before the crowd started pushing its way out through the opened doors. In moments, almost everyone had moved outside.

On the quiet stage, Merle threw up his hands in exasperation. "You believe this? There goes our show."

Faron handed his guitar to Merle. "Hold on to this, Merle," he said, moving toward the edge of the stage. "I better see if I can help."

Faron took off over the edge of the stage.

Not wanting to miss the action, Merle followed him out the door.

It was dark outside, but Merle could see a crowd forming across the highway, gathering at a chain-link fence. He hurried to join them, his eyes going to the fire burning in the grassy field beyond. The smell of jet fuel hovered in the air. Moving closer, he saw a crashed single-jet engine plane with a snapped wing and a smoldering fuselage. Flames flickered around the cockpit.

Someone shouted, "Look, the pilot's trapped! He can't get out!"

At that moment, Faron hopped the tall fence like some heroic TV cowboy and ran to the wreckage. Everyone watched in silence as the Singing Sheriff began helping the pilot from his seat.

"Man, he is going to get himself killed!" Merle called.

But moments later, Faron and a hobbling pilot came hurrying from the wreckage, met with the welcoming applause of the crowd.

Eventually the fire engines arrived. The fire was put out and the pilot was taken in an ambulance to the closest hospital.

Later that night, after the crowd returned to the Skyway Club, Faron, Merle, and several performers stood at the bar, toasting the night's last drink. Faron rehashed his story for the newcomers, laughing at himself and his foolhardy bravado, when the overhead lights came on just at closing time. The laughter stopped as everyone's eyes went to Faron.

Faron frowned, then turned to check himself in the mirror over the bar. He was covered head-to-toe in black soot. His canary-yellow Nudie suit was stained with greasy smears and most of the rhinestones had fallen off the sleeves. The suit was ruined.

Merle cringed. He knew how much Faron loved his suit, and he knew just how hard Faron had worked to get it.

After inspecting himself for a quiet moment, Faron turned to face his friends with a big grin. He wiped a smear of soot from his brow. "They didn't tell me this son of a bitch was fireproof!" He laughed. "If I hadn't been wearing it, well, hell, I could've died!"

The tension broke. Merle and the others collapsed into fits of laughter, all of them clapping Faron proudly on the back.

By 1951, with Webb in his corner, Faron was ready to leave the Skyway Club and other small venues for the Hayride.

Horace Logan gave him his first chance. The reception was immediate and overwhelming. Everyone agreed the Singing Sheriff—a name he'd given himself—fit right in. It didn't take long before agents with Capitol Records caught Faron singing on KWKH Radio and signed him on with a five-year contract. The sudden notoriety was Faron's ticket out of town.

Goodbye, Hayride. Hello, Opry.

Faron moved to Nashville to kick-start his career, but his rising star was thwarted by the Korean War. The United States Army drafted Faron shortly after he moved to Music City. Discouraged, Faron answered the call and made the most of his four years of service. He performed at Army posts and quickly made a name for himself. By the time he fulfilled his military obligations, he had become a kind of celebrity among fellow soldiers.

When Faron returned to Nashville, the Opry welcomed him back with open arms. He made a quick transition from Army soldier to Country Music singer. It didn't take him long to build an audience, and as the years progressed, he became an Opry mainstay, eventually rising to Country Music superstar status with a long-running career and countless hit records like "Hello Walls," "Goin' Steady," and "Four in the Morning." Moreover, Faron became instrumental in the success of other music artists, guys like Willie Nelson and Kris Kristofferson, who were both struggling songwriters when Faron recorded their songs. That's how Faron operated—he liked helping the underdog country artists.

One of those struggling artists was Merle. Faron and Merle stayed friends throughout the decades, becoming roommates in the late Seventies, when Merle lived in a downstairs bedroom at Faron's

Harbor Island home in Tennessee. In an interview during *Country Music Roundup*, Merle recalled those years with fond memories.

Merle was going through a divorce with his fifth wife (he often joked about losing track of his marriages because he stood at the altar six times over the span of his lifetime), and it proved to be a kind of "grab-your-shit-and-get-out" scenario. During this rough spell of a divorce, Merle was living with his old friend Bob Lockwood, a Nashville deejay, when Faron surprised him with a phone call. "Brother, I bought me this mansion on Harbor Island, and I want to rent you the bottom half of the house. I'm gone all the time. You come and you live with me. Just the two of us. We'll have fun."

Merle took him up on the offer.

Here's how Merle told it.

Those days I'd have a drink or two. Faron was a great cook. I mean, he could cook my favorite. Shake 'n Bake pork chops. Crowder peas with onions. Sweet potatoes. He knew how to cook, man. Like we were the original odd couple. He called me at the Hall of Fame Motor Inn Bar. And he said, "Hey, brother, are you coming home early?"

"Yes, sheriff! I'll be home at six-thirty, soon as the traffic dies down."

"Don't lie to me now. I got your favorite. Shake 'n Bake pork chops. I got some candied yams that are delicious. I got crowder peas, and I got onions— the little tiny onions, you'll like that—and I got some fresh sliced tomatoes."

I said, "Grrreat!"

"Now, what time will you be home?"

I said, "Six-thirty to six-forty-five."

He said, "Okay."

And about midnight the waitress said to me, "Merle, you got a phone call."

And this voice said, "Listen. You think I slaved over this hot stove, cooking you Shake 'n Bake pork chops, sweet potatoes, crowder peas? Don't even think about coming home on an empty stomach. You better stop at the Waffle House, because Byron Binkley's dog Fluffo is getting your meal. Goodnight!"

Faron was a good cook, but he liked to have his cooking appreciated, too.

Faron was a generous and goodhearted guy, always quick with a laugh, but his mischievous smile probably hid a lot of pain. In his later years, he became an alcoholic, although he famously commented, "I'm a drunk, not an alcoholic; alcoholics go to meetings." He drank so much that his friends worried about him. He once passed out in his front yard; his neighbor found him without a pulse and saved his life. Most of Faron's friends would have agreed that you couldn't find a nicer guy than a sober Faron, but a drunken Faron was a true terror. Evidence of his alcohol-induced tirades trace back as far as 1965, when he was arrested in Nashville for assaulting a police officer.[11]

Faron also struggled with depression. Opry member Jack Greene said of him, "I don't think he was ever happy. It seemed like he was always looking for something he hadn't found."[12] After he retired in 1994, Faron withdrew, pushing friends and family away, growing more reclusive over the years. When his health worsened—emphysema, prostate cancer—his depression spun out of control, ending in his tragic suicide.

But there were good memories and lots of laughter on the day of Faron's funeral. Merle made sure of that. He told his stories, and he honored Faron's memory by painting a caring and generous portrait of Faron; a good man with a sad heart.

Among all his stories, Merle gave special emphasis to Faron's long-ago act of heroism, the day he pulled a pilot from a smoldering plane. He used this particular act as a kind of defining moment for Faron—a moment that reflected Faron's true character.

"No one ever acknowledged Faron's act of heroism," Merle pointed out to his listeners. "Not the firemen, or the club owner, or even the rescued pilot. The newspapers didn't even send a reporter for an interview. But Faron never sought recognition for his heroic deed, and he never complained about ruining his suit. That's testimony to Faron's character: he was a good man when it mattered most."

It was a good story to tell, and I can't help but wonder if Merle's story also suggested his quiet regret. In his last days, Faron had become that pilot, caught in his own downed aircraft, trapped in the cockpit while the engines smoldered. Only, no one came to his rescue; no one was there to drag him clear of the wreckage.

No one, not even Merle.

Elvis Presley

Would you believe me if I told you Merle was there the night Elvis Presley became famous? Consider this moment in time: an isolated phenomenon, the moment when the world discovered Elvis, and Elvis discovered his true potential. The birth of an American icon.

And Merle had a part in it.

I remember an afternoon in the late 1990s when I visited Merle at his office just off Music Row, an area southwest of downtown Nashville considered the heart of city's entertainment industry, with its countless record labels, publishing houses, recording studios, and video production houses. He ushered me inside with a proud grin. His office looked like you'd expect it to: gold records on the walls and framed photos of him laughing with famous people. Merle's office always had that Hollywood "Agent-of-the-Stars" look about it. I moved around the glass coffee table that was scattered with Country Music knickknacks and took a seat on the sofa. He circled around to the back of his desk and settled into his leather chair. We talked for a while about my life and college and girlfriends.

Then his eyes brightened and he snapped his fingers. "Hey, you'll like this," he said in his baritone voice as he opened a desk drawer and brought out an unopened CD. I went over and had a look. *The Louisiana Hayride featuring Elvis Presley's Debut.*

I raised my brow. The Hayride? I'd heard him talk about the Hayride several times before, but I'd always assumed it was an outdoor event. The picture on the CD showed me something completely different: a huge brick auditorium with cars jam-packed at the doors.

"I didn't realize it was an actual place," I said. In truth, it wasn't at all what I'd had in mind.

"It was a *show*." He flipped the CD over in my hands and pointed to the column of musical numbers. A roster of singers had performed that night. He slid his finger down to number eight. "Look at that."

Number eight read: "More and More" by Merle Kilgore.

I was awed. "You were there when Elvis became . . . *Elvis?*"

"Yeah, man," he said, eyes flashing. "I was *there!*"

For a short while in 1954, the Municipal Auditorium was just about the most important place in music history. I like to think powerful currents were at work here to make this happen. Shreveport drew many cultures and artists and it thrived with creativity and innovation. The Hayride served as the town's clanging bell, calling out for artists. Elvis Presley must have heard it. My grandfather must have heard it, too. And good thing he did. He got to see Elvis Presley change the world.

Merle was twenty years old when KNOE-TV cut funding for *The Tall Texan* show, forcing him to find a new job. Until then, his career had gained impressive momentum, with "More and More" still getting airplay, while big band Guy Lombardo cut a version and brought the song to another audience. Merle, meanwhile, had released his first record with Imperial Records and "It Can't Rain All the Time" gained a lot of attention. From his guest appearances on the Hayride, WSM Grand Ole Opry, and even the Ernest Tubb Show, Merle had become something of a star. But with his television show going away, he needed a new home, so he called Horace Logan and found work. The

Hayride wasn't a reliable source of income, however; it wouldn't pay him enough to sustain a family, and that's the kind of pay he needed because it wasn't just about him anymore. He was now married to Dot, and they were expecting.

So, he came up with a plan. Dot would stay with her mother in Monroe, and Merle would move to Shreveport to get the ball rolling. In addition to performing several times a week, including the weekends, he promised to seek out a second job. Then, after he'd saved enough, he'd bring Dot and the baby home. Dot agreed to his plan, although I'm sure she had her concerns, and Merle packed the car and headed to Shreveport.

He'd been a regular on the show for several months when a new guy arrived on Saturday, October 16, 1954.

Merle met him and his band in the front lobby of the auditorium. Right away, he understood why the Opry had turned the guy away. Elvis Presley looked helplessly out of place among other hillbilly singers with his hot-pink jacket, black slacks, and a greasy mop of hair that spilled over his brow. The guy even had a funny name. But Elvis had something going for him, too. His boyish good looks, his large eyes and scowling lips were the stuff of movie stars. He possessed an equally appealing charisma, being bashful, well-mannered, and humble.

The moment Merle introduced himself, Elvis knitted his brow and asked in a thick drawl, "Kilgore? You wrote 'More and More' for Webb Pierce, didn't you?"

Merle grinned. He already liked the guy. "You're going to do just fine," he said, leading Elvis by the shoulder to the long corridor running alongside the auditorium. When they reached the backstage area, Merle offered to show Elvis to his dressing room. But Elvis had something else in mind.

"Say, ah, Merle, I heard Tibby Edwards is playing tonight," Elvis said, referring to the Hayride regular with a Cajun accent. "You think I could meet him?"

"Well, sure," said Merle. "But don't you want to see your room?"

Elvis shook his head. "Nah, I think I'd rather meet Tibby."

"Suits me. And you're in luck. Tibby's a good friend of mine. We share the same dressing room."

Merle led him to his dressing room, giving the door a brisk knock before poking his head inside. Tibby was there, standing at his mirror in just his under-shorts and a button-up shirt.

"Tibby," said Merle, "put your pants on. Elvis wants to meet you."

Tibby frowned. "Who's Elvis?"

"You know, he's got that new song out called 'That's Alright Mama.'"

The song apparently didn't ring a bell with Tibby, but he waved them inside anyway.

Elvis hurried over to Tibby and vigorously shook his hand. "Sure is nice to meet you, Mr. Edwards," he said. "I'm a big fan of your music."

"Is that right?" Tibby said with a smug grin. "Well, I hear you're—"

But Elvis became distracted. He hurried over to the coat rack where Tibby's flashy jacket hung from a hook. "Man, that's some kind of jacket," Elvis muttered. He looked at the men behind him. "I love this artwork."

"That's a Nudie suit, Elvis," said Merle. "They're expensive, but man, they look good. You should think about getting one."

"A Nudie suit," said Elvis as he ran his fingers along the sequined wagon wheels and cactus trees embellishing the fabric. He shook his head and whispered, "Man. That's all right."

Only then did Merle notice Elvis's black-and-white shoes. A coating of white polish failed to hide the original pink underneath. *Ooh, a home job*, thought Merle. Elvis had evidently painted them himself. Perhaps he'd found pink toes a bit much. Merle didn't say anything.

In a way, those shoes represented the life of the music artist. You spent your last dime creating an image for yourself. You painted over your flaws and your insecurities. You dressed up your pains and disappointments with a showman's grin. But no matter how thick you applied that final coat, a part of you always seemed to bleed through.

Believe it or not, Elvis didn't do so hot on the Hayride stage—not at first.

Here's how it worked: the Hayride did live shows several times a week and on weekends. For each show, there was a lineup of ten or more acts, similar to the Grand Ole Opry's show setup (in fact, I'm pretty sure the Hayride got the idea from Nashville; then again, they were all borrowing from the Old Southern musical roundup in the tradition of barnyard dances). Each performer got two onstage appearances, once early in the show and then once again later.

Elvis got his first performance early in the hour. And he flopped— that's the consensus, anyway. Elvis certainly didn't get a welcoming reaction from the crowd. Maybe he was too nervous and too wound-up, and so his moves came off as aggressive and stiff. Merle didn't know what to think. Down in the audience, the girls were backing away from the stage, apparently worried that Elvis might pounce on them.

Elvis knew he'd missed the mark. He returned backstage, and Merle and Tibby Edwards sat with him in his dressing room and offered ways to overcome his stage fright. Ultimately, there was nothing to worry about, Merle assured him. "You've got another chance and you are going to kill it!" Horace Logan claims that Merle and Tibby had a lot to do with Elvis' success that night: "I don't know what they said back there," he recalls in *The Louisiana Hayride*, "but Merle gave Elvis a good pep talk."

When it was Elvis' turn later that night, Horace introduced him on stage to the crowd by saying, "I hope you're ready to witness music history."[13]

Elvis hurried out to stand nervously beside the Hayride manager, his knees noticeably trembling. Horace tried to calm him by clapping a hand on his shoulder and asking, "You ready for this, Elvis?"

But when Elvis replied, his voice quivered with uncertainty, amplified by a hundred speakers across the auditorium. "Y-yes, sir," he said. "Uh, I suppose if you are, then we are, too."

Horace walked away, leaving Elvis standing alone at the microphone stand. The band started with a driving guitar riff, a chugging bass lick. Elvis collected himself, arms hanging at his sides, fingers wiggling, feet planted in a wide stance, and then he sang "That's Alright Mama," and everything changed. He broke free from the chains of insecurity to become a whirlwind of confidence. His moves were unlike anything the Hayride had seen before, with hip thrusts and pin-wheeling arms. The guy danced with a sexualized energy, as if he'd learned all his moves in the bedroom.

The crowd unraveled. The girls screamed and tugged at their hair. The floor trembled from thousands of stomping feet.

That tremble was felt all across the world. Think of the classic black-and-white footage of the first A-bomb test fire, the shockwaves kicking up mountains of dust, the goggled spectators watching from distant trenches, their awe evolving into shock as the explosion surprised any and all expectations.

A similar thing happened that night. And Merle Kilgore was standing at ground zero.

Hang around somebody famous.

I'm sure that crossed his mind when Merle visited Elvis' dressing room one Saturday afternoon to check in with the Hayride's newest celebrity. Saturdays at the Municipal Auditorium often looked the same, buzzing with performers who whiled away the hours hanging out backstage, playing cards or writing songs or joking with friends. But not Elvis. When Merle stepped into the room, he found Elvis buzzing restlessly about, practicing his moves in the mirror.

"It's gonna be a big crowd tonight!" Merle told him, hoping to lighten the mood. It didn't help. "Everybody's talking about it."

Elvis scratched the back of his neck. "Yeah, that's great. Say . . . I'm hungry. I get hungry when I get nervous. You know where we can get a burger?"

Merle shrugged. He had nothing better to do. He agreed to drive. They hopped into Merle's Cadillac and headed toward the center of town when he noticed Elvis' darkening eyes.

"What's on your mind, Elvis?" he asked him.

"You're gonna think I'm crazy, but something's telling me to ask you this." Elvis looked at him. "What's your mama's name?"

The question came out of left field, and for the moment, Merle just looked at Elvis with his brow knitted. "It's Gladys. Why?"

Elvis' eyes widened. He shook his head and laughed to himself. "I knew it! Merle, that's *my* mama's name. That's something else, ain't it? Our mothers have the same name."[14]

There it was again—the flash of psychic intuition surrounding all great artists, at least, in Merle's world. Merle raised his brows at this. An idea struck him. "Say, Elvis, my folks live just down the street. Why don't we stop by for a minute and say hello? I'm sure my mom would love to meet you. She'll be glad to fix us lunch."

Elvis thought it over for a moment and then nodded. "Yeah, I suppose we could spare a minute. I'd like to meet your mama, 'specially since she's got the same name as mine."

They reached the house on Clemmont Street, a small shotgun cottage with wood siding and a postage stamp-sized porch. They stepped inside and went to the kitchen at the back of the house, where they found Gladys standing over the sink, scrubbing pots and pans. She turned, dried her hands with a dishrag, and offered a smile to the boys. She wore dark curls and horn-rimmed glasses.

"Oh, hello, boys," she said agreeably. She shot a glance at Elvis, quickly sizing him up.

"Mother, I want to introduce you to someone," Merle called with a wide grin. "This is Elvis Presley, the Hayride's newest star. He wanted to personally meet you."

"Real nice to meet you, Mrs. Kilgore," said Elvis, his voice pleasant and thick with a Memphis drawl. He stepped forward with a bashful smile and offered his hand.

Gladys looked down at it for a moment before shaking it. "Pleased to meet you, too, El . . . Eh . . . what did you say your name was again?"

"E-Elvis."

"Please to meet you, Elvis."

Merle bristled at the peculiar way she said his name. His mother was a sweet woman, a kind-hearted and devout Christian, but she had an edge to her, and sometimes her prim and proper ways came off as slightly . . . judgmental. Gladys was famous for speaking her mind. Should she spot something that challenged her notion of the world, she told you pointblank—most times without meaning to offend, even if it usually did. As a teenager, Merle found that bringing his girlfriends to meet Gladys Kilgore was an exercise in embarrassment.

He only hoped she'd step lightly around Elvis. But already he noted the potential volatility of this situation. He could almost hear her gears turning: *Elvis—what sort of name is that for a grown man? My goodness, do you wash your hair with Crisco oil? I see you painted your shoes; did you try to polish them first?*

"Mother, you won't believe this," said Merle, wearing a grin to hide his anxiety. "Elvis told me his mother's name is also Gladys. Can you believe that?"

Gladys' brows drew together, looking at Merle as if to say, *You poor, simple child.* "Gladys is a common name, Merle." She looked at Elvis and smiled. "But it's still a nice coincidence, isn't it?"

Merle cleared his throat, and for one uncomfortable moment, the three of them stood in quiet while Elvis scratched the back of his neck.

"Mother, Elvis and I were on our way to eat when I said we should stop here for lunch."

Elvis shifted nervous eyes from Merle to Gladys. "Ah, Mrs. Kilgore, I'd hate to put you out like that . . ."

She looked at him quietly and the lines softened around her eyes. "Well now, you wouldn't be putting me out. As it so happens, I have some porcupine meatballs. Would that be all right by you?" (For the uninitiated, this is a hearty Southern dish, meatballs packed with rice and cooked in a rich tomato sauce).

"Oh, yes, ma'am. That sounds fine. I've got a show in just a while, and I sure hate to sing on an empty stomach."

With a smile, Gladys flapped her hands at the men, shooing them toward the table. "You boys go have a seat and give me a minute."

The two shuffled over to the table. Merle felt sulky; his mother had a way of making him feel diminished somehow. They sat at the small kitchen table, and Elvis folded his hands before him and dropped his head, quiet with his thoughts. Beneath the table, his knees jittered anxiously. *Nerves*, Merle thought. He knew all about that; he was a great bundle of them right at that moment and couldn't help but think they should have just gone to Murrell's Café for lunch.

Several minutes passed and then Gladys brought them two steaming plates of meatballs and glasses of milk.

Elvis smiled and said, "Thanks a lot, Mrs. Kilgore!" before launching gleefully into his plate. He gobbled half a meatball down in one bite, then gulped down his milk in a single swallow.

Gladys hurried off to the kitchen and returned with a milk bottle. Then she stopped directly behind Elvis, frowning down at the back of his neck. She gave a reproachful shake of her head. Merle nearly choked on his meatball. Here came the offensive comment. He saw it in her eyes.

Touching Elvis on his arm, she said, "Darling, you really must do something about the back of your neck. It is *covered* with acne."

With great effort, Merle swallowed the plug in his throat and bellowed, "Mother! Don't say that about his neck!"

"Well, it's true!" she piped back innocently, as if meaning no harm in stating the truth.

Elvis scratched the back of his neck and blushed. A half-cocked smile of embarrassment touched his lips. "Yes, ma'am, I get that occasionally."

She set his glass of milk on the table and sat down in the chair next to him. "A little soap and water would clear that right up, you know. Looks like you could stand to wash your hair a little more often."

"Oh," he said, dropping his gaze to his empty plate. "Yes, ma'am."

"And maybe not put so much grease in it."

"Well, ah, you see, I have to use Pomade," his said timidly. His eyes darted to Merle before fixing on Gladys. "It's for the look, you see."

"You boys with your 'looks,'" she said superciliously. "I don't see any sense in slicking your hair like that. A man should look clean and well groomed. That look never goes out of fashion. You ought to try it sometime."

Merle covered his eyes with a hand and moaned to himself.

He and Elvis finished their lunch and hurried back to the Municipal. Merle drove the first few miles in silence, too embarrassed to think of anything to say. When they hit Main Street, he looked over and said, "Real sorry 'bout that, Elvis. My mother gets like that sometimes. She's a school teacher, you know."

A wistful smile came to the corners of Elvis's mouth and he

shrugged. "Nah, don't worry, Merle. She's just speaking her mind. Nothing my own mama hasn't said a hundred times before."

Merle nodded. He supposed that was true. Maybe all mothers were sort of like that. They saw straight through the act. They didn't fall for the glitz and glamour like everyone else. Elvis was just a man in Gladys' eyes, even if he was an idol to everyone else.

Elvis quickly outgrew the Hayride, but his contract with KWKH kept him shackled to Shreveport, at least on designated show nights. Like most performers, he leveraged his uncommitted calendar days to travel to nearby locations and perform for other audiences. On several occasions, he invited my grandfather along, an incredible opportunity even with its inevitable downsides: most times the squealing Elvis fans just wanted to see *Elvis*, meaning all other performers were subject to harassment. (In years to come, Hank Snow would be famously booed off stage; even Faron Young was subjected to such humiliation and vowed never to open for Elvis.) Luckily, Merle didn't suffer a shutdown, though I'm sure he faced some pretty tough crowds.

It was New Years of 1955 when Merle opened for Elvis at the Red River Arsenal NCO Club in Texarkana, Arkansas. Sometime after that, Elvis asked my grandfather to join him on a double date.

Now, opening for Elvis is impressive; double dating with him, doubly so. Unless, of course, you're a married man with a pregnant wife who thinks you're busy preparing a home for your family when, in reality, you're running around with other women. Then it's . . . well . . . not nearly as impressive. But I'm not here to judge my grandfather. Instead, I'll offer this: for a twenty-year-old with irreconcilable aspirations of becoming famous, a double-date with the most famous guy in town must have presented an incredible temptation.

Nonetheless, Merle never included a moral struggle when telling his Elvis stories, and so I won't propose one here.

"Beautician students," Elvis told him, "two of 'em—so you won't have to worry about gettin' an ugly one. I just need you to keep the friend busy."

Elvis drove them to a nearby campus, evidently a clandestine operation, considering how Elvis killed the headlights and slowed the car to a crawl. They parked in front of a dormitory. Moments later, two giggling girls hurried from the shadows and hopped into the car. Elvis squealed tires as they fled the scene.

"What do you girls wanna do?" asked Elvis, his girl tucked in close, one arm draping her shoulders. He looked in the rearview mirror, meeting Merle's eyes in the backseat. "Y'all want a bite to eat?"

Elvis' proposal was met with unenthused mumbles. When he didn't get an answer, he made the decision himself, swinging into the first roadside diner he could find. He parked the car, said, "Be right back," and then hurried into the restaurant. He returned a few minutes later with a large sack of food.

"I got some burgers for everyone," he said magnanimously.

The girls looked less than grateful. The redhead in the front seat scowled at her friend in the backseat. Elvis noticed and looked offended.

"What's the matter?" he said. "You don't want burgers? They're real good. I've eaten here before."

The girls weren't impressed. They shrugged and shook their heads.

Elvis shrugged. "Fine. Suit yourself." He looked irritably at Merle. "What about you? You not hungry either?"

It would have been foolish to protest. Merle raised his brow. "Are you kidding me? 'Course, I'm hungry. I'm starved!"

Elvis passed him a burger and Merle gobbled it down. It really was a tasty burger. "Oh man, that's good!" he said, wiping the grease from his chin.

Satisfied, Elvis nodded. "Told you so." He dug into the bag and mumbled, as if to himself, "What makes 'em so good is the onions. I told 'em to double up."

Merle swallowed slowly. *Double onions?* he thought. *On a first date? Are you kidding me?*

They caught a movie and then drove back to the university campus. Elvis parked on the corner just past a streetlamp. Everyone got out, and Elvis motioned Merle over toward the back of the car where they could talk privately.

"Listen, Merle," Elvis said under his breath. "Here's the situation. See, the girls share a single room, so me and my girl will go up first. Meanwhile, you and your girl can get acquainted in the backseat. When we're finished, we'll come down, and you two can go up."

Merle glanced over at the two girls giggling into each other's ears, and then shrugged. "Fine by me."

Elvis went and fetched his date and took her by the hand and dashed toward the dorms. Left alone, Merle smiled at his date, and then the two hopped into the backseat of Elvis' car. When she wasn't looking, he breathed into his cupped hand and checked his breath. *Ooh*, he thought again. *Double onions. Are you kidding me?*

But there was nothing to do about it. Besides, his date didn't seem to mind. She jumped him the moment he shut the door. The two became a tangle of arms as the windows steamed over. This went on for a while, until their lips were raw and their clothes were crumpled.

Then someone knocked on the car. Shocked, Merle snapped his head around to find Elvis' scowling face in the rear window. He looked disheveled and unhappy, with lipstick smeared across one cheek, his hair a mess.

Merle opened the door and poked his head out. "Elvis, what's going on?"

"You better send your girl on up," Elvis said with a scowl. "We're leaving."

Flustered and confused, Merle asked his date to leave. She opened her door and hopped out, then smoothed out the wrinkles in her skirt before hurrying across the dark lawn. She never even told Merle goodbye.

"Why did I just do that?" asked Merle, fixing his jacket.

"You might as well get in the front seat." Elvis stepped around to the driver's side and got in. "Your friend ain't coming back."

Elvis gassed the car, and the tires shrieked as they headed back to town. Merle didn't bother pressing Elvis for answers; the singer looked flustered, with his shoulders bunched, his hands white-knuckling the steering wheel, and his head tipped forward.

It wasn't long before Elvis started talking.

"It was the strangest thing," he muttered. "We got into bed and started kissing, when all of the sudden, she just stopped."

"Stopped? What d'ya mean?"

Elvis glanced over at Merle, showing a worrisome expression. He seemed truly bothered about this. "She gave me this real serious look and said, 'Sorry, Elvis, I just don't feel it. This ain't gonna work out. Maybe you and your friend better leave.'"

"She said *that?*" Merle frowned, trying to make sense of it. He'd always assumed Elvis had a kind of mesmeric power over women. They nearly always threw themselves at him. That a girl would kick Elvis out of bed seemed unimaginable.

They drove into town and found a small motel with a neon vacancy light in the window. They checked in and got a room that probably smelled like stale cigarette smoke with the typical layout, complete with a sofa and a little table. And a single bed.

I doubt the two even shared an uncomfortable look at the thought of rooming together. After all, this was 1954, and for Hayride performers, sharing rooms and even beds was just the norm; they did anything to save a buck. Merle climbed into the bed and turned off the lamp. But Elvis wasn't tired. He kept pacing the room, even when Merle covered his head with a pillow. All he wanted was sleep. But Elvis paced. And the floor was creaky.

Merle finally had to say something. "Say, Elvis," he said, propping himself up on his elbows. He tried to be pleasant, but it sounded forced. "You going to sleep, or what, man?"

Elvis, standing in a square of moonlight, spun around, his face a grimace. "I just don't understand it, Merle. I mean, I been playing it over and over in my mind. I can't figure out why she didn't want me."

Merle sighed. *Elvis is taking this too seriously.* So a girl got scared at the last moment and ran him off—so what? That kind of thing happened all the time. But maybe it *didn't* happen to Elvis. Maybe this sort of rejection was new to him. Who knew the sort of impact it might have on his mind? *Hell, it could unravel the guy, strip him of his confidence.* What if a thing like this could ruin the man's career?

"Maybe I'm losing my touch," said Elvis. Now he was tugging at his hair. "Was it me? You think she just didn't like me?"

Merle slid his feet over the side of the bed and sat up. "Elvis, I know exactly what happened."

Elvis turned a hopeful gaze toward him.

"The girls didn't eat any burgers," Merle recalled. "Remember? They didn't eat anything."

Elvis shrugged. "Yeah, so?"

"Well, my burger had a double order of onions. What about yours?"

"Sure it did. I ordered them all that way."

"And *there's* your answer! Onions, man! She couldn't take the onions on your breath. She smelled onions and it grossed her out."

Elvis cupped a hand over his mouth, huffed, and then sniffed the air. "You really think so, Merle?"

"Ah, man, I know so." Merle failed to mention that his story had a glaring hole in it; he'd eaten the same burgers, after all, and his date never mentioned his breath, but he kept that to himself. "Girls hate onion breath. It drives 'em away every time."

"No kiddin'?" Elvis' face relaxed some. The corners of his mouth curled in a little smile. "Yeah, I think you're right, Merle!"

"Good. Now come on into bed, Elvis. I'm beat."

The Hayride management knew they couldn't keep Elvis. In just a short time, he'd gotten way too big for their small venue. For that reason, Horace and the other executives gathered together and made the decision to let him break his contract. This was April 6, 1955. It was probably the right thing to do since Elvis belonged to the world. But the Hayride wanted one last favor—a promise from Elvis that he'd return for a final show. To Elvis' immense credit, he did just that. He returned to Shreveport to headline the biggest show Shreveport would ever see.

My grandmother remembers Elvis' return on December 15, 1956. She still has the ticket from that night; it remains intact. According to her, by the time Elvis came back, she and Merle were once again living together, along with their newborn baby, Pamela. They found a babysitter for the night and then rushed off together to the fairgrounds, where Elvis was performing at the Hirsch Youth Center. When they arrived, they fought their way to the back entrance where smaller crowds had gathered, obviously motivated by the same bright idea.

But no one was getting inside. A thick-armed doorman made sure of this. He was busy turning someone away when Merle and Dot approached.

"I'm here to see Elvis," Merle told him with his showman's grin.

With his arms crossed over his broad chest, the doorman only shook his head and said, "Nobody's getting inside. That's my orders."

"Tell him Merle Kilgore's here," Merle announced confidently.

The doorman didn't budge. "Sorry. But like I said—"

Just then, Elvis's head peeked around the doorframe, his familiar eyes gleaming, and that's all my grandmother saw of him.

"Hey, Merle's all right," Elvis told the guard. "Let him on back."

Elvis disappeared from the door, and Merle beamed a smile as he pulled Dot toward the backstage door. But they went only a few feet when he stopped abruptly and swung around to face her. "Ah . . . Dot . . . I'll see you after the show."

He planted a kiss on her forehead, and before my grandmother could protest, he hurried inside.

I can see her clearly across the decades that night, wearing a nice evening gown, her hair in curls, lips painted bright red, and standing all alone amidst a crowd of strangers, abandoned. It's a sad image, a forlorn foreshadowing of things to come, and I'm sure Webb Pierce's words echoed in her ear: *"You can't have a family and a music career, Merle. It's one or the other. You have to decide."*

Johnny Horton

There's a guitar stored deep in the archives of the Country Music Hall of Fame Museum in Nashville, a loan from Merle's private collection. Long ago, Merle got the guitar from Country Music legend Johnny Horton, the Singing Fisherman, who'd wanted to say farewell after having a premonition of his own death.

"Merle, I'm going to die, and I want you to have this."

My aunt, Kim Kilgore—Merle and Dot's youngest of three children—once told me a story in 2008 about that guitar, how Merle kept it hanging on the wall of their home in Madison, Tennessee. She told me of how she and her dad once heard the guitar strum itself, just a few clumsy chords, but enough to scare them both.

It's possible they imagined the whole thing. But then, if you knew Johnny Horton, you might think differently. The search for the afterlife was an obsession for him and, ironically, he got his answer all too soon when a drunk driver ended his life. The world was a strange place from Horton's perspective, and strange phenomena surrounded him, mostly because he invited the unknown into his life. For that reason, his guitar came to represent for Merle an affirmation of a world beyond our own. In that light, it seems at least appropriate that the instrument should play itself.

I can't help but wonder if anyone working at that museum ever hears noises from the archive vaults—noises like clumsy chords played on a guitar. Then again, I'm sure there are plenty ghosts haunting those archives.

In 1955, at an Elvis Presley concert held at a high school gymnasium in Bono, Arkansas, the floor collapsed beneath the weight of several thousand roaring fans. A similar incident occurred in Shreveport, only this time, the industry itself collapsed, and many of its struggling artists fell through the shattered floorboards, especially the Hayride singers standing at the epicenter. After Elvis left in pursuit of greater fame, he inadvertently took the audience with him. No one seemed to care about Country Music in his absence.

Then came the final hammer-blow: In January of 1956, Elvis recorded "Heartbreak Hotel" at RCA Studio B in Nashville, and the song nearly moved the entire Country Music industry off its moorings.

Around the time Elvis left the Hayride, Merle and Dot moved into their new Bossier City home, a small house with a single-car garage. Of course, the house also meant a hefty mortgage, so Merle picked up a day job in the shoe department of the local Sears and Roebuck in addition to his evenings at the Hayride. While it put Merle in a financial bind, purchasing that home turned out to be advantageous to his career, leading to a friendship that would forever change the course of his life.

It all started when he spotted an unlikely neighbor walking past his home.

Her name was Billie Jean Jones, the surviving widow of Hank Sr., and an irresistible knockout. She'd already earned a notorious reputation on the Country Music scene. Before Hank, she'd dated Faron Young. But she ended that relationship on the night when she and Faron ran into Hank backstage at the Opry. It was love at first sight for Hank; that night, he cornered Faron, showed him a gun, and according to Robyn Young in a 2014 interview, said, "Hoss, she's coming home with me."

Billie Jean cut a striking figure, and Merle, standing beside his Cadillac, noticed her right away. He called out to her, and she laughed when she recognized him (long ago, before she'd married Hank Williams, Sr., or dated Faron Young, she'd been Merle's date at Senior Day at Byrd High School). They struck up a friendly conversation at the foot of the driveway. Billie Jean quickly filled his head with gossip, from her ongoing courtroom battles with Audrey Williams over Hank's estate and her brief singing career under the moniker of the *Widow of Hank Williams* to her recent marriage to Johnny Horton. She'd married him only a year after she'd buried Hank.

That Johnny Horton lived just down the street intrigued Merle. He'd often crossed paths with the Hayride performer, but they rarely got beyond a friendly nod or handshake. Still, Merle knew plenty about him. A Hayride favorite and a regular since 1952, Johnny Horton was tall and friendly, with smiling eyes and a boyish grin. He wore cowboy hats and Western shirts with sequined fish and Indians sewed onto the breast pockets and sleeves. The guy was genuine, and he set the moral standard for the other entertainers; unlike most of the Hayride acts, Horton promoted himself as a teetotaler and an unabashed Christian. He was also an amazing fisher. His work with Bacon & Edwards, a local tackle company, and his endless hours spent at the lake earned him the name the Singing Fisherman. Most importantly, Horton had real talent, even if he hadn't yet reached his full potential, and Merle was eager to meet him.

Billie Jean and Merle ended their conversation with plans of getting together, and just a few nights later, they made good on their promise. They all got together at the Horton household, and Merle and Johnny Horton liked each other right away. The wives—Dot and Billie Jean—also struck a quick friendship. It wasn't long before the four of them were best of friends.

In this context of the post-Elvis era—a time when no one seemed interested in anything but Rockabilly, and Country Music faced an identity crisis—friends were an invaluable commodity. Everyone at the Hayride was broke; lately, the Municipal Auditorium looked like a ghost town on weekends, and poor ticket sales meant there wasn't much wealth to spread around. The performers who stuck around took a real beating.

But Horton faced the hardships with a boyish playfulness. Besides, money didn't matter much out on the water. That's where Johnny Horton liked to be, fishing on his johnboat. He soon dragged Merle out with him, and the two spent endless afternoons on Caddo or Cross Lake. Horton's skill as a fisherman went unmatched. He could cast a line with impressive accuracy, aiming his lure like a bullet. He was so good that he even made it part of his act. He'd take his fishing rod onstage with him and position himself at one end. An empty coffee can was placed at the other end maybe thirty feet away. Then he'd snap the rod back and forth, sending the lure whispering across the stage in a long, quiet arc until it plunked into the can. The crowd loved it, and Horton never missed.

They didn't call him the Singing Fisherman for nothing.

So Merle and Horton made fishing at the Springhill Paper Company millpond a regular activity. I can only imagine how odd of a pair the two made, with Horton dressed in short sleeves and cargo shorts and Merle dressed in slacks and sports jackets; Horton relaxed and in his element, and Merle complaining about the heat. Still, it must have been hugely entertaining to watch Horton fish. While Merle snagged more tree limbs than bass, Horton caught enough to fill barrels at a time. The fish just sort of exploded out of the water and dropped into his bucket.

He got a kick out of Merle's endless amazement. In turn, Horton pretended to know esoteric fishing secrets. Sometimes he'd stick a finger in the pond and then stick it in his mouth, tasting the water with dark, considering eyes. Then he'd select a lure from his tackle box with a confident, "Yup, this here will do the trick," as if he could tell what lure to use just by the flavor of the water. It was no wonder that fishermen dropped out of local fishing tournaments when they heard Horton was competing.

Merle and Horton had just put the boat in the water at Glenita Stewart's pond in Bradley, Arkansas, when Horton first mentioned his interest in the occult.

"Merle, do you believe in the afterlife?" he asked.

The question caught Merle temporarily off guard. "Well, sure," he said after a long moment. "You mean, like, Heaven and Hell?"

Horton shrugged. "Not exactly. I mean the spirit realm. You believe we go somewhere after we die?"

"I suppose anything's possible," Merle said with a shrug.

"I believe it, Merle," Horton went on. "I had a vision once."

"Is that right?"

"It happened after I rolled my Oldsmobile. Almost killed me. And right then, through the cracked windshield, I saw a bright figure." He fixed Merle with a knowing gaze. "It was Jesus. I saw him just as clear as I see you now." He waited a moment for dramatic effect. Then he said, "I want to introduce you to someone. He's a spirit medium."

"A medium? Well, what's a medium?"

Horton leaned forward. "Someone who contacts spirits."

"You mean talks to the dead?"

"You got it, Chief."

Merle shook his head, miffed at the idea. "Aw, man, come on. That stuff's not real."

"I'm telling you, Merle. It's real."

The conversation didn't stop there. During the drive back to Bossier City, Horton spoke at length about the paranormal—ESP, divination, spirits, and so on—but Merle didn't buy everything he was hearing.

"The guy's name is J. Bernard Ricks," said Horton as he parked the car in Merle's driveway. "He's the spirit medium I told you about. I'll take you to meet him tomorrow. What d'ya say?"

Anything for a friend.

The next day Merle rode along with Horton to meet the psychic, bracing himself for the weirdest possible experience. But the truth proved just the opposite. Bernard Ricks lived in a modest-sized home with a manicured front lawn and shutters on the windows. The man who greeted them at the door looked surprisingly average—a middle-aged man in slacks and a button-down shirt, slightly heavy around the midsection. Ricks ushered them inside. The sitting room was bright and neat, with photos of family on the walls and fresh-cut flowers in a vase. Nothing about Ricks gave the appearance that he cavorted with the spirits of the dead.

After introductions, Ricks settled into a loveseat, and with his hands on the armrests and his chin resting on his chest, he went into a trance. He spoke in a quiet voice. "Oh, Merle. Tomorrow a phone call from your mother. Your aunt who lives in Oklahoma will pass away at approximately one o'clock. She's an elderly woman, and she will have a peaceful passing."

Merle played along, not wanting to hurt anyone's feelings. "Ooh. Okay," he said.

But the conversation didn't end there. Bernard started singing a church hymn, and it made an eerie and almost embarrassing impression on Merle. When the singing psychic finished, Merle checked his watch and said, "Oh! Look at the time. Johnny, we best get on back. You know how Dot hates it when I'm late."

On the drive back, Horton seemed eager to hear Merle's reaction. "Well, Chief?" he said. "What'd I tell you? That guy's something, ain't he?"

Merle shrugged. "I don't know. He seems a little strange, don't you think? I wouldn't waste a whole lot of time with that guy."

Once home, Merle didn't give Bernard Ricks another thought. But the following morning he received a call at the radio station that he managed. It was his mother. She called to tell him that a distant aunt had died. Immediately after the call, he dialed Horton's number, eager to tell him the news.

Johnny Horton swept Merle up into his fascination with the occult, and in return, Merle fed Horton's obsession. When they weren't studying at the feet of Bernard Ricks "the Singing Spiritualist," they were practicing on their own.

Inspired, Horton had a great idea. He transformed one of his home bedrooms into a Spook Room—a room designed as a kind of spiritual radio station. They hung black velvet sheets on the walls, emptied it of all furniture except a round table with a crystal ball centerpiece and a black table skirt, and added a few chairs and lots of candles. This was a room designed with a purpose in mind: to create a more conducive atmosphere for séances by blocking outside psychical interference.

They spent a lot of time in that Spook Room, seeking affirmation of an afterlife, and they often invited friends from the Hayride to join in. It didn't take long before everyone at the Hayride knew about their grim hobby. All around town, Horton and Merle's paranormal hobby became the hot topic. Fueling the fire, they got a whole train of cars to follow them to Crocket, Arkansas, where they promised to expose an actual ghost. In a 2008 interview, Billie Jean recalled the story, how all those cars gathered in a clearing near the railroad tracks long after the sun went down. Standing before a crowd of rhinestone-glittering cowboys, Horton told the tragic story of a porter who died there long ago when a train struck him. Then Merle and Horton left the group and hurried out to the moonlit tracks.

To everyone's amazement, a glowing green orb that bobbed like a paper bag caught in the wind confronted the two men. About twelve others saw it, although no one knew *what* they saw. When the light vanished, the group cheered loudly, and Horton and Merle hurried back to join them.

But not everyone cheered. Dot and Billie Jean were terrified, and the moment Horton and Merle returned to the car, Billie Jean demanded that they take her home before everyone saw that she'd wet her pants.

Investigating the paranormal was obviously not for everyone. But it certainly piqued a lot of interest, including a Hayride singer named J.R. Cash, who invited himself over to participate with Horton's crazy pastime.

Johnny Cash had just recently arrived at the Hayride, but he'd already shaken up the place. Before Shreveport, he'd lived in Memphis, working as an appliance salesman and writing songs in his free time. Sam Phillips at Sun Records had taken interest in him, recorded some of his songs, and scored big with the locals with "Cry! Cry! Cry!" and "Hey Porter." Sam recognized Cash's potential, but he wanted the artist to smooth out the edges, find his style, and build a stage presence. For that reason, Sam sent him away to Shreveport.

Cash came out swinging for his Hayride debut on December 10, 1955. The performance left the crowd in a rabid state, and Horace Logan, the Hayride's manager, signed him on with a contract that very night.

Since then, all eyes were on Cash. The town knew the status quo: The Hayride needed new artists with mainstream appeal to save the show or else the ship would sink beneath the tsunami that was rock 'n' roll. Fortunately, Cash had a lot going for him, with a gritty, haunted style, a baritone voice, and songs that spoke to the working class and the hardships of a post-American dream. He had rhythm, too; his band, the Tennessee Two, carried him along on a distinct *boom-chicka-boom* that offered something new and fresh to the music.

He had plenty of fans. And as it turned out, Cash was a big fan of Johnny Horton.

For years, Cash had followed the Singing Fisherman's career, and he'd been eager to meet him from the moment of his arrival. Cash and Horton eventually got together, and the two had plenty in common. Fishing was among their top priorities. They also shared an interest in the paranormal. Once Cash learned about Horton's Spook Room, he immediately wanted to see it.

According to Ralph Emery in an interview with me in 2008, the day Cash came to visit, Horton also invited Merle, hoping to keep things interesting. The men sat at the table and played around with tarot cards and crystal ball readings. Cash watched the two men with quiet eyes, apparently unimpressed.

"We should try hypnosis," Merle suggested to Cash. "Johnny and I—we've been studying up on it. I can try and put you under, if you want."

To his surprise, Cash shrugged and said, "Sure, why not?"

They turned off the lights and lit a few candles, and Cash relaxed in a chair, while Merle coaxed him to "Sleep . . . sleep . . . sleep . . ." Then an amazing thing happened. Cash's body went suddenly limp, and in a somber voice, he intoned, "I'm in the land of the pharaohs. I see the desert. People in robes and sandals. I think I must have lived here a long time ago."

Merle gaped and he turned his gaze to Horton, conveying incredulity with his eyes. *Can you believe this? Do you hear what he's saying? By God, we've tapped the supernatural! We've uncovered evidence of a past life!*

But then Cash cracked up. His sudden belt of laughter chased away any possibility of ghosts. Looking at each other, Merle and Horton quietly stewed with their arms crossed, knowing they'd been duped. But they didn't stew for long. In moments, Merle and Horton's scowls gave way to grins. They couldn't stop themselves. They rolled their eyes and shook their heads. But eventually they gave in to Cash's contagious laughter, and soon all of them were sharing a good laugh at the expense of a few bruised egos.

As 1956 rolled out, many Hayride singers scattered. Those left behind sang to an empty auditorium. The ones who didn't leave town faced hard financial times. Country Music just wasn't a lucrative business anymore, and while the Hayride grew anemic, Merle and Horton clung to it like fleas on a dying dog.

But an empty bank account never kept Horton from living the high life. During a 2008 interview, Dot recalled how the Hortons bought everything on credit, from Billie Jean's fur coats to his new cars that he never expected to keep. Dodging bill collectors was just sort of the norm for the Hortons. Once, my grandmother dropped in to visit Billie Jean, only to find her running through the house and stashing her valuables—including packets of frozen meat from the freezer—because she'd gotten a call that bill collectors were coming. Billie Jean even wrapped herself in two fur coats before jumping into bed and hiding beneath the covers.

"Let the sons of bitches in, Dot!" she called out to my grandmother standing outside in the hallway. "They can take what they can find, if they can find anything worth taking!"

Hard times only brought out Johnny Horton's generous nature. He shared whatever he had, even when it didn't technically belong to him. Take, for example, the time he lined up all new tires for Merle's Cadillac.

"New tires?" Merle exclaimed, baffled. "You want me to buy new tires? You kiddin' me? I can't afford that."

"I didn't ask if you could afford 'em," Horton told him. "Any day now, the repo man's coming for my Cadillac, and I figure he can have the car, but I'm keepin' the tires, and I want you to have 'em."

They took both cars to a local mechanic and paid for a swap. According to Billie Jean, the shiny new Cadillac looked awfully suspicious with threadbare tires. The repo man noticed right away when he finally showed up one afternoon. Nudging a tire with the toe of his shoe, he said to Horton, "Man, you sure must've driven this thing to hell and back. Those tires are practically bald!"

Horton only scratched his chin thoughtfully and replied, "You might want to check that front end. Looks like it's wearing down the tires to the nubs."

These were hard times for everybody, but stardom did happen. It happened to Johnny Horton, and it happened with the release of "The Battle of New Orleans." The song was a mega-success, and Horton became a sudden *national* success. He had money; he had fame. The only thing he didn't have in abundance was *time*.

From the time Tillman Franks became Horton's manager, the two worked tirelessly to shape Horton's image and get him noticed. Franks, a longtime resident of the Hayride show—either behind the stage or in front of it—knew what audiences wanted; he knew the importance of a unique style. He also had an ear for popular music. He was a musician and a songwriter, and he brought some solid ideas to Horton. Together, they refined Horton's rockabilly image, and more importantly, they wrote great songs.

They went to Nashville in 1956 and used Music Row's Studio B to record "Honky Tonk Man." The song was an instant hit and earned Horton a lot of attention. He had a rockabilly style that kids liked. Johnny Horton was on his way to becoming a star.

The royalty checks started coming.

Horton was excited and he wanted to share his success with Merle, so he invited him to a small restaurant in Shreveport, a place they often avoided because of its pricey menu. When Merle arrived, he found Horton already sitting at a table, dressed like a celebrity in his dapper new sports jacket and white Panama hat.

"Man, you are all over the radio!" Merle said, beaming as he seated himself. "You finally made it!"

Horton gave a bewildered shake of his head. "I still can't get over it. I'm really fortunate right now, and I want to share my good fortune with you, Merle. So listen. I want you to get anything you want today. It's on me. The sky's the limit!"

"I accept!"

Merle and Horton both ordered lavish plates. They'd been broke for so long that eating this good was still new to them. When the food came, they ate like kings, and in the satiated aftermath, the waitress brought the tab. As promised, Horton plucked it from the waitress's fingers, and then he said to Merle, "Like I said, this one's on me."

Horton took off his Panama hat and began searching the hatband with his fingers. But his expression darkened when he found a folded piece of paper tucked behind the ribbon.

Merle asked, "What's wrong, Johnny?"

Horton sighed and tossed the hat onto the table. "I keep my money in my hatband, and now it's gone."

"Well, what happened to it?"

Looking disgusted, Horton slid the note over to Merle. It read: "I.O.U. $100. B.J."

"Billie Jean?" Merle asked.

"Billie Jean," Horton answered, saying her name as if it somehow summed up all the problems of the world.

Merle paid the bill, just over sixteen dollars, a substantial amount in 1956.

Horton was red-faced with embarrassment. "You'll get your money back, Chief," he declared. "I promise."

Later that night, Horton made good on his promise. But when someone knocked on Merle's door, he found Billie Jean standing there and not Horton. Merle opened his mouth, but didn't get a word out before she stuck a twenty-dollar bill in his hand.

"Here's your money, Merle," she said, then turned around and marched away without even a goodbye.

By 1958, Merle and Horton had witnessed enough paranormal phenomena to convince them of an afterlife. But so far, they'd only toyed with the Great Unknown. The first solid confirmation arrived when Bernard Ricks called to tell Merle his baby was dying.

It was a quiet night at home on Rodney Street. Merle—now twenty-four and settled into his role as family man in addition to radio manager for KZEA Radio—agreed to watch the kids and let Dot get away to spend the evening with Billie Jean. But Merle didn't endure his babysitting detail all by himself. He'd invited over friend and fellow deejay Ed Hamilton to drink a few beers and watch television with him.

The kids were all asleep in their rooms when the phone rang.

Merle answered with a polite, "Hello?"

A wheezing, breathless voice responded. "Merle? Don't hang up."

The man sounded like he'd just finished running a marathon. Merle snapped off the television and sat up in his chair. "Bernard? Is that you? What's wrong?"

"I'm having trouble breathing," Ricks gasped. "You need to check on the children. I think something's wrong."

"The kids? What're you talking about? They're fine. I just put 'em to bed a little while ago."

A ragged cough came over the line. "Merle, please listen to me. Go and check on the children. Do it now. Call me back once you've had a look."

Ricks hung up, and Merle just looked at the phone while Ed prodded him. Merle just shook his head and picked himself up. "I gotta check the kids. Be right back."

He went to the rooms, starting with Pamela and Steve, finding them both asleep, and then finally to the baby's room, where he expected to find Kimberly in the bassinet. Only now, it was empty. He frowned at this. Had Dot taken the baby with her? Yes, he supposed so.

Just as he made his way back to the living room, the phone rang. Merle snatched it up and listened.

"Merle?" It was Ricks again, still short of breath. "Did you check the children's rooms?"

"Yeah. Everything's fine."

"Oh." Ricks sounded baffled, maybe even a little uncertain. "I'm .. . I'm glad to hear that. I had a bad feeling . . ."

"Well, thanks for checking up on us," Merle told him. "We sure appreciate it. I'll let you know if anything changes."

"Yes. Of course."

After hanging up, Merle flipped the television back on and turned his attention to the program, but his thoughts wandered, returning again and again to Kimberly's empty bassinet.

Dot had said nothing about taking Kimberly with her.

The telephone suddenly rang. Merle picked it up. "Hello?"

"Merle, it's me again." Ricks again. This time he sounded as if someone had him in a stranglehold. "Check the baby. *Please!*"

"Dot's got Kimberly. They're over at Johnny's place. Everything's fine."

"Then call Dot this instant—tell her to check on the baby."

Now rattled, Merle hung up and phoned the Horton's. Billie Jean answered, and he insisted she pass the phone over to Dot.

"What is it, Merle?" said Dot moments later.

"Bernard Ricks called," Merle said, his voice edged with frustration, "and he wants you to check on Kimberly."

"Check on *Kimberly*? What are you talking about, Merle? Kimberly's with *you*!"

Merle ran back to the baby's room and turned on the light. This time he saw that the bassinet's mattress was canted, resting on something big underneath. He threw the mattress aside to find the baby, lying on her back, her face a bruised color.

He scooped her up in a panic, finding her fingers and toes cold to the touch and turning blue. Kimberly had stopped breathing.

Leaving Ed to watch the other two children, Merle rushed outside to the car, only to see Dot running up the street from Horton's house. They met on the lawn and Merle handed Kimberly to her and told her to get into the car.

The Bossier City emergency clinic was just down the road. Thanks to an advance call from Ed, the medical staff was waiting for them when they arrived. Several ER workers took Kimberly and rushed inside with Merle and Dot in tow. They all hurried into one of the medical rooms, where a nurse placed the baby on a metal table. One of the doctors began administering CPR, and Dot watched in horror as the baby's lifeless body swelled like a tiny purple balloon with each breath.

Then came a sudden cry from Kimberly. The baby was breathing again. Dot and Merle wrapped their arms around each other and cried.

Later that night at home, Merle called Bernard Ricks, and said, "You were right, Mr. Ricks. You saved Kimberly's life."

"It was the spirits, Merle," Ricks responded quietly. "The spirits saved your child. Not me."

The temptation to drink had always been there, partly because Merle had been singing in barrooms from an early age, and it seemed like all the Hayride singers drank to help loosen their nerves. But until now, Horton had steered him clear of a rowdy lifestyle, using his own father as a hard example.

"Chief, my daddy was a drunk," he'd tell Merle. "Alcohol robbed me and my family of a happy home. That's why I never touch the stuff, and if you ever get to Nashville, *please* stay away from pills and whiskey. Don't do like everybody else."

But the moment Horton's career took off, he and Billie Jean moved away, purchasing a big home on the Bayou, leaving Merle to fend for himself. It didn't take long before Merle succumbed to a different lifestyle, with friends who didn't mind throwing back a few drinks before a show.

Then tragedy struck for the Kilgores. Dot gave birth to their fourth child, a baby boy, but he died only hours after labor. They named him Johnny Gale Kilgore—a name to celebrate their friendship with Johnny Gale Horton—and then Dot and Merle buried their child on August 21, 1959. I don't know if this directly influenced Merle's drinking habits, but he started drinking heavily, and most weekends ended in a booze-induced whirlwind.

But he balanced his work and his social life. By 1959, Merle had his fingerprints on every aspect of the local music business. He'd earned considerable notoriety as a disc jockey, having worked at nearly every station in town, including KBSF, KCIJ, Kent Radio, and KZEA. Meanwhile, his contract with Starday Records (the label behind George Jones, Dottie West, and Willie Nelson) kept him busy in the studio, recording minor hits like "Dear Mama," "Love has Made You Beautiful," and "42 in Chicago." He even sang a few of these songs on the Grand Ole Opry.

With all the excitement of his success—from the parties to the radio and television broadcasts—Merle sprung the very trap that Horton had warned him about: the vices of drugs and alcohol.

One late spring evening, after a night of drinking with friends from the Hayride, Merle came home at some ungodly hour, and to avoid waking Dot and the kids, he stumbled into the den to crash on the sofa. Merle later told Dot that he fell into a dream, finding himself staggering through a forested landscape with sullen trees shrouded in fog. He heard someone singing and followed the sound to find a lone soldier dressed in a Confederate uniform, a kepi hat on his head, and a long rifle strapped over his shoulder. But he also had a snare drum, and he played it and sang a song as his grinning and somehow familiar eyes fixed on Merle.

Merle woke with a start the next morning. Dot—who relayed this story to me in 2008—stood over him, arms crossed, unhappy with having found him crashed out on the sofa in the den, dressed in his underclothes. There was a Wollensak reel-to-reel tape recorder parked on the coffee table, still running and making a *click-click-click* sound. Merle had obviously left it running through the night; one of its wheels—the take-up reel—was loaded with tape and spinning slowly.

Click! Click! Click!

"Merle, get up and put some clothes on before the kids see you," Dot told him. "And you left your machine on."

Merle, still swooning from his late-night drinking binge, gazed dumbly at the recorder, trying to remember what he'd worked on. After Dot went away, he rearranged the reels, fed the tapehead, let the machine rewind for a moment, and then punched the play button.

A song rang from the speakers. It was Merle's voice; he'd obviously written it in the middle of the night. But there was a big hole in his memory. He didn't remember *anything* except drinking with the boys. Everything after that was a blur. Merle hit stop, let the machine rewind to the beginning, pushed play again. It was his voice all right, but he didn't know the song. It had a plunky guitar intro and a catchy refrain: *You fought all the way, Johnny Reb, Johnny Reb. Oh, yeah, you fought all the way, Johnny Reb.*

Simple. Haunting. Meaningful. It was good—up there with his best—and he couldn't even remember writing it. Stranger yet—the song was complete. It had an easy composition; a few verses, a chorus. No way could he have written that in his sleep. Someone or something must have helped him.

Merle called Horton, told him about the dream and the Confederate soldier, and then told him about the song. "It's unbelievable," Merle told him. "You've got to hear it. Johnny, I think the spirits wrote the song *through* me."

I'm sure the idea of a Country song written—at least in part—by a ghost snared Horton's immediate interest. He rushed over as soon as he could, and before long, the two were standing over the Wollensak, listening with wide-eyed amazement and shaking their heads in disbelief. "It's a heck of a song, Chief," Horton told him. Then he added, "It just puts chills on me."

Horton asked to borrow the tape. He had a recording session in Nashville over the next few days, and he promised to let a few artists there hear it, maybe strike up some interest. Merle was completely behind the idea. But before that, he wanted to make a change before anyone heard it. He'd noted an inaccuracy in the lyrics: "You marched into battle with the Grey and the Red." The colors were wrong. Confederates wore gray and *gold*.

Horton listened, then shook his head gravely. "Chief, you gotta keep it like it is. Trust me on this. It's perfect. Don't change a thing."

Off to Nashville Johnny Horton went with Merle's song in hand.

Days later Merle got a call from Horton. He'd been in Nashville for nearly a week by this point. Horton was obviously excited about something.

"Chief, it's me! I just got done recording at Bradley's Barn," he said over the phone. "And I want you to hear something."

Merle listened. He heard the plunkety-plunk-plunk of a banjo, supported by a rolling snare drumbeat. Then Johnny Horton's singing voice came clearly across the line: *You fought all the way Johnny Reb, Johnny Reb. Oh, yeah, you fought all the way, Johnny Reb.*

It was an incredible surprise—Johnny Horton had recorded the song, word for word. "Johnny Reb" appeared on the album "Johnny Horton Makes History" (1960) and went on to become a major hit.

Merle never solved the mystery of his song, but in later years, he made an interesting discovery. His great-great grandfather, Solomon Willis Kilgore, had served in the Confederate States Army, and even more curious, he'd played the snare drum, an important duty as the drummer signaled battle orders and kept the rhythm of the march. The coincidence was impossible to ignore, given Merle's interest in the occult, and he reached an inevitable conclusion: Great-great Grandpa Solomon Kilgore had ghostwritten "Johnny Reb."

As for the inaccuracies with the uniform's color, Horton embraced the error rather than change it. For the "Johnny Horton Makes History" album cover, he wore a red Confederate uniform, not likely signifying a color of the Confederacy, but more likely, the color of blood.

On July 28, 1960 Merle, Johnny Horton, and Tillman Franks all piled into Horton's Cadillac and drove to Houston, following sun-scorched roads, allowing hot, dusty air into the open windows. It was a road trip to honor the last living Civil War soldier, 116-year-old Walter W. Williams of the Confederate army.

It'd been Tillman Franks' idea. He had discovered Williams in an article in the Shreveport Sunday newspaper. He was delighted to read that Walter Williams considered "The Battle of New Orleans" his favorite song. That's when the idea hit Tillman: they could all drive up there together and give the guy a private performance. Of course, they'd also make sure to call every newspaper and television station available and let them know. It certainly made sense from a marketing standpoint. Horton's "The Battle of New Orleans" was still going strong. Plus, he'd just recorded "Johnny Reb," but they hadn't released it yet to the public. This could be a great debut.

"You can tell Walter Williams you wrote 'Johnny Reb' for him," Tillman suggested to Merle. "Just say you read about him in the paper and wrote the song that very day."

When they arrived at the home of Williams, a crowd of journalists and photographers greeted them.

The small home could barely hold their numbers. The three men shuffled into a cramped bedroom. The old man was there, lying in bed with ruffled white blankets draped over his frail frame. Williams seemed more skeleton than human. Amazing that he was still alive.

Williams' daughter, Willie Mae Bowles, sat beside her father's bed. At the sight of the three performers, her eyes filled with tears.

"Thank you so much for coming," she told them. "Daddy won't be able to see you, but he can hear you just fine. You'll just have to play it loud."

Cradling his guitar in his lap, Horton eased into a chair beside the bed, scooted closer, and then strummed a few chords before leaping into "The Battle of New Orleans."

The old man lay still for the first verse. But then his gnarled hands began flapping at his sides and the blanket shuffled at his feet. Willie Mae clapped her hands to her mouth and gasped, "He's dancing!"

After Horton finished his first song, he leaned closer to the man's ear and said, "Now here's a song that Merle Kilgore—he's here in this room—wrote just for you, and I just recently recorded it." Leaning back, Horton winked at Merle, then strummed his guitar and launched into "Johnny Reb."

The old man "danced" some more. Then tears gathered at the corners of his eyes. Merle felt tears in his own eyes. At his elbow, he noticed the cameraman was beginning to tear up, too. When Horton finished, Williams lay silent, and for one horrifying moment, Merle thought the old man had chosen that very moment to die. But then his chest rose in a feeble breath and his leathery fingers plucked at Horton's guitar strings.

Just as Franks had predicted, the event went over well with the public. Merle found news stories about Horton and the old soldier on dozens of newspapers. Record sales of "Johnny Reb" skyrocketed, settling at number ten on the Billboard charts, while selling more than 500,000 copies. "Johnny Reb," posing as a kind of companion song to Horton's "The Battle of New Orleans," further helped define Horton for his historic battle epics.

It was almost Christmas when Tillman and Horton, driving through Dallas, picked up a newspaper at a local diner. While Horton finished off his meal, Tillman flapped through the paper, then smacked it down on the table.

"Looky there," said Tillman, tapping a picture with his finger. "Poor old General Williams died last night. Says here the funeral services will be held on December 23. You know what we ought to do? We should cruise on over to the funeral home. We could perform a few songs right there over his grave."

"No way," Horton told him. "We've already used that old man enough."

In Ralph Emery's *The View from Nashville*, Merle recounts one of his strangest moments with Horton after a show somewhere in Spring Hill, Louisiana. The year was 1960, and Merle met Horton backstage. It was the last time Merle would see Johnny Horton alive.

Horton looked tired and nervous when he ushered him inside. "Chief," Horton said, "I got to talk to you."

"Everything all right, Johnny?"

Horton paced the room with a hand clamped hand over his mouth. "No, Chief. Everything is not all right." He went over and scooped up his guitar, the one he'd been playing earlier, and thrust it into Merle's arms. "Here, I want you to have this."

It was such a strange offering that Merle just shook his head and said, "You okay, man?"

"The spirits want me to give this to you," Horton told him. "Keep it at home. Put it on display at a museum. But don't you ever sell it, Chief. You hear me?"

"Would you tell me what this is all about?"

"The spirits say I'll be dead within the week, Chief."

"What?" Merle shouted. "Come on, Johnny. Quit fooling."

"No, Merle. I'm serious. They say a drunk is gonna kill me."

Merle said carefully, "You need some rest, man. Maybe the spirits are wrong. You know how these things go."

"I wish I believed that, Merle. But I don't." Horton paced the room for a moment. "You remember hearing how Houdini promised to send his wife a message from the afterlife? When he died, his wife promised a huge reward if anyone could deliver that message."

"That's right," said Merle. "Alfred Ford, the spiritualist, was the one who broke the code."

Horton nodded. "Yeah, that's right. I want to do something like that. If there is a spirit realm, then I want to contact you when I get there. Because I believe it, Chief. I believe it with all my heart, and that's why I'm telling you this. I've got something that they told me to give you—a message. I need you to commit it to memory."

"All right, Johnny. I'm listening."

Horton stared at him for a quiet moment and then said, "The message is: The drummer is a rummer and cannot hold a beat."

"The drummer is a rummer? Well, what the hell is that supposed to mean?"

"It doesn't have to mean anything, Chief," Horton said with a frustrated sigh. "Just remember it, okay?"

"Okay. Got it."

"Tell no one about this," Horton said. "I mean it, Merle. If you tell anyone, you'll doubt it, should you ever get the message."

Merle agreed, assuring Horton that he'd never say a word, and he left the club with his new guitar. He never forgot the message.

My grandmother remembers the night Johnny Horton died, November 5, 1960. The memory never faded; not only did she and Merle lose a good friend, but she also witnessed something strange and she took it as confirmation of the supernatural.

They'd been traveling all night, Merle, Dot, and the new agent, Buster Doss and his wife, Kay. Following an aggressive marketing campaign, Buster had Merle booked all across the Northeast, all the way up to Montreal. They'd just driven from New York when they decided to check into a hotel just outside of Chicago.

After settling into their rooms, the four regrouped at the hotel restaurant, where they pored over the menus. They were all hungry and they wasted no time when the waitress came to take their orders. The service was slow and the waitress dragged her feet. Merle complained about the wait.

But the moment the food arrived, Merle lost his appetite. Something came over him. The color went out of his face and he looked suddenly tired.

Dot frowned at him. "Merle, what's wrong with you? Why aren't you eating?"

"It's nothing," he said, shaking his head. "I just had a weird feeling. I think I'll go on up to the room."

This struck everyone as odd, considering how hungry he'd been just a few moments earlier.

Dot was annoyed. "Well, can we at least finish our food?"

But Merle only shook his head. "Come up with me, will you?" he asked her.

They excused themselves and hurried to the elevators. When they got to their room, Merle plopped onto the edge of the bed and buried his face in his hands. Dot didn't know what to do; he was acting so strange. So she just stood beside him and gently patted him on the back.

"Will you please tell me what's wrong?" she asked.

"Something bad's happening," he told her. "I feel just . . . just terrible."

Peeved with his odd behavior, she said, "Nothing *bad* is going to happen. You're just imagining it."

But Merle couldn't shake off the sense of dread. He drew Dot onto his lap and rocked her slowly, sadly, and Dot tried to sooth him by running her fingers through his hair.

The night eventually passed; somehow, they got through it.

In the morning, Merle looked much better as he hurriedly got ready for the day. He snapped the radio on. But there was no music, only words. That's when they both heard it.

"This just in: Johnny Horton is dead. He died last night in Milano, Texas; determined dead on arrival after he was involved in a head-on collision. The incident is still under investigation. With him was manager Tillman Franks, who survived but is in critical condition . . ."

Merle stumbled back against the wall and slid to the floor with his hands on his head.

"Oh, no. Didn't I tell you something bad was gonna happen?" he croaked. "Johnny died."

"No, you heard it wrong," Dot insisted. "They said *Wharton*, not Horton."

They didn't have to wait long before the deejay repeated the announcement, and this time they got the entire story.

Johnny Horton, the Singing Fisherman, was dead.

Suddenly it all made sense to her—Merle's loss of appetite, his overwhelming sense of dread, his odd behavior. Somehow, Merle had just *known*.

Johnny Horton performed his last show on November 5, 1960, at the Skyline Club in Austin, Texas, the same stage where Hank Williams gave his final appearance before his own untimely death. Horton was fidgety and paranoid, and he refused to leave his dressing room.

"I don't know why you keep booking us at these kinds of places," Horton grumbled as he wandered back to the dressing room. He had a good point; the Skyline Club was small, and Horton was becoming hugely popular, especially after his recent appearance on the Ed Sullivan Show.

"Then we won't come here anymore," Tillman said. "But I already collected $800 for this gig, and so there's no way of getting out of it."

"But I got a bad feeling about this, Ace," Horton insisted. "The spirits told me I ain't got much time left. Some drunk driver's gonna kill me."

"Nobody's gonna hit you in a car while you're up there on that stage," Tillman told him. "I can promise you that! Now come on. We got a show to do."

Horton gave in and did the show. He was in rare form and performed three sets that night. Everything went just fine. Afterward, Tillman wanted to find a hotel, but Horton had another plan in mind: he wanted to drive them back to Shreveport in one drive. Tillman argued with him, pointing out how tired they all were. It made more sense to just get a hotel and drive tomorrow. But Horton had his mind set.

"I can't, Ace," he told him. "Me and Claude King are going duck hunting tomorrow. I promised Claude I'd be there. Now, come on. You don't have to drive anyhow."

"Fine then," Tillman told him. "If you think you can get us home without falling asleep at the wheel, then be my guest."

They loaded Horton's Cadillac Fleetwood. Including all their gear, they were crammed in tight, with Tillman's upright bass shoved into the backseat and Tommy Tomlinson, a fellow guitarist, lying beneath it, preparing to sleep the whole way back. Tillman rode shotgun to keep Horton company.

Horton drove them through the night on dark country roads. Tillman eventually dozed off.

Sometime later, roaring along Highway 79 into Milano, Texas, the road swept Horton into a narrow bridge that carried the Cadillac high above the railway tracks below. Headlights appeared from the other end of the bridge. The lights belonged to a truck, and as it barreled toward them, it swerved to one side of the road until it slammed the guardrail and sprayed a fan of orange sparks before lurching to the opposite side of the bridge and smashing into the opposite railing.

Horton wrestled with the wheel, but there was nowhere to go. He met the oncoming truck head-on. He died before the ambulance arrived.

In the aftermath, medics determined that the driver, who'd survived the crash, had been driving while drunk. Everyone, especially Merle, recognized the sad irony here. Horton had always rebuked alcohol, blaming it for his broken childhood. And now, it had taken away his life, just when things had started getting interesting.

Johnny Horton's funeral service was held at Hillcrest Cemetery in Haughton, Louisiana, just east of Bossier City. Numerous friends and family gathered beneath the aluminum-framed marquee. Even Tillman Franks managed to come to the service, although he'd left the hospital in a wheelchair against his doctor's orders. Merle and Johnny Cash served on a group of pallbearers who brought Johnny Horton's coffin to its burial place.

"When I heard he'd died," Cash told Merle, "I locked myself in a barroom and cried."

After the service, Cash found Merle and said to him, "Merle, when you're ready to play the big time, you come see me in Nashville. I'll help you out the best I can."

Merle gave an appreciative nod. "Hey, that's great, Johnny. I've had Nashville on my mind lately. I might just take you up on that offer."

But I think Merle was too overwhelmed to take Cash seriously. Horton's last words to him still echoed in his mind. "*I think I'm going to die, Chief. If something happens to me, I'll try and contact you . . .*"

Merle didn't get the message at the cemetery or later that night at home. In fact, Merle spent the next several years waiting for a sign from Johnny Horton. He even returned to Hillcrest Cemetery a few times to stand over Horton's grave and ask for a sign. "Okay, Johnny," Merle would say. "I'm here. Come on back and give me the message."

But his hopes diminished over the years. No ghostly visits. No messages from the afterlife. Eventually, Merle let the notion go that Horton could cross the Great Divide between life and death. Johnny Horton was gone and that was the end of it.

All Merle could do was honor his memory by making a promise, to not drink for a year. It was a big promise for a would-be alcoholic.

It was 1967, some seven years later, when a small group of New York spiritualists gathered for a séance in their Greenwich Village apartment. With the curtains drawn against the city lights, they sat at the table as flickering candles glowed in their eyes. It was a quiet gathering of middle-aged men and women, dressed in suits and evening gowns, all sober-minded as they held hands and prayed.[15]

The group was hopeful that night. After meeting once a week for several months, they'd come to expect exciting things from their ceremonies. Only recently they'd met a spirit, a man they called the Cowboy, who'd visited the group six times over the past year.

"Spirits of the dead, hear our call," moaned a heavy-set woman, her head bowed. "Show yourself to us. Show yourself . . ."

All about the room, the tiny candle flames flickered. Then he appeared. Tall and lean and glowing like the moon. They called him the Cowboy because he wore a white Western suit and a cowboy hat. By now, they were all familiar with his gentle, boyish face and his smiling eyes. Still, his presence stirred a visible shudder from the group, all except the old woman, who never scared easily.

The Cowboy had unfinished business. The group wanted to help him, but communicating with him proved difficult. Sometimes they felt him rather than saw him. Sometimes they heard his muffled, disembodied voice. Other times he spoke through the old woman, using her the way a ventriloquist uses a wooden dummy. But the sessions proved tedious and slow going. It'd taken three months to get his name: Johnny Horton . . . or was it *Wharton?* They spent another two months trying to piece together the specter's strange message, a kind of adult nursery rhyme. Then he tasked them to deliver the rhyme. The Cowboy had even given them a name: Merle Kilgore. Unfortunately, none of the spiritualists had ever heard the name before.

Tonight the apparition visited them again, and when he talked, his voice sounded like the wind rattling dead leaves. Meanwhile, the old woman bent over a piece of paper and scribbled frantically with a black pen; only she seemed to understand the apparition. Everyone at the table looked at her, waiting for her to speak.

Finally, her watery eyes raised and met their gazes. "Merle Kilgore again," she whispered. It was always the same. After a pause, she tipped her doughy-white face back so that it hung like the moon, and asked the quiet room, "Who is Merle Kilgore?"

No one at the table dared look over their shoulder at the apparition. It was best to see him from the corner of the eye. They all sensed him moving closer. His icy presence brought the temperature down ten degrees or more.

When the ghost failed to answer, the old woman asked again, this time more forcefully. "Who is Merle Kilgore?"

And then, just as quickly as it had appeared, the ghost vanished.

In the quiet aftermath, the group shifted restlessly in their chairs. One of them stood up and turned on the lights. The tall man decided drinks were needed. Then they all sat looking at each other with their arms folded and their brows bent. Someone lit a cigarette.

"Kilgore," said a middle-aged woman with blonde curls. "I tell you, I know that name from somewhere. It's familiar . . ."

The tall man returned to the table with a decanter of brandy and poured them all glasses. "I tell ya, it's just fantastic. The Cowboy looked remarkably clear tonight."

A short, balding man reached for one of the glasses with a shaky hand. He spilled half of his drink before downing it in one gulp. Drawing on his cigarette, he let out a long sigh and said, "That Cowboy sure gives me the creeps." He laughed unevenly and asked, "How about we liven things up with some music?"

As the others carried on, he turned in his chair and snapped on the radio, an Admiral Transistor 8. The radio hissed and then a charismatic deejay intoned: "That's going to wrap up tonight's program. In closing, I'll leave you with a final song, written by songwriter Merle Kilgore, whom I had the pleasure of meeting this past weekend in Nashville, Tennessee. This song made the Billboard top ten when it was released. Its singer, the legendary Johnny Horton, died only a few years later. Ladies and gentlemen, this is 'Johnny Reb.'"

The bald man's eyes became as big as saucers and he looked at the others, but somehow they all missed it, even the old lady who prided herself on hearing voices from the dead. The group kept on talking, and so he turned around and cranked up the radio's volume. "Johnny Reb" filled the room, and the others finally shut up and stared at him, their brows drawn in quiet dismay.

The tall man gave him a puzzled look. "A favorite of yours? Had enough of Gershwin?"

But the bald man only smiled and he snapped his fingers to the beat of "Johnny Reb" as his friends watched him with growing suspicion. He let the whole song play right on through . . .

At the Kilgore house, a ringing phone woke Merle from his sleep. He rolled over in his bed and groped in the dark until his fingers happened upon the handset on the nightstand. He jammed it against his ear and cleared his throat. "Yeah, who is this?"

"Eh, hello . . . Mr. Kilgore?"

The voice sounded hesitant and unfamiliar, and Merle checked the clock on the nightstand. It was after midnight. "This is Merle."

"Mr. Kilgore, my name isn't important," said a thin voice with a proper Boston accent. "I'm part of a spiritualist group who meets once a week in Greenwich Village."

This got Merle's attention. He sat up in bed and said, "I'm listening."

"Mr. Kilgore, we, eh, that is, my spiritualist group, have been meeting with a certain spirit for over a year. It has been very difficult communicating with him. We got his name after many months, and then we got your name. But still, we didn't know. You must understand that we are not familiar with Country Music, and so these names didn't mean anything to us."

"Go on," said Merle. "I'm listening."

"Well, this spirit of ours—he dresses like a cowboy, all in white, and says his name is Johnny Horton."

Merle caught his breath. For a moment he couldn't think. He couldn't hear over the thumping of his heart.

"Ah, Mr. Kilgore?"

"Yeah," he managed to say. "I'm here."

"Well, like I said, we Northern spiritualists aren't much of Country Music fans, and so the names meant nothing to us. But luckily, this evening I heard your names on the radio. It was terribly strange. We had only just finished the session, when I turned on the radio and there you were, both names together. I got in touch with Bob Lockwood at the radio station, and he gave me your number. I hope you don't mind."

"Oh," was all Merle could muster.

"Mr. Kilgore, there's more. The spirit of Johnny Horton said to give you this message, and the message is: The Drummer is a rummer and cannot hold a beat.'"

Merle dropped the phone. Then he sat in the dark for a long while. "Johnny?" he said to the dark and empty room. "I got your message. I believe you now. There *is* another side, and I hope to see you there one day. Only," he added, "not anytime soon."

1952 Merle Kilgore

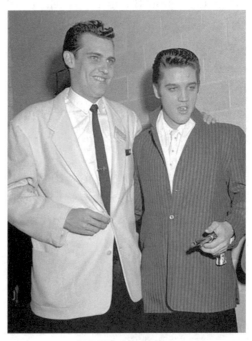

1954 Merle and Elvis

1955 Merle and Johnny Horton

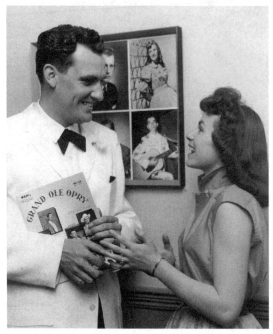

1959 Merle Kilgore First Appearance on Opry

1950s Merle and Kitty Wells

1963 Lefty Frizzel, Merle Kilgore, Faron Young, and Abe Mulkey

1968 Merle Kilgore and Johnny Cash

Hank Williams Jr. gives Merle Kilgore Boogie King suit

1972 Merle, Webb Pierce, George Jones, and Walter Bailes

Merle Kilgore and Hank Williams Jr.

1972 Johnny Cash, Merle Kilgore, & June Carter Cash

1976 Claude King and Merle Kilgore

1976 Judy and Merle Kilgore

1985 Merle Kilgore, Jerry Lee Lewis, and Hank Williams Jr.

1985 Waylon Jennings, Hank Williams Jr., Merle Kilgore, and Johnny Cash

1989 Frank Gifford, Hank Williams Jr.and Merle Kilgore

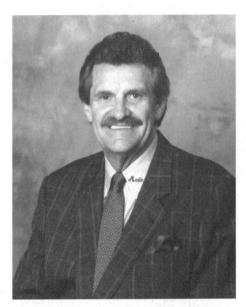

1994 - Merle Kilgore

1996 Merle Kilgore and Lee Ann Rimes

1998 Willie Nelson & Merle Kilgore

2001 Bill Anderson, Eddie Arnold, and Merle Kilgore

2002 Pam Anderson, Merle Kilgore and Kid Rock

2002 Ronnie Dunn, Merle Kilgore, and Kix Brooks. "Are you shitting me?"

2004 Hank Williams Jr., Mark Rickert, and Merle Kilgore

2004 Martina McBride, Merle Kilgore, & John McBride

2012 Steve Kilgore with the bronze statue of Merle that is located at
the William Morris Talent agency in Nashville.
Photo by Silver Stephens copyright March 6th, 2012.

clifton clowers

"Wolverton Mountain" was one of Merle's most popular songs. In the early Sixties, it launched Claude King's career and stayed on the Billboard charts for nine weeks. It also got picked up by several other important artists, including Nat King Cole and Hank Williams, Jr.

Not many people remember it now, but in its time, "Wolverton Mountain" made a lot of people happy. People sometimes tell me stories, like this guy who had a special childhood memory of riding horses with his father, trundling across a hillside and singing "Wolverton Mountain" as loud as they could with no one close enough to hear. It's so popular that it got a mention in *Trivial Pursuit*; I discovered this one night while playing a game with friends and finding the question: "Where did Clifton Clowers live?" And you know a song's become famous when it gets a parody. The hilarious Country Music duo Pinkard & Bowden, the team behind classics such as "Mama, She's Lazy," and "I Lobster but Never Flounder," took Merle's classic and spun it into "Three Mile Island," referring to the 1979 nuclear reactor meltdown in Dauphin County, Pennsylvania. In this version, the bears and the birds "are bigger than houses, and all the fishes are growing hair."

But the irony is, when Merle first wrote the song, there was only one person in the world who cared, and only because Merle wrote it for him.

A drive in 1959 from Springhill, Louisiana, to Conway, Arkansas, gave Merle some much-needed alone time. He'd kept the windows down, allowing the fresh October air inside, and traveled at a good clip along the miles of empty highways, flanked by great expanses of countryside. He had his reasons for driving all the way to Wolverton Mountain, but most importantly, he wanted to celebrate Uncle Clifton Clower's sixty-ninth birthday. Besides, driving alone for all these miles gave him a chance to clear his head; over the past few years, he'd faced hard times, losing a newborn son and a best friend.

I suspect Merle had a great deal to process on his drive to the mountain. Wolverton Mountain (a minor misnomer, since that great ripple of earth better fits the definition of a ridge) held a special place in his heart. It was there, at Uncle Clifton's home, that he'd spent many childhood summers with his cousins playing in the sorghum fields, getting lost in the woods, or swimming in the cool streams. Having grown up in the city, Merle became a fish out of water on that woodsy mountain terrain. His cousins would laugh themselves to tears when he tried to milk a cow or climb a tree or fish in the creeks when they were kids. But they also made sure to teach him the right way of doing things.

It was Uncle Clifton who gave him the greatest lesson—he taught Merle about music. Each night after farming with his team of long-eared mules in the sorghum fields, Clifton retired to his creaky front porch rocking chair to play his mandolin. His music would ring out across Wolverton Mountain, and Merle would sit at his feet, listening with bright eyes, his imagination ablaze. At the end of one night of music like this, Clifton stopped playing and looked down at Merle, who sat on the porch floor with his face in his hands. Clifton said, "You like that sort of music, don't you?" When Merle nodded, Clifton got up, disappeared into the house, and returned with another mandolin, this one older and less polished. "You like it?" he asked, handing it to Merle. Of course, Merle was thrilled. "Well, it's yours," Clifton told him. "It's missing a string, but it carries a tune."

It was an inspiring gift. Merle accepted it with disbelief in his eyes, then hurried away to teach himself. His cousins remember how he would sit on a low branch of a walnut tree, his legs dangling, the mandolin cradled in his lap. He'd strum and sing for hours, and when his cousins giggled at him, he'd say, "You just watch. One day I'm going to be a big Country Music singer. You won't be laughing then."

Memories like these were whirling around in Merle's head on that long ride that day in 1959, when inspiration struck. He imagined a melody, and he sang to an empty car, drawing on his past, when life was much, much easier. By the time he reached Conway, Arkansas, he'd written a new song.

He reached Wolverton Mountain later that day, grinded his way up the rocky road, and reached the small home at the top of the ridge. In the distance was Uncle Clifton standing beside his two long-eared mules in the sorghum field, just like old times. Merle fetched his guitar from the backseat and marched into the tall green stalks, calling, "Hey, Uncle Clifton! I wrote you a song on the way up here."

Clifton looked surprised. "Well, what'cha waiting for? Go on and play it."

"Right now?" Merle frowned. "I haven't learned it on my guitar yet."

"Then sing it a cappella."

Merle considered it, shrugged, and then launched into a playful song with lyrics that danced suspiciously close to his uncle's life. A story unfolded; a stranger had come to Wolverton Mountain to fetch the girl he loved. But first, he had to face her father, Clifton Clowers, the irrational mountain man who threatened to kill any man who tried to take his daughter away. To make matters worse, Clifton had the help of all the mountain critters to alert him when a trespasser entered his territory. But not even the fear of death could stop the bleeding-hearted hero from climbing the mountain and taking the girl for his wife.

A grin stretched across Clifton's face as he listened, surprised to discover that he'd become a character in Merle's song. His nephew had a few things right, such as Clifton's trophy marksmanship, having gained experience in WWII as a combat veteran. But Merle had also taken a few artistic liberties. Clifton Clowers rarely, if ever, resorted to violence or objected to boys dating his daughters, Virginia and Burlene. For that reason, the song was a kind of joke, and Clifton picked up on it right away.

"Well?" said Merle once he finished singing. "What d'ya think?"

Clifton thought quietly to himself, nodded slowly, and then said, "I think you wrote yourself a hit, nephew."

Merle thought so, too. But I suppose they were both wrong in some ways, and both right in other ways.

A year later, in 1961, Merle got a call from Al Gallico, a general manager with New York-based publishing house Shapiro Bernstein. Al had a job offer.

Shapiro Bernstein, Al explained, had decided to open a BMI-affiliated publishing company in Nashville called Painted Desert Music. This would mark the publisher's first foray into the Country Music genre; the industry had a lot of buzz lately, and they wanted to get in before it exploded. Al Gallico had been assigned to helm the project, and he wanted Merle to manage it.

For Merle, taking the job meant leaving his Shreveport roots and moving to Nashville. It also meant moving the wife and kids to uncharted territory. Still, Al's offer was impossible to turn town, and Merle accepted. In the winter of 1961, he moved his family to Tennessee.

Music Row, the Grand Ole Opry, WSM radio—Nashville was the heart of it all. The city moved with the synergy of major record producers, publishing companies, record labels, and recording artists, all coming together to make commercially viable music. On any given day of the week, enormously talented singers and musicians booked sessions at the Quonset Hut or the RCA Studio B on 17th Avenue. Nashville had proven to everyone that Country Music had more life in its bones and it would not be silenced by the emergence of rock 'n' roll. All this provided Painted Desert Music with a rich environment in which to thrive. As operations manager, Merle had his plate full. First, he had the company's catalog to bolster—the bigger Painted Desert's stockpile of potential hits, the better chance the company had to sustain itself. Merle's job demanded that he keep a flowing pipeline of songs, and that kept him walking the streets, discovering unsigned artists and buying up rights to unpublished songs. All this required some intensive campaigning. Merle became a constant surveyor, keeping an ever-attentive ear to the ground, waiting for new talent to arrive in Nashville. Music Row nightclubs became something akin to untapped oilfields. As a result, names like Eddie Rabbit (who crashed on Merle's sofa for a few weeks) to Glen Sutton (a songwriter who later developed the "countrypolitan" sound with Billy Sherill) became just a few of Merle's discoveries. By day, Merle's office echoed with unproduced music blaring from his radio speakers. Every so often, he would hear an inspired cut and then run down the halls shouting, "I just found the next hit! This one's going gold before we even get it on the air!" The celebration parties always followed.

But his work didn't stop there. After building Painted Desert's catalog, he had to turn around and pitch those songs to professional recording artists, knowing that the right artist could take a mediocre song and turn it into a hit record. The challenge was to get the recording artist into his office to hear his songs; they just didn't have the time. So Merle assumed a kind of hawking, aggressive sales strategy, oftentimes drifting up and down Music Row like a back-alley pusher, and the moment he spotted a country star, he'd run up and start singing and strumming an imaginary guitar.

"Well what do you think?" he'd ask with a hopeful grin as the artist usually regarded him with something between amusement and concern. But Merle was too brash to ever back down. "You should record it. It'd be a *smash!*"

After a few years of this, Merle had become an unmistakable fixture in the Nashville music scene. Not only did he stand out from the crowd, with his towering frame, his deep voice, and that frenetic sense of humor and enthusiasm that got him recognized by the Grand Ole Opry with the WSM DJ Award, but he'd also become a prominent business figure, rubbing elbows with all aspects of the industry. It helped, too, that Al Gallico took special pride in Merle and provided an education that would serve him until the end of his days.

The office work never got in the way of Merle's dream of becoming a star. In fact, the business gave him a foot in the door to plug his own songs. He had plenty of material by this time, with a private catalog of more than a hundred songs, and in his gut, he knew that at least one of those songs was an unsuspecting million seller.

Merle's luck changed when an old friend gave an unexpected call at the office.

Tillman Franks was in town and he wanted to meet Merle for lunch. Merle laughed with surprise; he hadn't seen Tillman since moving away from Shreveport. He asked Tillman about his family and why he'd come to Nashville. He ended the conversation with a cryptic statement. "I'm working on a special project," he told Merle. "It's a secret. But I'll tell you more when I see you tomorrow."

They met the following afternoon at the Noel Hotel on Fourth Avenue North and Church in downtown Nashville. Tillman arrived with a surprise guest, Claude King, the tall, quiet Hayride singer from Shreveport. Claude and Horton had been best friends and fellow fishing buddies, and Merle had spent countless afternoons on the johnboat with them; Claude had also been an exceptional fisherman. In jovial spirits, Merle, Tillman, and Claude made their way to the hotel restaurant, where they ordered lunch before getting down to business.

"Claude here is recording a new album," Tillman revealed, pointing out that he had taken on the role of Claude's manager. "That's the big secret. We're almost finished. But we need one last song. That's why I wanted to see you today. Claude and I talked about it. We want to help you out; give you an opportunity to throw something on the album."

Merle perked up in his chair. He had plenty of songs in his briefcase. But when he went for them, Tillman raised a hand.

"Hold on," said Tillman. "We're looking for a specific kind of song; we're looking for a *mountain* song."

"A mountain song?" It was an awkward request, but something clicked at the back of Merle's mind.

Tillman, mistaking Merle's tone for doubt, squared his shoulders and said, "Well, sure. Folksongs are popular right now."

Merle didn't need to be convinced. He already had something in mind, and it was as if he'd been waiting all along for this moment. Leaning forward, he grinned and said, "Boy, have I got a song for you!"[16]

That Claude King wanted a mountain song for his album was beyond coincidence. Merle left the men sitting at the table and hurried off to use the phone at the hotel service counter. He dialed his home number. Dot answered.

"Listen, Dot," he said anxiously, "I need you to go through my box of songs and find that one about Wolverton Mountain."

Dot asked, "What do you want with that awful song?"

She, like many others, never had much hope in the song. But Merle never stopped believing. From the moment he'd sung his song to Uncle Clifton, he'd had faith that "Wolverton Mountain" had a world of potential.

Things hadn't worked out the way Merle imagined they would. Once back in Shreveport, he'd plugged "Wolverton Mountain" all over town. But it soon became apparent that most people in the business didn't share Uncle Clifton's enthusiasm. In fact, they didn't seem to care for it at all. Billy "Crash" Craddock, the up-and-coming artist of "Boom Boom Baby," was the first to reject him. Merle had spotted Crash at a local diner one time and followed him into the men's room. Once Crash locked himself into one of the stalls, Merle serenaded the unsuspecting recording artist with "Wolverton Mountain," signing it just outside the toilet.

"That's your next hit!" Merle shouted, breaking the silence that followed.

The toilet flushed. Crash came out and quietly washed his hands at the sink. Then he turned to face Merle standing in the corner.

"I think I'm gonna pass on that one," Crash told him, and then added, "Hell of a try, though."

Johnny Horton had been next. Horton had listened with mild interest until Merle hit the second verse, then Horton's expression soured. He interrupted with waving hands. "Cla-cla-Clifton Clowers?" he said with an offended grimace. "Man, you should change that name." Then he added: "Merle, that's the *worst* song I ever heard you sing."

Merle even sang it to fellow Hayride singer George Jones. George never even let him finish. "Stop right there," he insisted with a scowl. "I *hate* mountain songs."

Merle took the harsh criticism on the chin like a seasoned boxer, with hardly a flinch or a bruised ego. He never got upset, and he never budged from his belief that "Wolverton Mountain" had legs. He simply shrugged and said, "No kidding? You don't like it?"

Merle hated to quit, but the endless rejections had worn him down, and he finally threw in the towel. "Wolverton Mountain" went into his shoebox of duds, where it stayed for a long time.

But the time was right—Merle knew it in his bones—and he waited anxiously that day at the hotel restaurant to hear Dot's voice tell him that she'd found his song.

"Merle? You there?" It was Dot. "I found that song of yours."

He breathed deeply and shook his head. "Okay, then. I need your help. You recite the lyrics to me—word for word—and I'll write them down."

She followed his instructions, and Merle wrote down the lyrics on a sheet of hotel memo paper. Afterward, he raced back into the restaurant, waving the page of handwritten words over his head.

The men finished their lunch. Claude and Tillman shared a room in the upper floors of the hotel, and they all went up. They handed a guitar to Merle, and he sang "Wolverton Mountain" while they listened with amused grins. When the song ended, Claude told him, "Let me work with it for a minute. Maybe I can tweak it a bit."

Merle vigorously shook Claude's hand. "You won't be sorry about this," he said, then added, "It's gonna be a hit!"

Claude shut himself away with the song and his guitar while Merle and Tillman waited downstairs in the lobby. As soon as Claude came down, they all headed to the recording studio a few blocks over, where Claude recorded the song in one go. Tillman gave his stamp of approval. The song came out just fine.

"Wolverton Mountain" found a place on the B-side of Claude King's single "Little Bitty Heart," a song that Tillman felt was a surefire hit. During the following weeks, they sent the record to hundreds of radio stations, and it received positive—if somewhat lukewarm—reviews. But it wasn't until a deejay working at a Milwaukee pop station discovered "Wolverton Mountain" and decided he liked it better than the A-side track. He liked it so much, in fact, that he let that record spin continuously throughout the day. The station's phone started ringing off the hook.

The deejay telephoned Tillman the following day, crying out, "You put the wrong song on the B-side. 'Wolverton Mountain' is your hit!"

The deejay was right.

In 1962, "Wolverton Mountain" soared to the top of the Billboard charts, where it stayed for nine weeks. Additionally, big band musician Guy Lombardo picked it up and made it a crossover hit. Suddenly, the song that no one liked became the song that everyone was singing.

When Judy Kilgore and I drove to Wolverton Mountain for research, we met with members of the Clowers family, distant relatives of mine. They welcomed us inside and fed us home-cooked meals. I even met Burlene, an inspiration for the daughter of the fictional Clifton Clowers, only now the "pretty young daughter" had grown decidedly older.

I spent the day ambling along dirt roads, my hands in my pockets, listening to the cousins tell their stories. They had fond memories of Merle, and we all laughed a lot. At the top of the ridge that overlooked an especially lush ravine, we stopped to consider a furrowed area, overgrown with weeds. One of my distant cousins said, "This here's the place," referring to the home of Clifton Clowers, long ago laid waste by a fire.

I turned to find a walnut tree with gnarled, low-hanging branches. I smiled to myself, envisioning a young Merle Kilgore in jean overalls, a lanky boy with gangly legs and knobby knees, big ears and freckles, a mandolin tucked into his lap. I saw him clearly, all by himself, singing his heart out while the kids below giggled up at him.

Just you watch. One day. I'm gonna be a big star.

As the sun drifted low, Judy and I made our exit, and the road carried us past an old cemetery with tooth-like headstones. I whistled Merle's song under my breath, feeling his presence, and considered him in a new perspective. I was closer to him now that I'd visited this place.

My understanding of "Wolverton Mountain" has since changed. Merle had picked a fine place as the subject for a song. He'd fallen in love with Country Music here; he'd become enchanted by the idea of fame. You can hear all this in his song if you listen closely. Sure, on the surface, "Wolverton Mountain" is a quirky fairytale romance, but dig deeper, and it's a song about chasing a dream and making it a reality, even if the whole world tries to stop you.

johnny cash

"Are you *shitting* me?"

To his dying day, that was Merle's gimmicky one-liner, a real crowd pleaser among Country Music movers and shakers. Whether making an appearance at a party or showing up for an important CMA board meeting, Merle delivered his famous zinger without fail.

All it took was for someone to ask him, "Merle, how the hell are you?"

As an answer, he'd flourish both hands, showing the rings on his knuckles, and wiggle each finger to make the diamonds sparkle. Then he'd move in closer, giving a conspiratorial wag of his brow, and say, "Are you *shitting* me?"

It was funny. He acted as if he had the inside scoop on success; as if the rings said it all, and I suppose they did.

But to really get the joke, you had to understand a few things. Merle came up with his *Are you shitting me?* shtick in the late Fifties, a period when singing on the Hayride didn't pay the bills. That was a bad time for Country Music, the decidedly *post*-Elvis Presley years, when good-ol'-country-boy music faced the brink of extinction, and rock 'n' roll became all the rage. As a result, nobody was going to the Hayride, or paying for shows, and entertainers like Merle were always broke.

Like his fellow singers, during times of lagging business, Merle headed to the local pawnshop to hock his things for cash. The first to go were always his gold rings. It must have been difficult for him, considering his love of jewelry. How much he loved his dazzling accoutrements became something of a joke among his friends. Merle rarely went a day without wearing his "bling" (his later term of endearment), and should he happen upon a bad part of town, he'd tell his friends something like, *Oh, Brother, we better hide our bling before go inside the Walmart.* His rings were his pride and joy, from his weighty golden star, a gift from his wife Judy, to his fat horseshoe diamond ring, a gift from Hank Jr. In fact, Merle purchased his first ring, a golden lion's head, with the money from his first royalty check, the payoff of "More and More." Rings were important to his self-image, and in his eyes, they made the man.

Merle loved his rings, and so it pained him to pawn them off. He never wasted a moment to buy them back when he got paid.

In good times, he *wanted* people to ask him, "How are you doing, Merle?" Because that's when he'd show his rings and shout back: "Are you *shitting* me?" The rings signified money in the bank, and that meant he was doing just fine. *Yes, Amen.*

Johnny Cash knew Merle's one-liner better than anyone. You bet he did. He and Merle were old friends, and they'd traveled endless miles together. Cash knew why Merle flashed his rings and how it signified good times. But Cash also had a wry sense of humor, and toward the end, he gave Merle's catchphrase a sad and clever twist.

June Carter Cash had just passed away, and Johnny had fallen ill and checked himself into a hospital. When Merle dropped by during visiting hours, he found Johnny looking sallow-faced and haggard in his hospital bed. The Man in Black was now faded charcoal.

It saddened Merle to see Johnny this way. Merle had come to cheer him up, but now he didn't know if he could pull it off. This was a hard time. Not only for Johnny, who'd shared a celebrated and popularized love story with June, but also for Merle, who suffered his own grief. June had been a good friend, and she'd contributed to his personal success, and on the day of her funeral, Merle had helped carry her casket. No, this wasn't easy for anybody.

"Brother, how are you doing?" Merle said, standing next to the bed, patting his friend's hand. He already knew the answer. But he asked it anyway.

Cash gave him a sullen smile. Then he flourished his left hand, knuckles up, and let the light shimmer against his wedding band. In a strained voice, he said, "Are you shitting me, Kilgore?"

My grandfather couldn't help but appreciate the spin on his catchphrase. For all these years, the flash of rings and those four resolute words meant a declaration of personal triumph (*Are you shitting me? I'm fabulous! Do you even have to ask?*). But Cash had turned the phrase inside out. Today it meant just the opposite. *June's gone*, is what the phrase meant. *Of course I'm not okay.*

I'm fairly certain that Merle never saw Cash again, not alive, anyway.

Johnny Cash acted as a guiding light for Merle at one time.

Merle's first years in Nashville during the early Sixties were difficult, and the entertainment world felt mercilessly unstable beneath his feet. Still, Merle had a number of positive things going for him, like his job as manager of Painted Desert Music and royalties from his songs, including Claude King's most recent homerun, "Wolverton Mountain." But at any moment, the ground threatened to collapse and swallow him whole.

He hoped to change all that when he visited Johnny Cash, who'd by now grown into a Country Music superstar.

Almost two years had passed since they'd last met at Horton's funeral, but Cash acted as though it'd been only a matter of weeks. All smiles and beaming eyes, he ushered Merle into his hotel room, giving him the welcome of a long-lost friend.

"Kilgore, that new song of yours is a damn smash!" he said (Cash always referred to Merle as 'Kilgore').

Merle never had any use for modesty. "It's been number one for about five weeks now," he told him. "Made my uncle a star, too. You know, he lives up there on that mountain. He says there's a line of cars up and down that driveway. He can't do anything without someone running up to him and asking for an autograph. But you know something? I think ol' Uncle Clifton likes all that attention. He's the one who turned me on to Country Music. It's funny. I wrote him a song for his birthday—a joke more than anything—and now it's selling a million records."

"You still working for Gallico?"

"Oh, yeah," Merle went on. "It's been fun, but I'm getting antsy. I want to start touring again. I'm spending too much time behind a desk. I miss the stage."

Cash understood. "Any place in mind?"

"Nothing yet," Merle told him. "But a lot of doors are opening up for me. A lot of doors. I'm putting feelers out there. I want to make the right move."

Merle was obviously baiting Cash, and I'm sure Cash knew it, because he finally just came out and asked, "You want to be on my show, Kilgore?"

Merle didn't even hesitate. "You better believe it!"

A lot had changed since Johnny Cash left the Hayride.

Back in his earlier Shreveport days, Cash had still been new to the music business, younger and maybe a little stiff, having recently been discharged from military service as a code interceptor with the

United States Air Force, intercepting Soviet transmissions from a base in Landsberg, Germany (incidentally, Cash had been the first to transmit the news of Joseph Stalin's death). But now, coming back, Cash seemed like a different man, with a fully realized style and unmatched charisma. Here was a man in control of his destiny, who refused to follow the trampled, foot-worn path of other Country Music recording artists.

Cash had done the unthinkable in 1958 when he'd flown the coop, leaving the Opry for California, where he launched a traveling road show, featuring a variety of performers, musical styles, and comedy routines. The Carter Family, George Jones, the Statler Brothers, and even Carl Perkins were all part of the show at one time or another. Now Merle also had a place on that show. This was the chance of a lifetime.

Around this time, Merle and Cash discovered a common interest in the party lifestyle. Amphetamines, or *speed*, became the drug of choice for both men. They fueled each other's addictive personality, egging each other into taking handfuls at a time. There for a while, I think these drugs defined their friendship. (Someone once told me that Merle got Cash hooked on speed, but I can't know for sure, and I'm not sure it matters.) High on amphetamines, they succumbed to wild behaviors, from trashing hotel rooms (they once snuck a crate of chicks into a hotel and set them free on every floor by way of the elevators) to playing gags on each other. When you hear about Cash's early hell-raising years and his pill-popping frenzies, Merle was often right there with him.

The drugs explained a lot of what they did. They threw caution to the wind, downed handfuls of speed, and drank straight from the bottle. The amphetamines would suck them into a tornado and then spit them high into the vast reaches beyond sobriety. Oftentimes, they out-partied everyone around them, writing and drinking and singing songs until the sun came up.

One story—or at least variations of it—concerning pills, a cow, and Merle's wacky delusion kept coming to my attention while I interviewed folks around Nashville. Robyn Young, Country Music Hall of Famer Carl Smith, NSAI (National Songwriters Association International) Executive Director Bart Herbison, and even Judy Kilgore told it to me. Nonetheless, the story went like this: One night, Merle and Cash got so high on speed that they stumbled outside in the predawn hours, seeking out an old friend at a neighboring farm. Their "search" started from a conversation they'd had back at the house.

"Kilgore, you know what Horton once told me?" Cash had said. "'When I die, I'll come back as a cow.'"

They'd had a good laugh and then their eyes flashed with a shared idea. Maybe Horton *hadn't* been joking after all. That led them to the farm.

Stumbling outside, both dazed on amphetamines and sorely sleep-deprived, Merle and Cash hopped the fence of a neighboring farm, where a small herd of cows dotted the hillside. Cash lumbered over to the first cow and asked it, "Are you Johnny Horton?"

The cow blinked, fluttered an ear to chase away a fly, and Cash just shrugged. *Nope. Not this one.* Merle went to the next cow. "Are *you* Johnny Horton?" Still nothing. The two men made their way up the hill, moving from one cow to the next, asking the same question: *Are you Johnny Horton?*

Then, with a final: "Moo twice if it's you, Johnny," Merle got the response he'd been waiting for—a low, resonant *mooo!* that conveyed a confirmation. Merle turned to Cash and waved his arms, shouting, "Come over quick!"

Cash hurried over. "What is it?"

"I think I found him!"

"How can you tell, Kilgore?"

"Just listen." Merle put his hand on the cow's neck and whispered into its ear. "Moo if it's you, Johnny."

The cow gave a sonorous *Mooo!*

"See what I mean?" Merle shouted. "I'm telling you, it's him! And he just helped me write a song, too. I'm not lying. Here, I'll sing it to you . . ."

That was how they were, spontaneous and imagination fuelled while on drugs or alcohol. They were a fit. And it didn't end with cows.

While Merle made a promising fit for the show, Cash quickly recognized a slight problem. Merle and Cash looked too much alike. As young men, they were both tall and slender, both with black hair and deep-set eyes, and both sang in low baritone voices. Then Merle developed an impeccable Cash impersonation, assuming Cash's nervous shuffle, catching a cough in one fist, and lowering his voice so he could fool even June at times. He did Cash *better* than Cash could.

Cash, always the prankster, often put this to good use. Just for fun, he'd have Merle call June and schedule a date, or call the band members and drum up confusion. Once, goaded along by Cash, Merle called Saul Holiff, Johnny's manager, who'd been sleeping in the neighboring hotel room, and said to him, "Hello, Saul, this is Johnny. We've got a problem. You know the courthouse flowers? Well, they're not there anymore. Kilgore and I ran over them in the car. The sheriff picked us up and we're in jail. We need you to come bail us out."

It was two in the morning, and Merle and Cash roared with laughter when they heard Saul rush from the room.

Cash got a big laugh whenever Merle impersonated him. Over the years, at various parties, he'd called on Merle, saying, "Show everyone here how you do me." No one got a bigger kick out of it than Cash. Sometimes Cash would just call in the middle of the night and say, "Kilgore, do me." This always cheered him up.

Merle had fun with it, too, and sometimes the gag was on Cash.

Once, while Cash was away on the road, Merle called Johnny's housekeeper, Ms. Kelly, and in his best voice, he said, "Ms. Kelly, this is Johnny. You know all those trees on the hill to the side of the house? I want all those trees cut down."

The housekeeper sounded alarmed. "You *do*?"

"Yeah," Merle went on. "Call somebody. Have them cut 'em all down. I want a tennis court put there."

When Cash got home from his tour and found all the trees gone, he immediately confronted the housekeeper. "Ms. Kelly, what the hell happened to my trees?"

Ms. Kelly gave him a funny look. "What do you mean? You called me. You said you wanted them all cut down so you could put a tennis court there."

"Well, I don't remember that," Cash said to her, then shrugged. "But it's a hell of an idea."

The tennis court was there till the end.

They had fun with their similarities. But it just didn't work onstage. Oftentimes, the fans got them confused. They couldn't tell Merle and Cash apart, and the tour didn't need *two* Johnny Cashes. That's pretty much what ended their touring together.

It was probably for the best. Those guys lived a dangerous lifestyle. Sometimes the jokes went too far.

During a Vegas tour and showing at the Golden Nugget, Cash nearly killed Merle with a fire hose. It had started when the bus's cooling system went out. Merle was miserable. As soon as the bus reached the hotel, he hurried to his room, wanting to cool off in front of the air conditioning. He was out of luck. His room was oven hot. So he called room service and barked his complaints, and a few moments later, someone knocked at his door. Merle answered, wearing only a towel. Instead of a maintenance worker, he found Cash standing in the hallway, his arms behind his back, hiding something.

"You cooled down yet, Kilgore?" Cash asked him.

"Are you kidding me? I'm burning up!"

"Well, I hate to hear that," said Cash with a conciliatory shake of his head. "That's why I came to help you."

"Help me? How? You gonna fix my AC?"

"Nope. I had something else in mind."

Cash flashed a wolfish grin and revealed a fire hose nozzle. Then he pulled the release lever. A powerful jet of water hit Merle in the chest, spinning him in circles until he slammed against the sliding glass doors at the other end of the room. His towel vanished in the torrent, swept away like a leaf in a hurricane.

In the doorway, Cash stood with his hands on his knees, rumbling with laughter, unaware that he'd nearly sent Merle flying through a pane of glass.

On May 10, Cash's 1962 road show ended with an important final stop at New York's prestigious Carnegie Hall. This was a time of burgeoning interest in folk music, especially in the North, and Cash hoped to leverage this opportunity to generate awareness for the Country Music industry, which really didn't have an audience in a place like New York City. Having Cash sing in Carnegie Hall was big for the entire industry.

This sort of high-profile show required Cash to scrub the list of performers. The show only had room for headliners, and unfortunately for Merle, he didn't make the cut. I think he was okay with that. He didn't make a fuss about it. From a slip of newspaper that I found in Merle's scrapbook, he tells the reporter how he'd already packed his bags and was ready to leave when Cash's manager, Saul Holiff, surprised him over breakfast one morning by asking, "What songs are you planning to sing tomorrow at Carnegie Hall?"

Merle shrugged and shook his head. "I'm not scheduled to sing."

This got a rise out of Saul. He smiled. "Johnny didn't tell you, did he? Well, he put you on the list himself."

Merle dropped his cup in surprise and coffee and glass went everywhere.

It was like that with Cash—the guy couldn't pass up an opportunity to blindside Merle with a big fat surprise. Still, it beat getting blasted by a fire hose.

The night of the show, Merle got a knock at his dressing room door. He answered to find a delivery man bringing a hand-tailored costume: a Confederate uniform, complete with boots, cap, and a Confederate Cavalry Civil War sword to wear on his hip. A note was pinned to a front pocket of the ensemble. It was from Cash. *Wear this onstage tonight when you sing "Johnny Reb."*

The Carnegie Hall opened its doors to an impressive crowd that night, surprising everyone, except maybe Cash, who'd brought a production team along to record the show for a live album. Unfortunately, that never happened. Prior to the show, Cash caught a cold, and a sore throat left his voice in bad shape. The crew decided to nix the live album, but Merle didn't let that steal his thunder. He marched across the stage, in his gray Confederate uniform, and facing his predominately Yankee audience, he sang "Johnny Reb" as good as Horton ever managed. His stirring performance moved one guest to shout "*Yee-haw!*"—the battle cry of the Confederacy. The guy was in one of the upper balconies, and when he shouted, he sent his dentures flying like a cannonball over the unsuspecting audience below. From stage, Merle watched as a woman sitting on the ground floor fell out of her chair, wounded from a blow to the head—a final casualty of war.

In this time of touring with Cash and sharing the stage with enormously talented performers, Merle tapped into true songwriting magic. The result was one of the biggest hit songs ever written, "Ring of Fire."

Merle shares co-writing credit with June Carter Cash. But conspiracy theories began to surface the moment Merle died, and no one was left who could answer the question: Who wrote "Ring of Fire?"

There are several versions. There's Merle's account (I'll get to that one), there's the movie version that has June Carter writing the song all by herself, and then there's the *New York Daily News* article published in 2007 that throws everything into question. It's no wonder why many Country Music fans regard the origin story of "Ring of Fire" as a controversial topic. It's not quite a "Who shot JFK?" or the Apollo 11 moon landing, but it's intriguing all the same.

Still, it's Merle's story that I grew up hearing, and so that's the version I want to tell first.

It started on Cash's road show. Merle had made a new friend, another Country Music artist. Her name was June Carter and she'd been born into the iconic Carter Family, an influential troupe of American folk singers with musical roots reaching all the way back to the 1920s. June herself began singing on the Grand Ole Opry as a preteen. Later as an adult, she won over her audiences with a playful spirit, a snappy sense of humor, and an undeniable gift for music making.

Neither knew it until years later, but Merle and June shared an interesting bloodline connection that made them cousins. Not only was June's grandmother Margaret a Kilgore before marrying into the Carter family, but June's uncle A.P. Carter had also married a descendant of the Kilgore clan (the daughter of Margaret's sister). So she had Kilgore monkeys all up in the branches of her family trees, as the saying goes.

Maybe their genetics played a role in a certain musical compatibility? Who can say? But I think June recognized something right away. It was she who suggested they team up and write together once the road show came to an end.

"Now, Kilgore," she said (like Cash, she always called Merle by his surname), "when we get back off the road, let's pick out a few days in the week when we can write some stuff and get recorded," she told him. "I got a lot of good ideas."

They shook on it and stayed true to their commitment. They both lived in Madison, a town just north of Nashville and no more than a few miles apart. Each day, they met at June's home and wrote until they reached burnout. During this time, they produced a steady flow of songs, and Anita Carter, June's sister, even recorded a few singles, including a duet with Hank Snow called "Promised to John." Anita was something of a fan, and she wanted them to write her more songs.

Then came the big payoff for the songwriting duo. It began as a slow afternoon. Ideas came and went, but nothing gelled. Both were getting frustrated.

"Let's go back to the basics," Merle proposed. "Do we have anything to start on—an idea maybe? What about a title? Hank Williams always said it's important to have a title."

A shadow danced across June's eyes. She disappeared into the back room and returned moments later with something in her hands. "Kilgore, I want you to take a look at something. Maybe this can give us some ideas."

She showed him a book of Elizabethan poetry. "This book belonged to my uncle, A.P.," she told him (A.P. was one of the original stars of the Carter Family). "He even underlined a phrase." She handed Merle the book and pointed to the words: *Love's burning ring of fire.* "I think A.P. wanted to write a song around that line," she added.

Arching his brow, Merle said, "Ooh man. That's powerful! Let's work on it."

From such an inspired title came an easy flow of ideas, with both artists drawing from separate sources of inspiration. Merle called on his muse, the memory of high school sweetheart Ginger and the broken heart she'd left him with, while June drew from her troubled love for Cash. Their ideas came together, and in just a short while, they'd nearly completed the song. But then the session came to a screeching halt.

"Mire?" Merle intoned, frustrated. "What the hell's that supposed to mean?"

June looked genuinely offended. She'd mentioned the word as a possible rhyme for *fire*. "Well, you know, sometimes you get stuck in a mire. Haven't you ever heard that word before?"

He threw his hands in the air. "No. I'm from the city!"

"Well." She folded her arms and gave him a wounded look. "You get stuck in the mud, you get mired."

"Oh, I don't know how this fits in a love song."

"I fell down in the deepest mire," she explained.

"But 'mired' is not an affectionate word. Sorry. I just don't like it."

And that was the end of it. It was the sort of disagreement that compromised their creative flow. Besides, they were both burned out. There didn't seem to be a solution in sight. For that reason, they agreed to call it quits.

Merle drove home, overjoyed with the work he and June had accomplished. But he was worried. He didn't like leaving without a finished project. Too often this meant the kiss of death for creativity. Still, when he arrived home, he couldn't wait to tell Dot the news.

"Me and June just wrote ourselves a hit!" he told her. A ringing phone interrupted him from saying more. He picked up to hear June's voice, wound tight with excitement. "Kilgore, get back over here! Anita just called. She's wrapping up her album today and she needs one more song. I fudged and told her we'd just finished one called 'Love's Ring of Fire.' If we finish that song by this evening," June nearly hollered, "we can get it cut on her album!"

He returned to his car and headed back to June's place, working out the song in his head as he went. June did the same on her end. When he arrived, they both got to work, and it didn't take much longer to nail down a final product. They had a great song on their hands, and they both knew it.

In just a short while, they arrived at the Nashville recording studio to crash the session. Anita broke away from her work to listen to Merle and June's latest creation. She and the others in the studio all agreed— it was a great song and it belonged on Anita's album. So they got to work recording it. June even called Cash to tell him. He came to the studio just as Anita and her production team were tying up loose ends.

After listening to the final product, Cash shook his head wistfully and said, "If she doesn't hit with that song, I'll cut it myself."

Anita's "(Love's) Ring of Fire" found release on her *Folk Songs Old and New* album *(1963)*. Well received and garnering plenty of attention, the song never reached its full potential on the Billboard charts.

Cash, I think, knew it better than anybody. Merle and June re-teamed with Cash at the Hollywood Bowl in Los Angeles later that year. After the show, Cash invited them both to his dressing room, and there he told them a secret. "I dreamed I was singing that song of yours—"(Love's) Ring of Fire"—only I heard Mexican horns." He played his fingers in front of his face as if to play a trumpet; he even made a trumpeting mariachi sound to give them an idea. "I'm gonna do it just like I dreamed it," he said. "I'm putting in the Mexican horns."

Merle and June gave each other a private look. *Mexican horns?* It seemed almost absurd.

But Cash took his idea to the studio and brought the pieces together in a way that only he could have envisioned. And it worked.

In 1963, "Ring of Fire" appeared on *Ring of Fire: Best of Johnny Cash* and became an immediate success. For seven weeks in a row, the song stayed at number one on the charts, the biggest in Cash's career. The song propelled Cash's career, helped to solidify his Man in Black persona, and paved the way for Cash to slug out another string of hits. Not only did it ramp up Cash's flagging career, but it also cranked up Merle's notoriety. He became a songwriter with the Midas touch, sought after by recording artists and record labels hoping Merle could turn vinyl into gold.

That's how Merle told it. I never questioned his story, not while he lived, and I never had any reason to. But the tale has recently come under fire, and things seem less simple beneath the interrogation lamps—especially when you consider that Merle's version of the story is not the only one out there.

I'm not sure why there are so many stories. Aside from Merle's telling, you've got *Rolling Stone Magazine*, in the same issue that named the song in its top 500 all-time best, arguing that June wrote it while driving to Anita's house, wrestling with herself and her love affair with a married man known to the world as Johnny Cash. But more stories have surfaced as of late, versions that are somewhat alarming and possibly damaging to history. In Vivian Liberto's 2008 biography *I Walked the Line: My Life with Johnny*, she (Cash's first wife) fueled the flames of controversy by insisting June had nothing to do with the song, that Cash wrote it while camping and then gave co-writing credits to June because he felt sorry for her and wanted to offer her financial help. According to Vivian, Cash told her this, point blank.

Supporting this claim is an article in the *New York Daily News* entitled "No Cash for Johnny Cash Daughters over 'Ring of Fire.'" Here, a famous fiddler named Curly Lewis argues that June had nothing to do with the song. In his version, Merle and Cash wrote "Ring of Fire" while on a fishing trip. How could Curly possibly know this? Because he was there, watching the whole incredible thing unfold right before his eyes.

Curly's story goes like this: They'd all gone fishing in Casitas, California, just he and Merle and Johnny, and they'd jammed themselves into a small boat, fishing poles out, with the sun beating down on their faces and the water lapping at the hull. Somewhere along the way, Merle and Cash started singing and tossing out melodies, riffing on each other's ideas, and Curly just sat there, listening in awe. I don't know if Merle and Cash caught any fish that day, but *my oh my,* they nabbed a hit of a song clean from the ether.

A song so good, in fact, that Cash looked at Merle and said, "Kilgore, we just wrote ourselves a hit."

So why doesn't Cash share songwriting credits with Merle?

Well, according to Curly (remember, Vivian shares this story), Cash gave songwriting credits to June to avoid losing a cut to his soon-to-be divorced wife Vivian. By giving June his portion of the songwriting credits, he protected his share of the royalties. If this is true, I suppose his plan paid off pretty well. After all, Cash *did* divorce Vivian, and he did later marry June, and in that way, I suppose, his portion of the royalties did eventually come back to him.

But this is Curly's story, remember, and I never heard Merle mention it (though I'd love to hear what he'd have to say were he alive today). Do I believe Curly and Vivian's stories? No, I can't say I do, and neither does Merle's widow Judy, or his ex-wife Dot (who remembers the day in 1963 that Merle came home after spending the afternoon with June, writing the song), or his children, who doubt their father would keep such a secret from them.

But I also can't say that I know the truth. There are so many stories. Merle had his poetry book, and June had her secret love affair, and Curly and Vivian had, well, something else in mind, maybe. Nonetheless, I'm fairly certain the truth lies somewhere in between it all.

Either way, I don't think the song would have ever existed if Merle and June had never met, or if Cash and June had never fallen in love.

In late February of 1968, after Cash proposed to June during a live performance in London, Ontario, they called to share the news with Merle. They also wanted to ask him for a favor.

"Kilgore?" It was June. "Johnny has something to say to you."

"All right," Merle said, happy for his friends. "Well, then put him on!"

There was a pause and then Cash's baritone voice said over the line: "Ah, Kilgore, what are you doing on March 1st?"

Merle frowned. "I don't know, John. Let me look at my calendar." It was a joke; he didn't have anything so important planned that he couldn't drop for Johnny Cash. "Absolutely nothing."

"Oh, yeah you are," Cash returned. "You're going to be my best man at the wedding of June Carter and J.R. Cash."

"Me?" Merle nearly dropped the phone. After a moment he added, "Is everybody out of town?"

Cash rumbled with laughter. "No. That's not it at all. We're having a private wedding; we don't want it to get out of hand. We're going to sneak up to Franklin, Kentucky. There won't be more than ten people there. No press. Nothing. And we decided that you're our old war buddy. That's what June called you. She said that we gotta have you in our wedding. And I agreed."

March 1, 1968, at a chapel in Franklin, Kentucky, Johnny Cash and June Carter exchanged vows, igniting a love affair that was soon romanticized by popular culture. This was a monumental moment in the world of entertainment, and again, Merle found himself standing at its epicenter, this time as best man to the moment, there to pin a rosebud boutonniere to Cash's lapel.

Merle wore a sharkskin suit to the wedding. It'd been snug several days earlier when he'd rented the thing, but on the big day, with his body all bloated from his medication and a night of hard drinking, he could hardly squeeze himself into it. To make matters worse, the church was stuffy and he'd gotten all sweaty. As a result, the sharkskin suit clung to him like plastic wrap.

It was too late to change clothes. Everyone was waiting in the pews, and Cash had already entrusted him with the ring, which Merle kept tucked away in his front pocket, and this would all be over soon.

The ceremony began. Following the wedding music, Johnny and June took their places at the front of the church, and the preacher read a significant passage from his Bible and then nodded to Merle, cueing for the ring.

As practiced, Merle stepped forward and reached for his front pants pocket, when panic set in. His suit seemed to be shrinking by the second and his pockets had all but sealed themselves shut. He couldn't get at the ring. With fingers that felt as big as pork sausages, he pawed at his pants. His heart thudded in his ears but a hush fell over the church.

Cash gave him a pointed look that said, *Get on with it, Kilgore!*

Merle made a desperate decision. Hooking his fingers into the seam of his pocket, he tugged until the fabric gave a terrific *rip!*—loud enough to reach the folks in the back pews, causing heads to turn in his direction. But Merle was so relieved he didn't care. He handed over the ring with a nervous smile.

It was that same ring, I suppose, that Cash showed to Merle during their final meeting on that mournful day some three decades later.

The universe often acts with a sense of irony. Take for example how Johnny Cash outlived June Carter. Who would have ever thought that she'd be the first to go? After all, she'd all but saved Cash from himself in the Sixties. The Man in Black had no right to outlive her, considering his early years of hard drinking and drugging, oftentimes with Merle at his side.

But here's a little known secret: all these years, Cash had been hiding from the Angel of Death. That's what he told Merle, anyway, when Merle came to visit him at the hospital (over the years, as the men grew older, they paid each other plenty of hospital visits).

"I never use my real name when I check into the hospital," Cash told him. Sitting up in bed, he snapped off his bracelet and handed it to Merle.

"I use a pseudonym: Malcolm Kilgore," Cash told him.

Merle fingered the plastic bracelet, considering it. Just as Cash said, the name Malcolm Kilgore was stamped on the plastic.

Cash smiled. "If the Angel of Death comes looking for me, he won't find me."

Merle cleared his throat, his superstitious sensibilities alerted. This new information—that Cash cheated the Angel of Death by using *his* last name—made him uneasy. Still, he made sure not to let it show.

"I know where the name Kilgore came from," he told Cash. "But where did Malcolm come from?"

Cash brightened at the question. "Malcolm IV, King of Scots!"

In retrospect, I suppose the name-change gimmick worked. Maybe it kept Cash alive for decades more than he deserved. Still, you can't run from the inevitable. Several months after June's death, at age 71, Cash checked himself into Baptist Hospital in Nashville where, on September 12, 2003, the Angel of Death finally found him.

In the aftermath, Merle personally called the hospital, asking the lady at the front desk an odd question: What name had Cash used to register himself? The front desk lady, hesitated, then put him on hold. When she came back, she told him. J.R. Cash. Cash had used his official name.

I suppose he was done hiding.

In 2005—the same year that Merle died—Cash's definitive film "Walk the Line," starring Joaquin Phoenix and Reese Witherspoon, hit the theaters.

Everyone in the Kilgore family was excited. We couldn't wait to see how the filmmakers would treat Merle's character, given his importance to Cash's story. But we were all in for a surprise. Merle was completely left out of the script. We were more than disappointed; we were hurt. This seemed so unfair to Merle's legacy, an irresponsible rewriting of history. There on the big screen was June (played by Oscar winner Reese Witherspoon), writing "Ring of Fire" all by her woeful self, and Merle nowhere to be seen. I suppose you can't fault the screenwriter for romanticizing the story and making it more compelling, but it was a lousy way to remember my grandfather.

But to director/co-writer James Mangold's credit, he does attempt to explain Merle's omission from the film on the Blu-ray's audio commentary. To introduce a bigger-than-life character like Merle Kilgore in a single scene wouldn't have made sense, Mangold pointed out. Merle was just too big for a quiet cameo. So the creative team agreed to leave Merle out.

HƏNK WILLIƏMS, JI.

Dark sunglasses, cowboy hat, unkempt beard—Hank Williams, Jr., is a Country Music icon.

For years, Hank Jr. carried the Country Music heavyweight title of Entertainer of the Year. He's won every award conceivable, produced unimaginable record sales, knocked out endless Billboard chart toppers. There are museums built around his name. I think you get the point. Though he hit his peak in the Eighties and Nineties, his music continues to find its way into mainstream media. To this day there's always someone singing his songs in Nashville, especially on karaoke night, and the music always gets a rise from the crowd ("Hank, why do you drink?" croons the would-be singer, then holds the microphone out to the bar, and the crowd roars back, *To get drunk!*; "Hank, why do you roll smoke?" *To get stoned!*).

Hank Jr. became a country-rock phenomenon, with all the flash of big money, wild parties, tour buses, and platinum records. His music videos showcased rock stars and girls in bikinis, while his musical style captured the rebellious spirit of the age. For someone who continues to pack auditoriums with screaming fans, there's no denying that Hank Williams, Jr., ascended to superstardom, becoming one of the most important figures in Country Music.

How he got there is the amazing part.

Hank Jr. has an impressive history, as good as any work of fiction, starring a country singer on a journey to find himself and his music, and who nearly finds death instead—ultimately completing his transformation. Hank told the story himself in his 1979 autobiography *Living Proof: The Hank Williams, Jr. Story*, co-written with Michael Bane. The story was so good that the USA Network picked it up in the early Eighties and produced a made-for-television movie that aired in 1983 starring Richard Thomas, best known as John-Boy Walton from the 1970s television drama *The Waltons*. For those of you who never read Hank's book or watched his movie, you're in luck.

There's no way for me to tell Merle's story without also telling Hank's.

Arguably, Merle and Hank Jr.'s story begins all the way back in 1949, when Harry S. Truman was president, the Red Scare had worked its way into the American collective conscious, and Hank Williams, Sr., stood at the threshold of becoming a megastar.

In the months following the world's most important footrace—a race that began with two teenage boys in the back parking lot of the KWKH building and ended with Hank Sr. directing Merle to "Grab it, Hoss"—my grandfather was in the inner circle of someone famous.

Hank Williams, Sr., apparently took interest in Merle. Why else would he continue to allow Merle to carry his guitar? After a while, it'd become almost routine. Only fourteen years old, and Merle had the best job in town. Best of all, carrying Hank's guitar came with a backstage pass to Shreveport's Municipal Auditorium, practically the epicenter of Country Music—outside the Opry, of course.

It was during all this—in the early spring of Hank Sr.'s career—when Randall Hank Williams was born. On May 26, Merle heard the news just like everyone else. It was *big* news: Audrey Williams had given birth to a nine-pound baby boy. Hank Williams had become a father.

In the following days, Merle, thinking himself a privileged guest (after all, he did carry Hank's guitar), paid a visit to the hospital delivery room in Bossier City, hoping to catch Hank Sr. and congratulate him. But he achieved more than that. Hank Williams was so glad to see Merle that he gave him an escort straight to the nursery where they stood at the bank of windows, gazing down into a dimly-lit room of tiny cribs. Hank pointed out his son from a roomful of crying babies, and together he and Merle smiled.

That's him right there, Hank told him. *That's Randall Hank Williams.*

I can almost see them, their reflections floating in the glass, each wearing big grins, while Hank taps at the glass, saying, *That's Bocephus.* (Incidentally, Hank Sr. borrowed the nickname from a ventriloquist dummy owned by Grand Ole Opry comedian Rod Brasfield; the name stuck, and "Bocephus" remains to this day a distinctive and memorable moniker for Hank Jr.).

It makes for the perfect beginning. You could even say that Hank Williams, Sr., christened this friendship between his son and young Merle. I also think it makes good scene. Two generations—Hank Sr. and Hank Jr.—separated by a pane of glass that catches Merle's reflections. There are hints of a great design, or an underlying structure, that binds Merle to the Williams family.

Hank may have set their friendship on course; but if anyone deserves kudos for bringing together Merle and Hank Jr., that credit goes to a mother's intuition. Had Audrey Williams not reached out to Merle in the coming years to ask for his help and involvement in her son's life, the two men might never have come together. Who knows how that would have changed things? I don't think I would have written this book.

It was the end of the 1950s, and those cosmic cogs turned once again to find perfect synchronicity, goading Audrey into contacting Merle. He was in his early twenties and working his way up in the music business. He'd established himself as a songwriter and a radio deejay *and* a family man with a wife and three children. Managing Shreveport's KENT Radio paid him a salary, but it also gave him ulcers. He was working at the station when he got the call.

"Hello! KENT Radio!" he barked into phone (and I like to think that maybe he heard, far in the distance, the sudden clatter of wheels setting into motion).

"Merle Kilgore?" asked a female voice, somehow familiar. "This is Audrey, Audrey Williams. Do you remember me?"

His eyes opened wide. "Well, of course!" he nearly shouted. How could he forget? She'd been married to Hank Williams, his hero and an American legend. That Audrey had decided to call him was beyond flattering. She actually *remembered* him, the kid who hung around the Hayride, fawning over all the stars. A lot had changed since then. "What can I do for you, Audrey?"

"Merle, I need a favor." For the next little while, she explained her latest business venture, a traveling Country Music road show. They were making their way to Shreveport. "I need your help. I want you to promote the show for me. Can I count on you?"

Merle didn't hesitate to help. I'm sure he would have done anything for Audrey. She was practically Country Music royalty, given her status as the ex-wife of a legend (and Merle's personal idol). He was so excited to help that he made her two promises: not only would he promote her show, but he would also find a guest singer—someone with real box office draw. The moment Merle ended the call, he flexed his networking muscles and started dialing numbers from his little black book. By the end of the night, he'd locked in one of the hottest acts in the business.

The night of the show came. Audrey's parade of singers (including a guest appearance by a nine-year-old Hank Jr., who sang one of his father's songs) performed for a packed house. Then it was time to bring out Merle's VIP guest: Little Richard, the latest rock-and-roll sensation to hit the scene. The guy ran out onstage with an electric guitar and cranked out songs like "Lucille," "Keep a Knockin'," and "Good Golly, Miss Molly." Backstage, a friend approached Merle in the booming excitement to congratulate him on a spectacular show. Gushing with pride, Merle was all smiles until his friend said in a matter-of-fact tone, "By the way, that last guy—he put on a great show. He looked just like Little Richard."

Merle was taken back, shocked. "*What?* Are you kidding me? Didn't you see the show? That was him. That *was* Little Richard!"

The man thought about it for a moment, then shook his head. "No, I don't think so. I just saw Little Richard in New York. He plays the piano, you know? That guy back there—" he hooked his thumb in the general direction of the stage, "—that guy plays the guitar. That was definitely *not* Little Richard."

The guy was right. The following morning, Merle learned the embarrassing truth: he'd hired an imposter. No wonder he'd gotten such a low price for a major celebrity. I'm not sure if Audrey ever discovered Merle's mess up, but if she did, she never said a word about it. They parted ways with a handshake, happy with the show's success, and another five years would pass before their paths crossed again.

The year 1963 was an exciting time for Merle. Living in Nashville and carried along by the momentum of "Wolverton Mountain" and "Ring of Fire," he'd become a respected name in Nashville. By day, he worked with Al Gallico in the publishing business, making friends with the movers and the shakers of the industry. On nights and weekends, Merle worked county fairground shows and nightclub gigs on Broadway and Second Avenue. He exhausted every aspect of the business.

Eventually his local buzz earned him the attention of an old friend. Audrey Williams had located him in Nashville and called to touch base. During their talk, she mentioned her upcoming party and asked him to come see her. "Sounds fantastic!" Merle told her. "I'll be there!"

There was no need for her to give directions. Everyone in the music business knew where Audrey Williams lived.

Merle arrived at the party with Dot and their kids, and they were all excited to see the house on Franklin Pike. It was *famous*. The home of Hank Williams was practically a historical landmark, a must-see attraction for Nashville tourists. Even the stars wanted to see it. Jerry Lee Lewis, Fats Domino, Ray Charles—they dropped by all the time, hoping to play a few keys on Hank's piano, hoping to feel the presence of his ghost. On the day of Audrey's party, the house was a scene of big names and big fun. With Dot and the kids occupied, Merle slipped outside, finding the pool area alive with music and laughter. I imagine Merle had no problem finding Audrey, she being the regal Hollywood type, poised in her foldout chair with her Greta Garbo hairstyle and dark sunglasses. When she saw Merle, she waved him over and demanded he sit next to her. They were all smiles as they caught up on the past five or so years since her traveling Country Music show had come to Shreveport. Then she stopped him and pointed to the other side of the pool.

"That's him over there," she said, pointing. "That's Hank. I want you to hear him play."

Merle pivoted in his chair to see Hank Jr., a handsome fourteen-year-old boy with broad shoulders and thick brown hair. He had an arm draped over the shoulder of a pretty girl and a revolver gripped in one hand (much to Dot's reproach, he'd been shooting at backyard targets all morning). The boy had changed a great deal since May of

1949, when Merle had first spied him through the Bossier nursery window. For starters, the poor kid had had a father then.

Audrey called out to her son, telling him to bring his guitar, and he did as he was told.

"Hank, this is Merle Kilgore," Audrey said to Hank as he moved over to stand before them. "He knew your father. I'd bet he'd love to hear you play one of your daddy's songs."

"Well, all right," Hank Jr. said with a shrug. He situated his guitar and started to play, launching into "Hey Good Lookin'" with an easy confidence. Everything about him—the tenor of his voice, the sway of his hips, the wagging of his knees—said *Hank Williams*. It was an uncanny impression of his father.

Merle sat up in his chair, his jaw hanging. Audrey had obviously failed to mention an important detail: Hank Jr. had been practicing *a lot*. With a grin, Merle looked to Audrey, pointing a finger at Hank Jr., and said, "That boy is ready!" Unable to hide his excitement, his voice carried across the pool area. "You need to get a band, get a bus, and get him on the road!"

Audrey folded her arms over her chest, nodding, while her mouth formed a satisfied grin. "All right, then," she said. "And you're going to open for him." She went on to explain her plans of a road show—*Audrey Williams' Caravan of the Stars*—with a star-studded lineup, including her son. "You can emcee for us. Open a few shows."

And . . . and there was more. Merle's job wouldn't end there. Hank Jr. needed a friend on the road. By touring with Hank and opening for all his shows, Merle could also keep an eye on the boy, serving as a kind of chaperone and keeping him out of trouble. Audrey knew the risks of living on the road; it was a life of temptations, and Hank would be surrounded by people pretending to be his friend forever. This sort of life had destroyed her first marriage; it had also driven her ex-husband to an early grave. For that reason, Hank Jr. would need a true friend if he were to survive out there.

I don't know why she chose Merle for this role. She hardly knew him, aside from their brief interludes over the years, but she certainly trusted him. Maybe she clung to the memory of Merle as the innocent fourteen-year-old boy who spent his summer evenings at the Hayride, hoping to carry guitars for famous people—a boy who'd been especially loyal to her husband.

Whatever her reasons, Audrey offered Merle a job on that sunny afternoon and she *insisted* he take it.

"If you don't accept," she told him, "then I'll have no other choice but to wait until Hank gets a few more years under his belt."

Merle's decision was *that* important. He owed it to Hank Jr. to accept, and he did.

Randall Hank Williams, Jr., was in many ways Audrey's creation. From early on, she held an unwavering conviction that her ex-husband's artistic genius flowed through Hank Jr.'s veins, and she spent years nurturing and cultivating that potential. In 1955, when Hank was just six years old, she started grooming him for the stage. That same year, she wrote a letter to the Hank Williams fan club; the letter was public, but her words were personal, written for her deceased husband, telling him about her son and how "One of these days before too long he'll be singing for you."[17]

She hired musicians and singers to come to the house and give her son lessons. Even her famous houseguests were potential teachers, and she rarely let them leave without sharing their wisdom. She personally brought plenty to the table, too. She taught Hank Jr. the nuances of his father's character, like his quiet smile and his magnetic personality. She also taught him how his father projected himself without raising his voice, and how he captivated his audience by moving his hips and knees and singing in what she called his "high lonesome" tone. All this was important if Hank Jr. was to carry out the act of impersonating his father.

"You're going to be just like him some day," she'd tell him.

It's hard to know what Audrey's true motives were. But critics speculated. Some joked she just wanted to bring her husband back from the grave. Others surmised she only wanted money. But it's highly possible, and probably closest to the truth, that she was simply looking out for her son, guiding him through the harsh entertainment business. Whatever the case, her son accepted his role as the reincarnation of Hank Williams.

In 1957, an eight-year-old Hank Jr. played his first show in Swainsboro, Georgia; in 1960, he played the Grand Ole Opry.

Now, in 1963—with Merle onboard—Audrey was ready to make major moves. Just a short while after that party at her house, Hank Jr. signed a $300,000-per-year contract with MGM Records.[18] Several local papers picked up the story, and the big publicity photo showed young Hank with pen in hand, moments away from signing. Merle is also in the photo, sitting beside Hank, wearing a business suit, flashing a showman's smile, and looking for all the world as if he was about to sign his own contract.

In a way, I suppose, he was.

During those early years, Audrey drove the business, and she kept her foot mashed against the gas pedal. She used the money that she'd won in an out-of-court settlement with Billie Jean. (The two women had battled it out for several years as they both considered themselves entitled to Hank's money. Still, in the end, Billie Jean relinquished the rights of Hank's estate to Audrey because she wanted the money, an alleged $30,000.) Audrey formed Aud-Lee Attractions along with promoter Buddy Lee, and they promoted the show—a Country Music review called *Caravan of Stars*, featuring a number of artists like Merle Haggard, Waylon Jennings, Duke W. Paducah, and even Audrey herself.

But the star of the attraction was always Hank Jr.

For Merle, opening for Hank Jr. was a side job at best. He still had his own career to think about. There was always the hope of writing his next smash hit or gaining national attention. He certainly kept busy through the Sixties. With Aud-Lee Attractions promoting him, his calendar was booked. He traveled year-round, with shows in Las Vegas, Topeka, Nashville, and even Frankfurt, Germany.

He had a lot going for him in the Sixties. He was tall and lean with a bright smile and smoldering good looks. He played a sufficient rhythm guitar and sang in an oak-barrel tenor that suited the smoky barrooms. With his songwriting credentials and his regular guest appearances on the Opry, he never had to look far for work. From his *Billboard Magazine* shout-out as one of the nation's top songwriters to his accumulation of BMI songwriting awards, he'd become a local big shot. He continued writing hit records for other artists; Claude King scored a moderate hit with "Tiger Woman" (1965) and Faron Young did even better with "She Went a Little Bit Farther" (1969). Merle's solo album *God Bless the Working Man* (1967) achieved modest success and even earned a nod from Paul Harvey on national radio. He stayed busy in Nashville; he always found places to sing. And there was invariably the hope of breaking into the national spotlight. Each time he cut a new album, there was that hope.

He also made his first break into Hollywood films. Several acting roles came his way, in addition to soundtrack offers. He played a reverend in *Sing a Song for Heaven's Sake* (1965) and cut the theme song for *5 Card Stud* (1967) and *Nevada Smith* (1966), starring Steve McQueen (though this track landed on the cutting room floor).

He took on his biggest role in *Second Fiddle to a Steel Guitar* (1966), a film that served as a measuring stick for his early career. As a movie,

Second Fiddle was all over the place: one part drama, one part slapstick comedy (with cameo appearances by Leo Gorcey and Huntz Hall of the famed Bowery Boys), and one part barnyard jamboree. This latter part makes up the bulk of the film and takes obvious inspiration from the Grand Ole Opry show. It showcased an impressive lineup of Country Music superstars, from Webb Pierce and Lefty Frizzell to Faron Young and Minnie Pearl, including Little Jimmy Dickens and Bill Monroe of "Blue Moon of Kentucky" fame. Merle played the host, master of ceremonies, decked out in a sparkling-gold smoking jacket and bowtie, his face beaming with a salesman's grin. In the film, he introduces each act with a tempered voice and all but oozes with easy affability. I'm not sure how Merle got the gig (the film's music director was Audrey Williams, and I'd bet she and Buddy Lee helped Merle get the part), but it must have amped up his career, made him feel like a star. For one shining moment, Merle Kilgore was in the club, standing shoulder-to-shoulder with the giants of show business.

From the starting gun, Hank Jr. was recognized as something special. He drew huge crowds to his shows. Much of his celebrity came by birthright; he was born to a famous country star, and that in itself attracted droves of Country Music fans, all curious to see the son of the hillbilly Shakespeare, all of them expecting a sort of Second Coming.

"Hank Williams was a saint," said Hank Jr. in *Living Proof*,[19] "and I was his chosen son."

Hank Williams, Jr., gave them their money's worth. "Hey Good Lookin'," "Jambalaya," "Long Gone Lonesome Blues," he sang all the classic Hank Williams songs, and he sang them so well that everyone was more than surprised. They were flabbergasted.

The audience's reaction was always the same. They watched at first with amused curiosity, maybe even suspicion, wondering how this was going to play out. But then Hank Jr. would launch into his act—an impersonation of his father, from the high-lonesome nasal voice to the subtle sway of his hips—and all those faces in the audience would crack, their expectant smiles dissolving into quiet awe. No one was prepared for such an uncanny imitation. They could almost believe the boy was channeling his father's ghost.

By the end of his show, Hank Jr. would have more than fans. He had *zealots*—an audience with rattled expectations, convinced that the legendary Hank Williams had returned from the dead.

Merle saw it with his own eyes. Once, while backstage during Hank's show, he spotted Grand Ole Opry star Red Foley—an old friend of Hank Williams, Sr.—slumped in his chair, looking almost ill with his hands trembling and his brow knitted. Merle hurried over to him, and the old man looked up with watery eyes. "I thought it was him," the old man croaked. "For a moment, I thought I saw Hank Williams standing there like a ghost. It scared me. It really did."[20]

Hank Jr.'s first year with MGM Records (a label that became a powerhouse by signing a deal with Hank Williams, Sr., in 1947) was a good one. He recorded his own cut of "Long Gone Lonesome Blues," one of his father's original classics, and it reached number five on the country charts. But Hank Jr. became a true star when he recorded the soundtrack for *Your Cheatin' Heart*, a musical/biopic starring George Hamilton as Hank Williams, Sr. The movie was a hit, and the album sold a million copies. Suddenly, fourteen-year-old Hank Jr. became the biggest thing in Country Music.

The novelty act worked; no one questioned that. But Hank Jr. couldn't be expected to impersonate his father forever. The fuse had been lit the moment Hank Jr. became suspicious of his limitations. There were shackles around his ankles, trapping him to a one-trick pony act. "Singing your daddy's song as a boy is great," Hank would often say in interviews. "Singing them as a grown man is hell."

Hank didn't stay a kid for long, especially while living on the road.

Before he had his driver's license, he'd become introduced to the clubs and barroom scene. He leveraged his association with Merle, Waylon Jennings, and a few other performers who were much older and who could show him the ropes. Merle turned out to be a somewhat bad role model. It wasn't all his fault; he'd held out against Hank Jr.'s persistence as long as possible. "No way, Hank," he'd say to the boy. "Your mama would kill us if she found out!" But I suppose Merle was just a big pushover, and eventually he started taking Hank Jr. with him to waste the night in smoky barrooms and drink, while also hooking him up with star-struck groupie girls. This was all a general introduction to the madness of the nightlife.

Hank Jr. transitioned easily into that world of honkytonk dives and booze. He hooked up with the girls and drank until he stumbled all over himself. Of course, the moment he started slurring his words, people would laugh and say, "Would you look at him? He's just like his daddy!" This was precisely the problem.

Hank Jr. was suffocating beneath the shadow of his father. From the outside looking in, everything looked just fine. But as his career blossomed, storms began brewing. All the publishers and MGM executives, and even Audrey, were excited about his success. But Hank Jr. was suffering from a psychological backlash. It was burnout. His 1966 single "Standing in the Shadows" hinted at this. He was only seventeen when that song made it to the Billboard charts; it painted the picture of a troubled young man working out some big psychological issues.

But the show went on. In 1969, Hank and Johnny Cash performed together at Cobo Hall in Detroit and achieved the highest-grossing Country Music show at that time. That same year, Hank's "Songs My Father Left Me" became his first country album to top the charts.

So now it's time to speak openly about Merle's less-than-glamorous problems with alcohol and pills—all of its hilarities, its seeming benefits, and ultimately, its destructive end results. My grandfather broke free of his addictions in 1976, around the time I was born, and once he sobered up, he never touched the stuff again. There were no meetings, no violent relapses. He just walked away from it and never looked back.

But there was a time—*Yes, Amen!*—there was a time that pills and alcohol played a major part in his party-hard lifestyle. Horton's warning about alcohol went to the wayside. Merle's signature drink was Tab and whiskey. The sauce helped him perform. He was a happy drunk (his words, not mine); it kept him loose and boisterous, while the pills kept the engine revved, even when his body threatened to collapse. He was the spokesperson for getting hammered. "Get on the whiskey!" was his evening show catchphrase; it's what he shouted from the stage.

So how was he ever going to quit?

It had started back in Shreveport, but Merle's drinking and pill-popping days kicked into overdrive around the time he teamed up with Audrey and Hank Jr. in 1964. That's when he found a party-all-night hangout at his booking agent's home. Buddy Lee had been a fairground wrestling promoter before moving to Nashville, but then he'd teamed up with Audrey Williams to form Aud-Lee Attractions. Buddy Lee kept his door open to all his recording artists, and so on any given day of the week, he got visits from guys like Kris Kristofferson, Waylon Jennings, and Johnny Cash. Back then, those guys all got wired on speed and stayed up for days and weeks at a time hanging out, drinking, and writing music.

They called it roaring, and during those chaotic streaks, they avoided drinking too much to preserve their buzz. They wanted to roar all night and create music. Everybody was looking for that next smash hit, and they used speed to chase the next song. When they came down, they came down hard. They crashed on sofas or on the floor, and Buddy didn't mind. These artists were the lifeblood of his business and he wanted to keep them happy.

Merle took special advantage of Buddy Lee's open-door policy. He became a regular guest, often crashing there for days and even weeks at a time, always wired and always downing handfuls of speed. Merle was a whirlwind, playing Sinatra or Spanish mariachi records and dancing around the room. He was the life of the party, fun and wild-spirited. He wrote songs on the fly, usually with other equally wired songwriters. He entertained everyone with his off-the-wall antics, like juggling a flaming Mexican bullfighter's hat with Buddy Lee (the living room ceiling had soot scuffs for years) or offering psychic readings. It was common for Merle to write through to the morning hours, skipping out on sleep, and greet the early-risers with a ghost-eyed grin, bristling with nervous energy.

People started to take notice. On a scorching hot day at Opry singer Carl Smith's pool party in Nashville, Merle arrived looking rather ridiculous in his white polyester suit while everyone else was wearing bathing suits and Bermuda shirts. Just for fun, Carl—who recalled this story to me in a 2009 interview (not long before he died)—walked up to Merle and shoved him. Merle was likely pretty loaded and was easily knocked off balance. Into the pool he went, making a splash big enough to draw everyone's attention. He flailed about until a few sunbathers wrestled him onto the ledge.

"You all right, Merle?" Carl asked, pushing his way through the onlookers, feeling bad about what he'd done.

Merle looked up at him with sour disappointment. "I'm fine, Carl. But damn it, you ruined my pills."

All this time, Merle was growing further apart from his family. Rita Lee (Buddy's wife) never forgot the day Dot called looking for her husband. Rita just sat there with her jaw hanging. Merle Kilgore

. . . *married?* She would never have guessed. He never mentioned a family. She'd just assumed, by the way he acted and how he sometimes crashed on the couch, that he was a bachelor without a family waiting for him at home.

But that family was most certainly waiting. Oh brother, they were waiting.

The time eventually came for Merle to dry out. Madison Rural Sanitarium and Hospital was a sprawling facility just outside of Nashville, tucked away on a cozy green hillside. He looked bad when Dot came for a visit.

With desperation in his eyes, he told his wife, "I can do without my pills. But I can't do without my music. Bring me my portable record player, will ya?"

Dot returned the following day with the turntable, the kind that folds up like a briefcase for easy toting, and Merle grinned like a ten-year-old on Christmas morning. He took his turntable and sent her away, saying, "Don't worry about me. I feel like a million dollars!"

Back inside his room, he investigated the turntable's hollow recesses, finding the pills he'd hidden there weeks earlier without telling his wife. He stayed bouncing off the walls for the next several days, charming the nurses, singing songs for fellow addicts. Meanwhile, the doctors all agreed: Merle's recovery was going remarkably well.

As for the speed, he relocated his supply to a potted plant on the windowsill. It seemed a fine hiding place until someone sabotaged his plans. He returned to his room one afternoon to find his pills reduced to slush at the bottom of the ceramic pot. One of the orderlies had decided to water his plant. It was a *fake* plant—a minor detail that had apparently gone overlooked.

Merle got out of the hospital, but recovery didn't take place for another few years. He had more miles to travel down that dark and lonely road. But one thing did change: his marital status. In the next year or so, he and Dot separated and eventually got a divorce. She took the kids, and Merle was on his own.

By the end of the Sixties, Merle's lifestyle was unstable. He had another failed marriage (this made number two), Dot and the kids were out of the picture, and his years of working with Al Gallico had finally come to an end. Fortunately, he found another job while hauling boxes of his things to his car.

Leon Ashley was a self-published recording artist who became a hot item in Nashville after releasing his own number one Country Music hit, something unheard of back then. Merle had a hand in this success. Just a year or so earlier, he'd stopped by Tootsie's for lunch when he overheard a couple of men in suits gabbing at a nearby table. Apparently, these men worked for a major record label, and they'd just signed on a new artist with a lot of promise: Leon Ashley. But they were concerned. Leon had a bad drinking problem and everyone knew it.

"I got a hit out of this son of a bitch," said one of the men between laughs. "But I don't know if we can keep the bastard sober long enough to get a cut out of him!"

Merle knew Leon had an office just down the hallway from Gallico. After lunch, Merle marched down to his office and told him everything he'd heard. Leon was so pissed that he cut ties with the record label, founded Ashley Records, and produced his own song. "Laura (What's He Got That I Ain't Got?)" became a smash hit, landing at number one on the Country charts in 1967, and years later would become a hit for other recording artists, guys like Marty Robbins and Kenny Rogers.

The day Merle left Gallico, Leon caught him in the hallway and offered him a job. Merle shrugged and said "Why not?" He started working for Leon that same day. Ashley Records became Merle's new home for a while; he left Columbia Records and signed on with Ashley's label.

While Merle rarely, if ever, worked a true blue-collar job, he certainly qualified as a blue-collar worker of the music industry. He was a working entertainer, and he traveled all over the world doing shows. He traveled with Leon or George Jones or anyone else willing to team up. He also toured with Hank Jr. and visited bigger towns (including London, where he opened for Hank at the Empire Pool—now the Wembley Auditorium—during a Country Music festival there). He also made regular appearances on the Opry. But by the time Hank Jr. left for his hiatus in Alabama, I think Merle was facing an unhappy realization: he was getting older, and his career was not taking off as he'd hoped.

But it happened for Hank Jr.

In 1970, Hank signed the biggest contract in the history of MGM Records. That same year he scored a number one hit with "All for the Love of Sunshine," recorded for Clint Eastwood's *Kelly's Heroes.* Hank's career was on the fast track now. City after city, the shows got bigger and bigger. When he wasn't touring, he was appearing on primetime television, on shows like *The Ed Sullivan Show, The Jimmy Dean Show, The Joey Bishop Show,* and even *The Tonight Show.*

From the outside, everything looked great. But Hank was struggling, wrestling with his own identity. The fans didn't help. They made backhanded comments like, "Oh, I just loved your daddy, Hank; I *loved* him. You're pretty good, but you'll never be as good as your father." They never let him forget it: Hank Jr. would *never* live up to his father's name.

He struggled with his music, too. He had ideas of doing his own stuff one day, if anyone would ever let him. From an early age, Hank Jr. had shown a deep interest in rock-and-roll. He liked the feel and the rhythm of the Delta Blues, artists like Lightnin' Hopkins, Jimmy Reed, Muddy Waters, and John Lee Hooker. To learn their styles, he brought a portable piano onto his tour bus and practiced rock-and-roll and boogie-woogie riffs until everyone around him was pulling their hair out. While still in high school, he'd even formed a rock band, Rockin' Randall and the Rockets. But this music was off limits to him. His mother was especially resistant. She saw his interest in rock-and-roll as a threat to her business. "You go out there, and you do your daddy's songs," she told him. "And that's *all*."

After several years of this, Hank Jr. had become bitter, convinced that all the booking agents, record labels, and managers only stood in the way of self realization. No one, it seemed, cared about Hank's personal development. Audrey was especially vocal on this subject. Just like the others, she wanted him to walk the path already forged by his father. It was safer and more secure that way. Audrey had put the greatest obstacle in his path, barring him from reaching his own musical identity. Eventually, a war brewed between Hank Jr. and his mother; he pushed, and she pushed back, and you can bet both were strong-willed people.

By Hank's twenty-first birthday in 1970, his resentment had festered into something like a cancer. He made his anger public during his party in Galveston, Texas. In *Billboard Magazine*, 2004, Merle remembers how, surrounded by a crowd of friends and music executives, Hank Jr. found himself goaded into giving an unexpected speech. When everyone turned to look at him, he blurted out, "All right. I'm going to tell all of you. From this day forward, there's nobody in the world ever gonna tell me what to sing, what to play, what to wear, or how to act. From this day forward, I'm doing it my way. Write . . . it . . . down!"

It was a declaration that would not come true for several years. But it was out there.

Hank's animosity manifested in self-destructive behavior. As it turned out, he was more like his father than he pretended to be. Throughout the early 1970s, Hank's drinking and drugging led him to dark times. He flung himself into chaos; it was nothing but dark barrooms, unfamiliar hotels, and strange women ending with drunken blackouts and big chunks of lost time.

It nearly killed him. When it didn't kill him, he offered a helping hand by attempting suicide by drug overdose. That was the last straw for Hank Jr.

Meanwhile, Merle was having his own identity crisis; he started to wonder if his image was to blame. For most of his career, he'd been mistaken for other country stars. How many newspaper articles had covered his shows, only to name him as Haggard or Cash? What he needed was a new look, something to separate him from other performers. He'd tried a few things already. For a while he'd worn a leathery Dracula cape and carried a coffin-shaped wooden guitar case, but he ended the act after someone (he suspected it was Marty Robbins) drove a wooden stake through his guitar case when he wasn't looking. Some joke. He was still groping for an image when a fan cornered him at the WSM studio.

At the time, Ralph Emery was the deejay at WSM (he would later become the nationally recognized television talk show host of Nashville Now). This was a popular show and a great platform for singers to promote themselves, considering how there were fewer than a hundred radio stations across the nation that played Country. The show ran into the late-night hours, and this made it convenient for Country Music artists since Tootsie's closed at two p.m. Ralph put just about anyone on if they came by at that late hour, especially Merle Kilgore.

Ralph particularly liked Merle Kilgore, impressed by Merle's tall stature, good looks, and bombastic personality. Ralph especially enjoyed his penchant for ghost stories and his tales of the weird and unexplained. Once, Ralph even invited Merle and a famous psychic to dinner at his home just to see what would happen. The result was a match of minds and psychic prowess that ended with a shared effort at spoon bending.

With Ralph's studio door always open to him, Merle made regular unannounced visits. It was good PR work, and it was always entertaining for both of them. Ralph never tired of quizzing Merle on-air about psychic phenomena. Merle set himself up. During a show, he'd claim to possess psychic abilities, and to prove it, he made three predictions to Ralph; things like *Your wife will ask about a bookshelf, you will get your own syndicated show, and the hedges around your home will all die.* All three predictions eventually came true; Ralph admitted he was most stunned when the bushes died, just as Merle had promised.

For one show, Merle boldly took his psychic act on the air, promising free live consultations. The station's phone rang nonstop; Ralph answered but turned the calls over to Merle. The first few were just what they expected: *Will I get married? Will I make lots of money? Will I get that job I applied for?* But then something strange happened—a man called with a question: *Has my wife been cheating on me?* Merle grew rigid, covered the mouthpiece with his hand, and then said to Ralph, "Pull it, man! Take me off the air!"

Ralph gave a puzzled frown and then moved hesitantly toward the mic. "Okay, that was fun," he said calmly. "Let's play a little music."

Merle finished the call in private (Ralph could hear only bits of the conversation), and after hanging up, Merle turned to him with wide, startled eyes.

"What was that all about, Merle?"

Merle went on to explain how he'd gotten a psychic impression, a glimpse of something bad; something that made his hairs stand on end. "I think I talked him out of it."

"Talked him out of what?"

Merle gave a great, heaving sigh. "I picked up on it right away. When he came on the line, I felt the vibes. *Bad* vibes. I thought, 'This guy's *angry*.' And then I knew why—some kind of love triangle." He looked at Ralph soberly. "That's why I told you to end it. I didn't want to talk the guy out of killing his wife while we were live on the radio!"

It was good copy whenever Merle came on the show, and that's why Ralph always made room for him. Merle got plenty out of it, too. One night during a visit to WSM in the wee hours for an on-air interview, he noticed a few visitors waiting out in the station's lobby to listen to the show over the ceiling speakers. Merle passed through there on his way out and noticed a father and his son. Suddenly, the boy stepped into his way, forcing him to stop.

"Are you the Boogie King?" he asked him.

"The Boogie King?" Merle grinned. No, he'd never called himself that. But it did have a nice ring to it. He wagged his brow and said, "Hey, I like the sound of that! I suppose I am!"

He was just being nice. But later that night after returning home, he dreamed of himself onstage, dancing to a boogie-woogie beat, a jazzy, bluesy rhythm driven by a piano. He woke up buzzing with excitement. He had a new sound; a new look, too. And he had a stage name: the *Boogie King*.

In the following weeks, he made his dream a reality. His first order of business was the suit. He spoke to Buddy Lee about it, but the promoter seemed less than enthused. "I just don't know. The *Boogie King*? I just don't know about that." But Hank Jr., also working with Buddy Lee, supported the idea. "You should try it out," he told Merle. "In fact, why don't you go on over to the House of Kershaw and buy yourself a suit? I'll pay for it."

The result was the Boogie King suit—big, flashy, and furnished with enough leather to upholster a Cadillac. It came with a long black jacket with great white lapels, a Napoleonic collar, with fleur-de-lis patterns along the sleeves and legs, and the words *Boogie King* written in rhinestones from the waistband to the flares of his bellbottoms. He wore white platform boots to complete the outfit. It was essentially an Elvis knockoff.

Nonetheless, that year Merle Kilgore posed as the Boogie King for *Country Music Magazine;* the photo showed him sitting in a wingback chair with a woman on each arm. For the final touch, he needed a theme song; he approached Gary Paxton with the idea. Paxton, the writer of such novel smashes as "Alley Oop" and "Monster Mash," came back with a wild romp of a song entitled "The Boogie King." The *Boogie King* album was released later that year featuring a mix of blues, country, and boogie-woogie rock 'n' roll.

Merle put on a crowd-pleasing, lighthearted show with his boogie-woogie beat and his frenetic energy. But I don't think anyone took it seriously, as evinced by Jerry Whitehurst, the bandleader on Ralph's show. In a 2009 interview with Ralph, he recalled that Jerry took one look at Merle's album and jeered, "What is this? The *Boogie King?* Are you kidding me? Are *you* the Boogie King?" Ralph and Whitehurst messed with him throughout the entire show, interrupting the commentary at any given moment to sneer, "Oh, hey, would ya look at that? It's the *Boogie King.*"

As hokey as the act was, it worked for a while. But by the early Seventies, the *Boogie King* fell into bad shape; he was now five times divorced, an estranged father, and had a liver that suffered from a rowdy lifestyle. To make matters worse, he developed colitis, an inflammatory bowel disease that kept him running for the restroom. Once, after Merle ended a show with a homerun, the crowd cried for an encore just as the disease struck him with an eye-crossing belly pain. He tried to duck out of the obligation, backing away from the microphone with a thankful wave, but they'd called him back with a unanimous cry for an encore. There was no getting out of it; Merle begrudgingly submitted to their demands and sang another song, all while his condition worked evil magic on his bowels. When he finished, he got another encore. Then another. The fans wanted a fourth; under his breath, Merle told them all to *"Go to hell"* and ran from the stage.

It wasn't a good time for Merle. To make matters worse, the medication caused him to bloat so badly that he could no longer squeeze into his Boogie Suit, and Merle was beginning to harbor serious doubts about his music career. And then came word that Hank Jr. was taking a year off. There seemed nowhere to go but down, and everything—including his health—was going to hell. As a result, Merle entered his early forties with weary mistrust.

Audrey refused to let Hank Jr. walk away without a fight. She and Buddy Lee had legal rights to his music for another year, and until their contract expired, they had legal control over anything he produced.

Staying in Nashville was not an option for Hank. He was desperate and broke and exhausted from the endless battle with personal demons. The nonstop nights of hard drinking had caught up to him. The doctor warned him: he was heading toward the same fate as his father. What he needed was a break from it all.

"Fine, then," he told his mother. "In that case, I'm taking a year off. I'll wait until that contract runs out, and after that, I'll do what I want."

He cut ties with Nashville, left his mother, and fired his manager, Buddy Lee. He was also contemplating divorce from his first wife of three years, Gwen Yeargain. It was 1974, and Hank was buried in debt. But he had a friend in Cullman, Alabama, named J.R. Smith, who was also a longtime friend of Merle. Hank had gotten to know J.R. over the years as he and Merle traveled to Pensacola to take boat rides on J.R.'s boat, fish, drink, and sometimes perform at a few honkytonks in the Florida Panhandle.

J.R. was pretty well off. Having recently retired from his own trucking company, he knew how to manage business, and he promised to help Hank with his finances. He also let Hank stay with him and his family in Cullman. Hank took up the offer. In the fresh country air, Hank found what he needed—a change of perspective.

Hank worked on his music in Alabama. He dug deep, looking for his own sound, somewhere between southern rock, country, and blues. Eventually, he had enough material to go to Muscle Shoals to record a new album. This was a significant location, the epicenter of new Country Music sounds, and it was producing albums that rivaled the stuff coming out of Nashville. The music was grittier, less restrictive. Hank Jr. was a welcome addition.

He worked tirelessly. The result was *Hank Williams, Jr. & Friends*. The album was the product of hard work and help from a string of influential artists—friends like Waylon Jennings, Charlie Daniels, and Toy Caldwell of the Marshall Tucker Band—who helped Hank realize his vision. The album was a statement, a bold new sound, sharing a feverish energy and drawing from multiple influences and styles, including southern rock and blues. The album challenged what Nashville Country Music had become.

The result was a critically acclaimed album (many of today's critics argue that the album is one of the best from the "Outlaw" era). Those artists couldn't have known this then, but they knew it was a strong piece of work. The folks in Muscle Shoals knew it. Hank was sure of himself.

The album was good. Maybe even a masterpiece.

It was 1975. Hank Jr. had just recorded *Hank Williams, Jr. & Friends*. The album was something special, and he felt certain it would change everything. This was his breakthrough record, a departure from his earlier work and style. This new music came from a place of honesty and sincerity, ringing with a style of his own making, comprised of his early influences, emboldened with southern rock and blues. It was a break from his father's style, and an even greater break from what his mother wanted from him. For this one, he'd cranked up the tempo and sang from a place of raw emotion. It was his most personal work to date and a declaration of artistic independence. From his perspective, none of his earlier albums mattered.

But Hank Jr. was nervous. His life had reached a major crossroads, a time when he suffered from an almost palpable uneasiness. He still had not made amends with his mother, nor had he completely made amends with his father, or even himself. Before releasing *Hank Williams, Jr. & Friends* to the general public, he wanted to reconcile.

He turned to the Montana Mountains for help. Up there on the peaks, he could find the serenity of fresh air and pine, with the earth and rock underfoot and the cool air in his lungs. The mountains gave him a sense of solidarity that he couldn't find in Nashville. Up there, he would conquer his fears and anxieties; or maybe he'd leave them alone and just get lost in the moment. Of course, he had practical reasons, too, like an upcoming hunting expedition in the McKenzie Mountains of Canada, and that sort of trailblazing demanded strong muscles and acclimated lungs. He had his reasons, and he went to the mountain.

On August 8, 1975, a day Hank recalls vividly in his autobiography *Living Proof*, he arrived at Ajax Mountain with his friend Dick Willey and Dick's eleven-year-old son, Walt. They spent the day climbing the jagged range, with its worn dirt trails, treacherous inclines, and rock-strewn crags. They talked about hunting and fishing, and Hank kept his mind on simple things; but the new album was always lurking in the background, and he even offered a sneak peek to his fellow climbers by singing them a song.

But on the way back, they came to a snowbed the size of a small pond with part of its perimeter shoring up to the edge of the mountain. Dick meditated on this for a long moment before folding his arms over his chest and shaking his head. "We can't walk across that."

Hank frowned. "Well, why the hell not?"

"For all we know, there's an icy lake underneath all that snow," said Dick. "We got no choice but to go around it."

It was a tough call. Skirting the snow meant walking dangerously close to the edge. Dick was perhaps the most experienced climber of the bunch, and so he went first, walking the ridge like a man on a tightrope, testing each step with his heavy boot, his breath forming clouds around his head. Every once in a while a footfall would send snow and pebbles rolling down the mountainside to his right. When he finally reached the other side, he turned and waved for the others to come, warning them to be careful.

Walt went next.

Then it was Hank's turn. He tightened the straps of his backpack, squared his shoulders, and started along the edge. The ice and snow crunched beneath his hiking boots. A frigid breeze scraped across his face like sandpaper. He chanced a few glances to the edge but forced himself to stay focused.

His foot came down on soft earth. The ground gave way. He took a breathless drop, reaching out for something to grab, but found only thin air. It wasn't a freefall—thank God for that. In just a few heartbeats, the slope of the mountain rose up to meet him. On his back, with his feet trailing behind him and his toes pointing toward the sky, Hank went shooting down the slope like a human bobsled. Trees and brush went rushing past him. Rocks and brambles grated at his back and arms as he sped by.

He managed to spin himself around. With his feet in front of him, he could at least see the earth dropping away from him, and that was a slight improvement. But then he bounced, rolled into a cartwheel, and was flung into a summersault with his arms flapping at his sides. Then he came down—face-first—into a slide to the finish.

The stretches of the slope were a blur. The rocky, hard-packed earth felt like a cheese grater against his chest. The slipping went on forever, and at one point, he dared to believe that he might make it. *By God, I just might!* But then he spotted the wedge-shaped boulder rearing up directly in his path. There was nothing he could do but brace for impact. Hank struck face-first against the rock.

There was a meaty thud and a burst of stars, and then Hank's vision dissolved into darkness. But he wasn't alone there. His father was waiting for him. Tall and dressed in a cowboy suit, Hank looked like a glowing angel. He smiled lovingly at his son and said, "Be your own man. Get up and do it your own way. Not mine."

There was more to it, maybe. But that was the gist of their conversation.

Do it your way; not mine.

Dick and Walt went skittering down Ajax's crumbly terrain to find Hank Jr. far below in a crop of jagged boulders, picking himself up from his incredible fall.

"I'm all right!" Hank shouted. "I made it. Oh God, I made it! Thought I was going to die!"

Dick may have felt momentary joy, but I'm sure he lost that feeling the moment he got a good look at Hank's butchered face—a face that had taken the full brunt force of stopping his tumbling fall. All that *gore*. The son of Hank Williams looked like a stage prop from a B-rated horror movie. His face was split open as if from an axe blow. He suffered a shattered skull that reached down to crack the roof of his mouth. His nose looked as if the world's strongest man had crushed it in with his thumbs. One of his eyes was hanging loose from its socket.

Hank saw the look in his friend's eyes and reached up with his hands, touching his own face. There were muffled sobs, caught behind blood-spattered fingers. *My face . . . Oh God . . . my face . . .* Hank thought as he realized the extent of his injuries. The shock hit him then. He was conscious, but desperately confused.

Dick wanted to help. He told Hank to sit down and then unbuttoned his coat to help him relax. It was the gray matter leaking from Hank's forehead that really bothered him. Dick tugged off his gloves with his teeth, then used two dirty fingers to poke at the brain matter, smushing it all back into the skull where it belonged. (Hank remembered hearing a wet, gurgling sound, only he heard it with more than his ears, and he doubts that he will ever forget it).

Dick made Hank as comfortable as he could and made an icepack out of snow and a ripped shirt. Dick turned to his son and said, "Stay with Hank. Keep him company and promise me—*for the love of God, promise me*—you'll keep him from falling asleep."

Then Dick went running for help.

It must have been devastating for that kid, to sit in the lonely cold, listening to the babble of a dying Country Music singer. Hank was out of his mind, dizzy with shock. It was cold up there, and rocky, too.

Meanwhile, toward the base of the mountain, Dick found help. The park faculty made some calls. Minutes later a medical helicopter came buzzing out of the sky, searching for Hank. It had to park several yards down the slope, and Hank cried in pain as they loaded him on a gurney and carried him to the helicopter. It was a rough but successful mission. They got Hank Jr. to the nearest hospital and patched him all up. Sort of.

They told him he had eight days—eight days for his brain to catch fever, and if that happened, there could be no help. An infection in the brain is like pumping corrosive acids into the cranium. You're just "shit out of luck," so to speak. Dick's fingers were dirty and he'd *touched* Hank's brain, hence the potential for disaster.

"We watch it for eight days," the doctors told him. "A week and one day. You get past that, and you're in the clear. But if you get an infection . . ."

Nothing more needed to be said. If an infection happened, Hank would likely die. So they all waited.

A week passed without Hank's brain catching fever, and he lived to tell the tale. But the doctors were convinced that a part of him—Hank Jr. the Entertainer—was as good as dead. After all, he'd suffered a fractured skull and a shattered face *and* a finger-poking to the gray matter by dirty fingers. No one believed Hank would ever entertain after all that.

Merle came right away. He still couldn't believe it. He'd seen Hank Jr. just a day before the fall. He and Helen had double-dated with Hank and Becky, his latest love interest. It'd been a good evening, and Hank had seemed truly inspired by Becky.

But now this.

Merle arrived at the hospital to find the world in chaos. There was a lot of confusion in the lobby. He found a group arguing with each other. Audrey was there. So was Gwen, Hank's soon to be ex-wife. Even Irene, Hank Williams' sister, was there. They were arguing over Hank's estate. Who gets the money should Hank Jr. die?

Merle was bothered by the whole affair.

He found his way to Hank's room. His friend was unrecognizable, with his head swollen to the size of a watermelon, wrapped in white dressings. A single black-and-blue eyeball stared from a hole in the crisscross of gauze. A plastic hose snaked from his throat to a buzzing machine beside the bed.

A nurse stood just behind Merle, talking. She said something about the likelihood of a dangerous fever and the possibility of brain damage, and something more about gray matter being exposed, and bacteria. Hank Jr. was still fighting for his life, she told Merle. He'd taken incredible trauma to his body and mind, and if he made it, there would be many more operations.

Hank's face was badly damaged. But the doctors would try. They would try to make him look *normal* again.

Hank's done. That's all Merle heard. It's what he kept telling himself. He felt despair at that moment. Not only had he nearly lost his best friend, but his own world was crashing down around him. Until that moment, Merle believed with all his heart that Hank Jr. would become a star, maybe even *important* for Country Music.

This was not what he'd envisioned. Sure, Hank might survive the fall, but *Hank Williams, Jr., the Entertainer* was gone forever. It was a crushing realization.

Behind him, the nurse kept talking, and while he'd missed most of what she had to say, he caught her final words.

"I don't know what he's supposed to do," she said, "but he's supposed to do something special. People just aren't supposed to have that type of trauma, and that kind of injury and that amount of blood loss, and live."

George Jones's Possum Holler nightclub became Merle's newest stomping ground. Merle took on the mantle as the *Singing host of the possum holler*. He'd picked up the job once Hank Jr. left for Alabama (before his accident), and I think Merle considered the job a temporary gig. After all, Hank was supposed to come back to Nashville after he worked things out in his head. There was going to be a comeback. Endless shows on the road. The Holler was just a stop on the way to bigger things. Or so Merle thought.

But once Hank Jr. fell and hurt himself, everyone's plans changed. It certainly threw a monkey wrench in Merle's calendar. He'd hoped to make a future at Hank's side, but now the future was uncertain. Hank was out of the picture, and Merle's career had hit a slump.

At least he had the Holler. George Jones's Possum Holler was a popular nightclub in Nashville's Printer's Alley. Big stars came to sing, and the sprawling showroom and dance floor gave guests room to get down and let loose. There was endless traffic of famous visitors who hung out in the VIP lounge. This was the Studio 54 of Nashville.

Part of the Holler's popularity went to the promise of seeing visiting celebrities; if they really lucked out, they saw George Jones perform. After all, the superstar owned part of the establishment, and his face was in neon lights and painted on the back stage wall. But George had a legendary drinking problem. On too many occasions, he came to the club, got wasted, and then skipped out on his show. Over the years, he gave more no-shows than actual performances, earning him the nickname "No-Show Jones." Obviously, whenever George did this, he pissed off a lot of the clientele, especially his co-owner, Shug Baggott. With too much to lose, Shug insisted George do his show, drunk or not. As a result, George often slurred his way through his songs and sometimes he even took a fall off the stage. An escalating drama ensued, with George resenting Shug for putting him onstage and Shug resenting George for missing his shows. Their soap opera-sized drama led to impossible stories, portraying Shug as a bully who sometimes duct-taped George to a dolly and then rolled him onstage, and George as a wet-brained drunk, too far gone to defend himself. But these were just barroom myths . . . most of them, anyway.

Merle hit a perfect pitch with the Holler. Big, bombastic, and explosive, he livened up the room with his rally cry of "Get on the whiskey!" He often promoted his own drink, "Folks, be sure to try the Chicken Whiskey. It makes the men cocky, and the women want to lay!" He sang, told stories, and made grand introductions for the guest entertainers. But most of all, he lightened the mood with his legendary wit.

While the Holler paid a slim salary, it allowed him to stay current in Music City, USA. He sang and entertained several nights a week; he rubbed elbows with stars on a daily basis when they came to sing, and with music executives and outside nightclub owners who came by to book him for their own businesses.

Consider this moment: a dark barroom and a big crowd on the dance floor, everyone watching Merle standing in the lights, dressed in a suit, with a big head of hair and shaggy, Elvis-sized sideburns. He's singing "Cold, Cold, Heart"—a typical inclusion for Merle, since he never fails to sing a Hank Sr. medley, or tell a Hank Sr. story, or mention how "Hank's cousins would tell that, down in Alabama on those dusty roads, Hank, as a kid, would walk barefoot, see his friends, and say, 'You want to hear one of my homemade songs?'"—when something stops him cold.

The music plays on, but Merle just stands there, looking confused. Then he looks over his shoulder at the house band. They look at him with something between confusion and alarm. There's Walt on the piano, Gary Boggs on the steel guitar, Zeke on the fiddle, Clyde with his lead guitar, and Ernie Rowell on bass. Robyn Young's there, too, standing just offstage. Merle signals them all to stop the music. The band is hesitant, but they follow orders. In moments, the music stops, and a hush falls over the audience.

"Ernie," says Merle. "Did you just touch me?"

Ernie glowers defensively, shaking his head. "I didn't touch you."

"Robyn?" Merle says, searching the back stage area for his lifelong friend, the son of Faron Young. "Did *you* touch my shoulder?"

Robyn shakes his head and mutters, "Merle, what the hell are you talking about?"

Merle ignores him, turns to the lead guitarist, and says, "Clyde? Did you touch my shoulder?"

Clyde's answer was the same. Nope!

Satisfied, Merle returns to his microphone and says in a deep voice, "Ladies and gentlemen, I apologize, but I had to verify it. Just now, I felt a presence. Someone touched my shoulder. And I believe it was the spirit of Hank Williams."

There are a few gasps. Most in the crowd look up at him, awestruck; a few stand and applaud. Before long, the rest of the room joins in and plays along, although I bet they're unconvinced. Still, it's more fun to just go along with it, and their faces light up, saying, *Can you believe it? The ghost of Hank Williams—right here in the Holler!* Everyone is impressed, except the band members, who just roll their eyes, each of them thinking the same thing: *Big Merle is so full of shit.*

I don't think Hank Jr. had a lot of friends as a young man.

He was born a rich kid with a famous father, and because of that, many people took interest in him, even at an early age. He was the son of Hank Williams, after all. But I'm sure it was difficult for him to know his true friends from the fairweather friends or the groupies or the people hoping to capitalize on his fame and wealth. But I don't think he ever had to wonder about Merle Kilgore. Hank knew and trusted him and leaned on him like a big brother.

I think that's why Hank Jr. came to the Holler, unannounced, to share the good news. Merle was his friend, and he wanted him to know it.

For the past year, Merle had visited Hank countless times in various hospitals. It seemed like Hank lived in recovery wards. Just this past winter, he'd gone to see Hank at a hospital in Virginia where Hank was holed up, preparing for yet another facial operation.

Merle had shown up early that morning, still half drunk, a lumbering giant in stage getup from the previous night and stinking of sweat. His limo driver, exhausted from the long drive, hobbled after him. The two men must have made a comical sight. They'd traveled through the night to get there, following a show in West Virginia and a big afterparty and lots of drinking.

He found Hank in good spirits. Propped up in bed, Hank was still somewhat unrecognizable with his scars and his dressings. The poor guy had made it through the worst. But he had a long way to go before he looked *normal* again. Still, Hank seemed happy to see Merle, even if Merle smelled like booze and swayed on his feet.

Merle said something positive, something along the lines of, "Brother, you'll be fine! Everyone in Nashville is worried about you. Man, you took a fall. But you *made it*."

But some thoughts went unsaid. The same unspoken thoughts were in everybody's heads after learning of Hank Jr.'s full injuries, things like: *You made it out, and that's the important part, and so what if you have bad facial scars and a cracked palate? So what if your music career is dead? At least you have your life. You're alive, and you have God to thank for that.*

Merle needed to sit down. "Brother, can I sit on the bed?"

Hank looked at him for a moment and then shrugged. "Sure," he said, moving to get up. "You can have the bed. Go on and lay down. You look like you need some rest."

It must have been difficult, and maybe even dangerous, but Hank picked himself up and shuffled over to the couch and sat down. Merle rolled himself out on the bed, where he passed out cold.

A little while later, one of the nurses came marching into the room and stopped just inside the doorway when she saw Merle's unconscious body splayed out on the bed. There was also a man sleeping on the floor. At the far side of the room was Hank Jr., watching her from where he sat on the sofa.

"Who is *that?*" the nurse wanted to know, pointing at Merle.

"That's my brother," Hank told her.

She looked down at the man on the floor and asked shrilly, "Well, who's *that?*"

Hank shrugged. "That's his driver. He's exhausted."

It had to be an odd scene for the nurse.

That day in the hospital had been months ago. Merle's mind was elsewhere as he sat at the Holler's bar, tired and sweaty from his last set. Someone tapped him on the shoulder. He swung around and looked at a grinning stranger.

For a moment, he didn't recognize Hank, with his face hidden behind dark sunglasses, a thick beard, and a cowboy hat with its brim jerked low over his brow. Only Hank's grin seemed recognizable. In spite of wounds that were still healing, he looked strong and determined.

After howls of surprised laughter, they ordered drinks, and Hank described his year-long journey through the depths of Hell. He reminisced about the hospital and the surgeries and the initial horror at seeing his reflection for the first time after the fall. He'd nearly lost all hope in that moment, gawking at the bathroom mirror, meeting the gaze of a disfigured stranger with a face sketched with long scrawls of stitches, a swollen head, and a snarl for a mouth. *I'm a monster. Oh, God—a monster.*

But the doctors did a fine job putting Hank back together. They fixed what they could and replaced what they couldn't. There were still the scars to deal with, but he found a way to hide those scars, both inside and out. What sufficed as "the new look" was also a disguise, and the disguise worked just fine, giving him a rugged appearance, the face of a nonconformist. That played right into his hands, as he meant to take on Nashville music as a Country Outlaw.

"Merle," Hank said, "we're getting ready to put the show back on the road. This time, I'm doing it my way, and nobody—I mean *nobody*—is going telling me how to do it."

Hank was confident; he believed every word of what he was saying. He'd returned from the outlands between life and death, and he'd brought back something fierce and unstable. It was in his eyes, and he was going to change the world with it. "I want you to pack your bags, brother. You're coming with me to Alabama. That's where we're going to start."

In Hank's mirrored glasses, Merle caught a glimpse of the future: gold records, cheering fans from all over the world, and tour buses with Hank's name on the side. Everything about him pointed to promise. Hank was going to be a star.

"Brother," Merle intoned as he finished his drink, "I thought you'd never ask."

This marked a significant moment in their relationship. Hank didn't have much to offer aside from a promise, but Merle didn't need much more than that. He accepted the risk, and their friendship became stronger for it. Hank was back in the saddle, and Merle was coming along for the ride.

It's strange how things lined up for Merle during this time. The universe was paying him close attention; the planets were aligning in his favor. First, there was Hank Jr., whose return was setting into motion major changes in Merle's destiny. Then there was Judy Williams, who entered Merle's life at perhaps the perfect time. After all, *somebody* needed to help him quit drinking.

Until then, Judy worked in New Orleans with Bob Harrington, the holy-rollin' evangelist who went by the name Chaplain of Bourbon Street and who presided over Audrey's funeral. As a single mother with two children, Judy had taken a considerable leap of faith in moving to Nashville to work with a record company promoting Gospel music. So far she'd found work as a waitress, a female wrestler, and now as a Nashville tour guide.

The Possum Holler was a single stop on her tour. Here, the tourists could order food and watch the show before their next destination. To pass the time, Judy hung out at the break table with all the other drivers and tour guides. With the table set near the kitchen, the area was loud with sizzling grease and clattering dishes.

She noticed Merle the moment he stepped into the break room. The Singing Host was dressed to the nines and hefting about a lot of extra weight, a side effect of medication and heavy drinking.

Merle walked past her to stand next to Ralph, the cook, who stayed busy over a sizzling stove.

"Well, Ralph," said Merle. "I left number five today."

Ralph, a scrawny man with an aged face and graying hair, frowned at Merle and said, "You mean your *wife?*"

"Yep. I'm out the door. I got nothing. A sofa and a coffee table. That's it."

Judy couldn't help but overhear; Merle was loud and noticeably irritated. He gave Ralph a derisive snort and swatted disgustedly at the air with one hand. "I'll never marry again. I'm done. No more wives!"

Judy didn't know him personally—aside from the fact that she'd seen him host the evening shows from time to time—but she couldn't resist interjecting. "You will marry again," she said.

He swung around to look at her. "No. *Never* again. I will *never* marry again."

But Judy didn't back down. "Yes you will. God has his hand on your life. You'll find the right person. And you'll marry again.

It was all a flirt, I'm sure. Judy didn't know it then, but she'd made an incredibly accurate prediction. The two were married within two years.

Bocephus

Hank Jr. made his comeback just over a year after his accident—only a short while after he'd stared at his ruined reflection and called himself a monster.

The fans didn't know how to take him at first. Some were shocked; others were flat out unconvinced. The general thought was, *Who the hell is this person, and what has he done with the real Hank Williams, Jr.?* The old guy—the guy with the clean-cut looks and colorful suits, the guy who sang with a smooth country tempo—was gone. So was the guy who catered to everyone's demands that he play his father's songs. This new guy looked nothing like the old Hank Jr.

Not only did he look different with his beard, sunglasses, and cowboy hat—his self-referred "Shadow Face" to hide the scars—but he also sang a different kind of music, touting songs from his latest album, *Hank Williams, Jr. & Friends*. His comeback was not only in opposition to his old style but to the Nashville music industry.

Hank, among other Country recording artists, had become antagonistic toward Nashville and its pervading *Nashville Sound*, the industry's latest trend. The Nashville Sound had started years ago and just wouldn't go away, emerging as a result of several factors. As money flowed into Nashville, the studio sessions came into higher production budgets, granting more polish to the recordings. Meanwhile, producers began looking for ways to commercialize Country Music. Chet Atkins, among other industry masterminds, devised certain hallmarks—

strings, easy tempos, pop beats—that gave the music a modern sound that appealed to the masses.

It worked; the new music took off. Nashville produced crossovers into pop markets. Country Music artists like Kenny Rogers, Glen Campbell, and Olivia Newton-John all had tremendous crossover hits. Country Music finally achieved a wide audience and brought lots of money to Nashville. It certainly made sense in the commercial world. But the backlash was a blurring between the line of pop and Country Music.

This frustrated a lot of the Country Music purists—artists like Jennings, Haggard, Kristofferson, and Nelson. They spearheaded the Outlaw movement and rebelled against the Nashville Sound. For them, the problem didn't lie with a particular aspect; it wasn't Kenny Rogers or the use of strings or easy tempos. The problem was the Nashville industry itself; it'd become stuck in churning out the same type of music: overproduced, watered down, and—to the Outlaws—pandering to the masses. Worse, big business had infiltrated Country Music and was changing it. The Outlaws retaliated by producing music that was rougher, more honest, and avoided the slick commercial polish.

Hank Jr.'s newest album *Hank Williams, Jr. & Friends* positioned him there among the Outlaws; his fans never saw it coming. His new style was a culmination of all his influences, with a backbone of southern rock, ringing with a rebellious spirit. When Hank returned to the stage after his accident, the crowds came in droves to see him. But at the tune of "Sweet Home Alabama," most of them scattered; an audience of 3,000 became an audience of 200. Sometimes they booed him. Those first shows were a disaster, and Hank faced incredible odds. It looked like his career was over. But he refused to back down. It was all or nothing, and if he had only 200 fans after the initial walk-out, then he gave those who stayed a three-hour show. It was only a matter of weeding out the posers from the fans.

Nor was he alone. Merle followed him into all that uncertainty, even when he didn't know what to think. His friends pleaded with him. "Merle, talk to him," they'd say. "All that great talent is just going to waste!"

Merle would only shrug and tell them the same thing he told everybody: "This ol' boy knows what he's doing. He's on to something."

"But *rock 'n' roll*? Are you kidding me? Man, this is suicide."

Merle ignored the naysayers. He trusted Hank's artistic genius, even if his music didn't exactly fit the mold. It'd become clear to him: Falling down Ajax Mountain had changed Hank Jr. in more ways than anyone knew. A part of Hank was still on Ajax Mountain, broken and bleeding against the boulders; but another part of him, maybe his higher self, had gotten up, and his face-off with death had ignited some sort of artistic awakening. Hank seemed inspired by his accident. Somewhere in all that pain, he'd discovered himself, and he returned to the world with a clear grasp of his own style and an unshakable confidence. His new symbol said it all: the phoenix, a symbol of regeneration, death and rebirth. The phoenix would signify the rise of his career from the ashes of his former life.

It happened within a three-year timeframe. Hank's shows began drawing bigger audiences, with fans who stuck around for the entire show. Gone were the old resentments and boos from the front rows. The new fans belonged to a younger generation, and they wanted only to hear Hank Williams, Jr., and so what if he had a famous father? They hardly knew anything about *that* guy.

Then Hank released his breakout album in 1979. *Family Traditions* launched two singles all the way to the top of the charts. Everything changed after that. Like Merle, Hank's fans soon arrived at a better understanding: the accident—the one that crushed Hank's face, cracked his skull, and nearly killed him—had also transformed him, miraculously, and in spite of the tragedy, or maybe because of it, Hank Williams, Jr., had become a superstar.

With Hank's career catching fire, Merle and Judy got married, a sixth and final excursion to the altar for him. They got married in Panama City.

Perhaps Judy came late to the game, or maybe she entered at just the right time. On his own, Merle had lived an indulgent lifestyle, and he'd taken a pounding for it. He didn't need a mountain fall to wreck himself—just a bottle. Lately, he'd slowed down a little, trading Tab and whiskey for blackberry wine, rumored to possess liver-detoxifying properties, and it seemed to help (until those moments when it didn't).

When Elvis died on August 16, 1977, Merle bellied up to the bar with all the other bleeding hearts. He left the bar in his Cadillac, and while he didn't hit anybody, run off the road, or spend the night in jail, he did manage to get lost in the backstreets of Nashville. He called Judy via the world's first car phone (yes, they had these in the mid-Seventies) and howled at her, "Judy! Where the hell are you?"

Judy answered back, "I'm home, Merle. You called *me*. Where are *you?*"

It turned out he was only a few blocks down the road from their home. Judy went for a walk and found him parked on the roadside, passed out behind the wheel. "You know how drunk you are?" she told him. "You're two blocks from home. I *walked* here. That's how drunk you are."

Months later, he felt a stabbing pain in his right side, like someone had kicked him in the ribs. Judy drove him to the hospital in Madison, where his doctor gave him bad news: "Merle, your liver is shot. No more drinking. If you take another drink, it could *kill* you. The party is *over*."

Judy visited him at the hospital. She asked to pray for him, and he humored her, even if he scoffed at the idea. Judy prayed, and it must have struck a chord, because Merle never had another drink. In fact, Merle did an admirable job in quitting. He never attended Alcoholics Anonymous meetings, nor did he remove himself from temptation. There's an old saying among recovering addicts: If you hang around a barbershop long enough, you're bound to get a trim. But leaving the bars and nightclubs wasn't an option; that was where he made his living. So he faced his addictions head-on, and he ordered Tab without the whiskey. But even in his sober years, he never gave up his rally cry: "Come on, everybody! Get on the whiskey!"

But sometimes it seemed the Devil himself had a vested interest in keeping Merle off the wagon. Take for example the time when a group of Hell's Angels bikers visited Hank's hotel room just before a show. Merle, still in recovery and visiting Hank, found himself suddenly surrounded by burly men in leather jackets, rowdy and howling praises to their hero, Hank Williams, Jr. They came bearing a gift—a bottle of Jack Daniels.

Somehow, the bottle found Merle's hands. He hesitated, not sure what to do, when a funny thing happened: the room fell silent as everyone turned to look at him with expectant gazes. Merle met their eyes with a nervous grin. How could he tell them that he'd stopped drinking? It would probably insult them and embarrass Hank. But then inspiration struck.

Pinching one nostril shut, he pressed his nose to the bottle's open mouth, and snorted, making the airy hiss of a vacuum hose.

"Merle?" said Hank. The room fell silent. "What the *hell* are you doing?"

Flashing a smile and wagging his brows, Merle held up the bottle and barked, "It's the newest thing, man! You snort the fumes, and it goes straight to the brain! Here—try it!"

He thrust the bottle to the closest man, who took it with a shrug, an uncertain grin, and then took a snort. Everyone laughed, including the biker, who nodded agreeably, and Merle had dodged a bullet.

Oh, but the Devil refused to let Merle go without a fight, and a few months later, Merle got a visit from another agent of the underworld. Merle had been playing at a hotel in Nashville and just finished a show, when he sat down at the bar and ordered himself a Tab. That's all. He was making a statement, possibly even testing himself. *I am bigger than the booze.*

But he didn't get a Tab. What he got instead was a martini.

Merle gawked, admiring the glass's delicate hourglass shape, the light sparkling on its rim. Back in the day, he'd loved martinis. It was his absolute favorite drink, especially with a splash of amaretto, giving a hint of almonds. This one looked especially tasty.

The bartender returned and apologized. "I'm sorry, sir. You ordered a Tab, didn't you?"

The man must have caught something in Merle's glance, because he leaned forward with a secretive smile and said, "Almonds. That's the *trick*," his voice dark and seductively smooth. "They like it when it tastes like almonds."

Merle gasped, clambered off his stool, throat constricting. That was a dangerously funny thing to say—the mention of almonds hit too close to home. Never in his life had he felt so incredibly thirsty. Almonds. It was as if the Devil himself was goading him on.

They like it when they taste like almonds . . .

The temptations subsided after that, until finally becoming a distant memory. The Boogie King had officially stepped down from his throne. I can't help but wonder if Hank Jr. had him in mind when he recorded "All My Rowdy Friends (Have Settled Down)" in 1981. Quitting drinking certainly prompted Merle to write "Happy Acres," a little jingle to capture the insanity of it all. He never recorded it, but it served a special purpose—a song for troubled friends on their way to rehab. That's when they called to hear it. Merle must've sung it to a hundred poor souls needing to hear it. Judy claims that even Keith Richards of the *Rolling Stones* called the house once, asking for Merle to sing it to him. No matter what day it was, no matter what time, if Merle got the call, he'd clear his throat and sing, "Happy acres! Happy acres! It's a party at the rubber room ball!"

By 1979, Hank Williams, Jr., returned to the top of the charts. Sure, he'd seen the top before, but this was different. He'd forged his own path to get here. He'd created his own success, his own music. The greater glory was here, standing before a crowd of 15,000 people, sweating beneath stage lights bright enough to drive away his father's shadow. Sure, he lost plenty of his old fans; he never expected most of them to follow. But he'd created a new crowd of fans, enough to keep his career thriving.

That same year, Hank released his first million-selling album, *Whiskey Bent and Hell Bound*. He also produced two country chart-toppers, "Family Tradition" and "Whiskey Bent and Hell Bound." This was just the beginning. He entered the 1980s as a Country Music superstar.

His next seventeen albums went gold. The later ones went platinum.

Meanwhile, Merle's opening show harnessed the excitement of Hank's growing fame, always ramping up the audience to match Hank's raucous energy. Finally, this was a place for Merle to test his boundless stage presence. Each show kicked off just the same, with Merle's towering frame—he weighed more than 200 pounds and stood six-foot-five—racing out onto the stage wearing blue jeans and a cowboy hat, brandishing his smile as he made way for Hank. He revved the engine, gassed it hard, and then shouted, "Are you ready people? Let me hear you! Hank Williams *Junyah* is coming to the stage!"

The bigger the shows, the bigger Merle's opening would be. "Ladies and gentlemen, if you didn't know by now, you're making history, with the number one artist in the nation, Hank Williams *Junyah!*" Then he'd launch into a song, singing, "I ain't gonna call him Junior, *Junior* anymore!" It was more of a proclamation than a song, pointing out the fact that Hank had overcome the shadow cast by his legendary father.

Merle's bit wasn't so much a show as an introduction, and once his mini-act reached a fever pitch and the crowd a cheering beast of pumping fists and howls, Hank would thunder onto the stage to deliver his knockout blows, giving a seamless transition between the two shows. Sometimes, Merle stuck around for a few songs, growling his praises into the microphone as Hank jammed on his guitar. "Yes-sah! Hank Williams, Junyah!" Sometimes Merle left by shuffling back, bowing and waving his arms in a kind of Arabic bowing out. *Salom! Salom! Salom!* That was Merle. Hank's pious and doting servant.

That's how Merle's act differed from a traditional opener. He did it all for Hank, not himself. Hank couldn't have a better sidekick. Or a better friend.

Merle's career was back on the fast track.

As Hank's right-hand man, he became a regular on television and at benefits and concerts. He and Hank appeared on Hee-Haw and That Nashville Music. He sang on the Opry, sang on the Johnny Cash Spring Special Live on CBS. There was also Marty Robbins's spotlight—the Acuff-hosted tribute to Faron Young. Then there were the major tours with Hank. The Coca-Cola Tour, the Wild Turkey Jamboree of Country Music, the Nashville Country Music Festivals. Vegas and the endless fairground concerts. He and Hank did a slew of benefits, teaming up with Bobby Bare, and Leona Williams, or Willie Nelson and Hank Snow to fight child abuse.

Over the next few years, Merle nabbed small parts—mostly

cameos—in several films, showing up in Burt Reynolds's *W.W. and the Dixie Dancekings* (1975), *Roadie* (1980) starring Meat Loaf, and Robert Altman's cult classic *Nashville* (1975). He even threw a punch at Tommy Lee Jones in *Coal Miner's Daughter* (1980), the Academy Award winning Loretta Lynn story.

But Merle played his biggest role in the 1981 made-for-TV adaptation of Hank Jr.'s autobiography, *Living Proof.* With a part in nearly every other scene, Merle had a chance to flex his acting chops, portraying the best friend, and the sometime guardian. There was Big Merle, dragging a drunken Hank from the swimming pool or busting down a hotel room to find Hank nearly dead from an overdose of pain meds. Merle had his best moment in a pivotal scene, when he drives up to Hank's log cabin, where Hank's been hiding from the world, his face badly mangled. In it, Merle tries to encourage him, tells him to keep singing and get ready for his comeback; but Hank doesn't want to hear it. He points at Merle's truck. "I don't want to hear it. Can't you see my face? I'm done, man. It's over. Now go on and get out of here!"

Merle's Range Rover kicks up gravel as he drives away, leaving Hank to watch from the front porch, bent with grief. Then he turns to find a guitar propped against a post; a gift from Merle. By now, the audience had already seen Hank smashing a guitar while in rehab, angered by the loss of all hope of becoming an entertainer. So Merle's gift had a great deal of significance. What's not disclosed is this: *That* was Merle's personal guitar.

The note said: "Hank, this is my guitar. Don't break it."

It's a fantastic scene, and while I'm sure it's somewhat overdramatized, the film shines a light on the depth of their friendship and how Merle played a vital role in Hank's career. Incidentally, while Merle was filming the movie, someone approached him, patted him on the back, and told him. "Say, man, you're doing a bang-up job. I met Merle Kilgore a long time ago, and you act just like him!"

The movie career was fun, but Merle continued making records.

He had a few more hits, including "Mr. Garfield," teaming up Johnny Cash and Hank Jr. and peaking at fifty-six on the Billboard charts.

Meanwhile, Charley Pride cut "More and More," and it hit number seven on the country charts. Then Merle and Mac Vickery wrote, "When You Get on the Whiskey, Let Somebody Else Drive," recorded by John Anderson, who took it to the Top Ten on the Billboard charts.

Throughout it all, Merle remained Hank's opening act, and by the early Eighties, Hank's fans had come to expect it; so did Hank. At the sixteen-year mark, the Country Music Foundation Library certified Merle as the record holder for the longest opening act in Country Music. As a token of thanks, Hank gave Merle a custom-made Martin D-41 guitar with pearl and gold accents and Merle's initials on the pick guard.

Hank's 1984 music video for "All My Rowdy Friends are Coming Over Tonight" made him a giant. He was throwing the biggest party in town, crowded with women in bikinis and a who's who of country singers, from George Jones and Willie Nelson to Kris Kristofferson and Waylon Jennings. Even Cheech and Chong made an appearance, tumbling out of a smoke-filled limousine. Merle got a cameo, too. You can see him for just a flash, standing next to Hank, wearing that big grin, a black vest, and a cowboy hat. Indeed, one of Hank's closest of Rowdy Friends. More than friends. They were partners.

And Hank was about to offer him the biggest gig of Merle's life.

Hank's private plane—a twin turbine with four seats and a great big Ruger phoenix painted on its side—soared high above Alabama, reducing the farmlands, lakes, and town squares to geometric shapes. Being Hank's best friend, in addition to the opening act, came with special privileges, like traveling in the jet. I've personally ridden in this plane; I was five at the time, on a special trip with Judy and Hank's second wife, Becky White, whom he married in 1977. I remember the small four-seat cabin, with comfortable leather chairs facing each other, clear light shining in from the oval windows, full and bright.

And I can see another moment in perfect clarity: the plane's small cabin, with Merle and Hank sitting across from each other. Merle was in his early fifties, in a plaid Western-cut button-up shirt, blue jeans, and snakeskin boots. He wore his snakeskin cowboy hat, a turkey feather sticking out from the hatband. I can see him with gold necklaces and big rings on his fingers. He, like Hank, never let someone take his photo without first brandishing his teeth in a mile-wide grin.

Merle had become an important part of the show over the years. His opening act had become a small but invaluable part of Hank's performance. Merle always did a great job in getting the crowd jazzed up. He shouted and sang and never took himself too seriously. While he'd achieved some great things in his music career, his big break never came, nor was it likely.

Hank said to Merle, "I'm moving to Paris, Tennessee, the whole operation, and I want you to come with me."

"Paris? What's in Paris?"

"I like it there. Daddy did, too. I want to get a house right on the lake. We'll launch the whole operation from there."

"Man. That's a big move. You sure about that?"

Hank nodded. "I've made up my mind. It's time for a few changes. In fact, I already told J.R. to take a long holiday. I'm not asking him back."

"*What?* Are you kidding? You let J.R. go?" Merle grimaced. His career depended on Hank's career.

Should the whole thing fall apart, who would he open for? He'd felt a similar dread several years earlier when Hank confessed that he wanted to take a year off. Without Hank, Merle was back in the nightclubs, The Possum Holler, or the Carousel. He'd be back in Nashville, playing gigs in smoky dives. The music business was an uncertain career; at least he had Hank to rely on. Hank was a certainty. But Hank was now without a manager, and that was a dangerous position.

"Well, do you have someone in mind?" Merle asked.

Hank tipped his sunglasses, showing Merle his eyes. "I was thinking of maybe putting you in charge."

"Me?" Merle nearly shouted.

Hank Jr. had clearly given the matter serious thought. His music career had become big business. Here he'd become a big star, with gold albums, tour busses, and sponsored tours; he had a staff, bookkeepers, promoters, producers, and attorneys. Obviously, Hank needed someone with business smarts to help run the show. This was no one-man operation; nor had it ever been. He'd had someone managing his entire career; if it wasn't his mother, then it was Buddy Lee or J.R.

"You want me as your *manager*?" Merle said.

"That's right."

"Well, I don't know, Hank. I mean, I just renewed my contract with Warner Brothers," said Merle, referring to his recent signing agreement with the label. "I don't even know if I can get out of that. Besides, they fronted me five thousand bucks. I already spent it."

"Five . . . thousand . . . dollars." Hank smirked, enunciating each word deliberately. He considered something, and then pointed to the pen in Merle's shirt pocket. "Hand me that."

Merle handed over the pen, and Hank scribbled something down on a napkin. "If you'd managed me last year, this is how much money you would have made."

He handed the note to him.

Merle read the figure written there, the neat dollar sign. He thought for a moment, then said, "Brother—I'll never sing again."

It was a promise that he would eventually keep . . . whether he believed it then or not.

On April 6, 1986, Hank Jr. made Merle senior VP of Hank Williams, Jr. Enterprises. That's a big job. Performing for a crowd of 15,000 must have been difficult; managing a multimillion-dollar entertainment juggernaut, even more so.

In the coming days, Merle helped move Hank's entire operations to Paris, Tennessee, a lush, green spot of land near Kentucky Lake. It was a place that connected Hank to his father, who had often gone there to fish, hunt, and escape from it all. There in Paris, Hank Jr. and Merle renovated a nightclub, transformed it into an office building with a neighboring souvenir shop and museum called Kaw-Liga Korners.

Merle was soon overseeing all operations, including concerts, recording sessions, and travel; he also monitored sales, promotions, and publicity. One of his first moves was to upgrade Hank's show to a state-of-the-art light and sound show with a $1.5 million stage. But above all tasks, his most important assignment was to fix a broken relationship.

Hank Jr. had a bitter past with Nashville. It wasn't just his disgust at the current state of Country Music and its overproduced Nashville Sound. It went deeper than that. He believed that Nashville—and more specifically, the Grand Ole Opry—sent his father to an early grave when they fired him from the Opry.

This had come as a major embarrassment for Hank Sr., who was at that time the king of Country Music. I suppose Hank had it coming. He'd become a raging alcoholic. He'd perform drunk, and everyone—including the fans—knew it. The Opry didn't try to help him; instead, they gave him an ultimatum: "We catch you drinking again, and we're kicking you off the show."

Hank Sr. promised he'd stop; he lasted about a week before breaking that promise. That time, he gave his show, and he looked bad. When he raised a knee, one of the managers spotted a whiskey pint bottle tucked into the top of his boot.

"That's it. He's out of here."

They booted Hank off the show that night, and in hindsight, it was a death sentence. After that, there was Shreveport, and depression, drugs, and death.

Hank Jr. resented Nashville for that, and in turn, the industry turned its back on him. By this point, Hank's music was all over the charts, hailed by critics and adored by fans. His shows were growing exponentially in size. For all that, when the big Country Music Awards (CMA) and Academy of Country Music (ACM) Awards rolled around, they pretended Hank didn't exist. He was practically blackballed from their nominations. By 1984, the major Country Music associations finally recognized him, but only with a music video award. During Hank's acceptance speech, he said, "You know, I do a little audio, too."

Hank concluded that he needed Nashville on his side. After all, what's Country Music without Nashville? Hank didn't just want recognition; he wanted it all, primarily, entertainer of the year.

So he hired Merle to make it happen. Merle had friends on Music Row, and he had history behind him. He'd worked in the business since the early Fifties as a performer, a businessman, a disc jockey, a songwriter, a publisher, a television host, and the list goes on. That gave Merle a lot of range. He could put on a show and run a business. He knew how to "shake and howdy" and schmooze people. He was the consummate politician.

Merle returned to Music Row on a mission to gain acceptance

for Hank Jr. This meant putting on a business suit and working his connections on his old stomping ground. Merle knew the business and the landscape; he rubbed elbows with the big-time players, sound studios, record labels, and publishers. He spent the better part of the year rubbing elbows and rekindling relationships, all the while sowing a single idea: *Vote for Hank.* Additionally, he started a campaign, sending mail-outs to all the voting members in the CMA and ACM. This was the first time that had been done. His idea is still used today.

"Oh, man, Hank's gonna be a smash," Merle would tell them. "You've got to hear his new album! I'm telling you, he's the entertainer of the year! Believe it!"

At first, his Music City friends cringed at the mention of Hank Williams, Jr. "Are you kidding?" they'd say. "I don't even like Hank. Why the hell would I vote for him?"

Merle would just shrug and say, "Well, do it for me!"

It was a smart move, bringing Merle on as general manager. In addition to having friends in Nashville, he was perhaps the most likeable man in Nashville, with his over-inflated charisma. He was without a doubt, Hank Jr.'s biggest fan.

I'll never sing again. Merle had made the promise just a year before, but he didn't keep it. He continued doing his opening gig, mostly because Hank wanted him to stay on the road and deliver his famous introduction. Merle had been doing it since the early Sixties, and the fans went crazy when he came out, singing "I ain't gonna call Hank Junior, Junior anymore!"

It all came to an end right before a show on New Year's Eve, 1986, in Tampa at the Florida State Fairgrounds. It was a big Marlboro show, and maybe ten minutes before Merle had to go on, he got a phone call. It was a lawyer. Merle had to make a $200,000 decision for Hank. It was a delicate situation; he could have won it, or he could have lost it, depending on which way he decided to go.

Merle knew better than to go to Hank and hit him with a $200,000 decision right before a show with 15,000 fans. Hank's mental state was a delicate thing before a show like that; Merle didn't want to put things at risk. So he made the decision on his own. He ended the call and then hurried for the stage to do his opening act. But he was rattled, wondering if he'd made the right decision (which, it turned out, he had).

Then he was onstage, standing before 15,000 fans, and suddenly, he could not remember Hank's name. His mind went blank. He just couldn't remember. Miles away, he heard his own voice, trying desperately to fill the empty moment while his mind worked it out. *What the hell is his name? Oh God, I can't remember!*

"Now, ladies and gentlemen," he said, "you know him; you love him. You know his father, one of the all-time legends, and, ah, ladies and gentlemen, he's made so many albums, and so many hits . . ."

He went on, blubbering in a panic, angry that after all these years he'd forgotten the man's name. But then it hit him; it came with the force of a bullet between the eyes, and he roared, "His name is Bocephus. *Yes-sah!*"

It was good enough. Merle raced offstage, wiping the sweat from his brow, and backstage he found Hank, grinning suspiciously. "What the hell's with you?" he asked, laughing. "I thought you were never going to bring me on!"

After Hank charged out onto the stage to meet his fans, Merle found a chair and a quiet spot, and collapsed. *He was laughing,* Merle thought to himself. *He thought I was putting him on!* Merle's shirt was drenched with sweat. His hands were shaking. How in hell had he forgotten Hank's name? What if the name had never come? Good

God, it'd almost been the biggest embarrassment of his life. That was the moment when Merle made the decision to end the opening act. He broke the news to Hank later that night.

Merle never forgot that swan song show; he understood its deeper implications. Until that moment, he'd become a split personality, the showman and the businessman. But those two selves could not coexist. It was one or the other, and he chose the other. From there on, Merle embraced his position as manager; he traded his blue jeans and cowboy hat for a suit and silk tie, and a leather briefcase replaced his guitar. In an interview, Merle once said, "When you step into the big chair, as I call it, all the weight of bank account spikes and countless other burdens weigh on your shoulders. Someone once asked me, 'What's it like to manage Hank Williams, Jr.?' Well, it's like moving General Patton and his army. You gotta make them both happy."

Some say the night of Merle's swan song show inspired him to make a name change for Hank Jr. From then on, he became Bocephus, not only to friends and family, but to millions of fans.

In just one year after Merle took the big chair, Hank got the recognition he deserved. During the CMA Awards and the ACM Awards of 1987, Hank claimed the coveted Entertainer of the Year Award, the heavyweight title of the Country Music industry. The year after that, he reclaimed the title from both the CMA and the ACM. Hank scored his last Entertainer Award during the 1989 ACM Awards, giving him a total of five to put on his shelf.

During the 1988 CMA Awards, Hank—dressed in a white Western suit, cowboy hat, and diamond-studded sunglasses—accepted his award, thanked the fans, and mentioned his longtime friends. He included Johnny and June Cash (whom he had to squeeze past on his way to the stage), and then he said Merle's name, and it's here that he paused to look out into the audience, to brandish a knowing smile at his manager—almost imperceptibly—as if to say, *We did it, brother.*

They made a good team. Hank Jr., a man of incredible talent, and Merle, a fantastic politician (he became an honorary state senator for Tennessee the same year Hank became Entertainer of the Year).

Only a few years after Hank reached the height of his stardom, with Merle as his executive vice president, the ghost of Hank Williams returned.

It was the summer of 1988, and Hank's tour led him to San Antonio, Texas, where he did a July show. The show took place just a few towns over from an old friend, Texas Big Bill Lister, an old honkytonk recording artist from the early Forties and Fifties, and possibly the last of Hank Sr.'s Drifting Cowboys still living. Bill was also a gunsmith and a collector, giving Hank even more reason to visit.

During an interview on *Nashville Now*, Merle told special guest host Tom T. Hall the whole story. He and Hank Jr. took a limo to Boerne, Texas, where Big Bill Lister, the lanky giant once nicknamed "Radio's Tallest Singing Cowboy," invited them inside and took them directly to see his guns. Hank liked what he saw; he got swept up in Bill's collection. Bill left him to it, pulling Merle aside, saying, "Come on into the den with me, Merle. I want you to hear something."

In the next room, Bill went over to an old record player and turned it on. A crackling hiss filled the room, followed by the high-lonesome voice of Hank Williams, singing a song that Merle had never heard before. He collapsed into the closest chair, gawking in disbelief, while Bill explained.

"That's a one-of-a-kind acetate recording of Hank Williams, Sr.,"
he said with a grin. "It's called 'There's a Tear in My Beer.'"

Just then, Hank Jr. hurried into the room, his face drawn in surprise.

"I can guarantee you this," Bill said. "There's no one in the world
ever heard that record, except me."

Big Bill's story began in 1952, when he played in Hank's band, the
Drifting Cowboys, and he had witnessed the night Hank. Sr. got fired
from the Opry. After that, Hank and his band scattered to the four
winds. Hank went to Shreveport and Bill went home to Texas. It was
there that Bill rekindled his honkytonk music career. After signing
with Capitol Records, Bill started work on a new album, but needed
more songs. That's when he called Hank for a favor:

"I need your help, Hank. They say I need a drinking song. If you
write me a song, Hank," Bill relayed, "why, I'd have it made."

According to him—and he was all they had to take it from—
Hank Williams had a special place in his heart for Big Bill Lister.
Which is why Hank told him: "I'll do it. I'll write you a song." As
promised, Hank recorded his song on an acetate—these were quick
demo recordings, really easy to make at the studio—and he gave it to
Bill, who raced to his own studio and recorded it. He released "There's
a Tear in My Beer" in 1952, but it fell on deaf ears.

It's an unusual story, and some have suggested an *unlikely* story
(Would Hank have written a song for Big Bill Lister without wanting
anything in return?), but since Bill and Hank are both now gone
forever, maybe the nuances of that reality don't matter. Maybe what
matters is this: The song found its way back to Hank Jr.

"My wife found it a box in the attic," Bill told them, pointing
out how fragile the record was. Acetates were especially popular for
recording studios in the Fifties. While they were similar to vinyl
records, they were cheaper to produce and made of far less durable
materials—basically a coating of wax over an aluminum disc. This

made acetates short-term and paper-thin quality; certainly never meant for long-term archiving. In fact, after a while, acetates started degrading after each play, as if self-destructing.

"You believe it? An acetate!" Bill said. "I'm amazed it still works. You know how hot that attic gets? It's been up there more'n thirty years. I've seen records melt like wax candles. But somehow the heat didn't get this one."

The men gathered around the record player, shaking their heads, looking down at the acetate with something akin to religious awe.

"I cut my own version of the song a long time ago, but it never hit for me," Bill mused, then shrugged. "I can play it again, if you want."

This earned a shout of alarm from Merle. "No, no, no," he cautioned. "Don't play that again. Let me make a call to some friends in L.A. They'll know what to do."

I'm not sure what Bill and Hank did after Merle rushed from the room—if they heeded Merle's advice or not—but I like to think Bill played it again. I'm sure Hank Jr. would've liked to hear it from the beginning.

Merle flew back to Tennessee with the acetate and careful instructions from Hank: *Guard this with your life, or you're fired.*

He made it home to Paris without incident. But the agents with Warner Bros. didn't take any chances. They arrived at Merle's home in a special climate-controlled truck, carrying a foam-padded case formed to fit the acetate. The rep took Merle and the acetate to the airport and flew him to a studio in San Francisco, where they made the transfer. Miraculously, after thirty years, the acetate had retained a surprisingly clear recording.

"It's like this was *supposed* to happen," Merle told them.

"I want to do a duet with my father," Hank Jr. told his producers. There was real commercial potential here. Not only did they have a rare recording, but Hank Jr. also had a great idea. "I want to make it a music video, too."

Cut to a scene of a house on a dark hillside in a thunderstorm—only, it's not a house but a sound studio—where Hank Jr. is recording his newest song, "There's a Tear in My Beer." Suddenly, lightning strikes, and strange things happen: a silhouette of Hank Williams, Sr., appears in the window of a shut door. Hank Jr. moves over to the door, presses it open, and then steps into the grainy past, where his father sings on the Grand Ole Opry. Overcome with joy, Hank Jr. joins his father, and together they sing a duet.

"You are on my lonesome mind . . ."

The production was impressive; a music video with a dash of movie magic and lots of blue screen studio work. The producers took historic footage of Hank Williams and dropped Hank Jr. right into the black-and-white frame. For one timeless moment, the two Hanks stood together, father and son, past and future, all on the same stage.

I'm sure the song gave Hank Jr. incredible peace of mind. For most of his life, he had plenty of psychological turmoil to work through being the son of a legend. As a boy, living in a kind of Hank Williams museum where celebrities made obligatory pilgrimages and brought endless gifts of praise, Hank Jr. had learned to idolize his father. But as a young man, Hank Jr. fought to separate himself from his father's image in a necessary battle of ego. Those years were all behind him. By now, Hank Jr. had become his own man, recognized by the industry as one of the greatest entertainers in the business, and in many ways, he was ready to stand beside his father.

All this was made possible by a song. This was a special opportunity, enabling Hank Sr. to reach across time and space to tap his son on the shoulder. "There's a Tear in my Beer" was a message in a bottle.

Merle recognized something almost haunting about all this. With his early interests in the occult, he was always the first to notice spooky coincidences. As a young man, he'd spent years exploring spiritualism, participated in séances, and sought out ghosts and psychic predictions. It was from where he got most of his stories. He recognized coincidences in everyday life, the synchronicities, not to mention he'd had confirmation with a message from Johnny Horton from the Great Beyond. So he knew a *happening* when he saw one. And this—the resurfacing of "There's a Tear in My Beer"—was one of those happenings; a subtle ghost story.

At the Tennessee Performing Arts Center in Nashville, they recorded the video for "Tear in My Beer." It was a magical experience, and Merle was confident that he felt *something*, a presence of some sort. There was certainly something strange in the air. I suppose that sense of magic found its way into the video. In 1990, "There's a Tear in My Beer" won a Grammy for best country vocal collaboration, in addition to the ACM Best Video Award, and garnered several other accolades.

The world of Country Music was blown away by such an unlikely reunion.

This became Merle's story to tell, along with all his other Hank Williams stories. Like a zealot, Merle spent most of his life telling stories about the legendary country singer. He had his reasons. As a child, coming into contact with Hank Williams, Sr.—such a highly charged character—had changed him forever. (A Bible story comes to mind, the one about the meek woman who pushes her way through the crowd to touch the robes of Jesus Christ; she was transformed, and Jesus noticed her, and I think a similar thing happened here between Hank Sr. and Merle.) That cross-current of energy—no matter how great or small a charge—blew a circuit and fused Merle to the Hank Williams's family tree. In some ways, Merle spent his entire life carrying Hank Williams's guitar.

Sometime in the mid-1980s, Hank Jr. entrusted Merle with

transporting several artifacts from the Hank Williams, Sr. estate to a museum in Nashville. This stuff was priceless—a cream-colored Nudie suit (its arms decorated with blue music notation) and a scrapbook of songs and handwritten notes. Arriving early to Nashville, Merle needed a drop-off point, and he chose my family home, just a few miles north of the museum, and charged my mother with caring for these priceless treasures.

Pamela, my mother, agreed to help. She'd known the name *Hank Williams, Sr.*, and she'd known a few of his songs, but at twenty-eight, she hardly grasped the importance of all this stuff. Still, she promised to keep it safe, especially when Merle told her, "Now listen. If the house catches fire, you grab these things, and you *run*. It's the first and *only* thing you grab!"

Everything went into the bedroom closet. But that night, Pamela's curiosity bested her, and she took it all out, placing each item on her bed. She explored the suit first, touching the fabric, considering the history woven into the threads. Then she flipped through the scrapbook, musing over the handwritten notes, song verses, and familiar song titles.

How neat, she thought. *How cool to be alone and in charge of a legend's private possessions.*

Not until years later did Pamela grasp the magnitude of those things. At her fingertips, she'd had a scrapbook of ideas that had forever changed popular culture, as well as the most famous stage costume in all of Country Music, the same suit that Hank Sr. had with him on the night when he'd died in the backseat of his Cadillac. She'd had it all to herself, the personal belongings of an American icon, arguably one of the greatest recording artists of all time, both a Country Music and Rock and Roll Hall of Fame inductee.

Ironically, that house *did* eventually catch fire. But Hank's stuff was long gone by then.

I find a deep personal satisfaction in knowing that Hank's belongings stayed for a short while in my childhood home. I remember seeing that jacket, covered in plastic, on a hanger in the closet and his book of songs on the nightstand. All that magic—and all that *history*—had graced my childhood, just for a moment. Maybe for that reason, I, too, have a personal connection to Hank Williams.

Maybe, for a moment, the ghost of Hank Williams also came into my life.

The senator

Once Merle started managing Hank, he wanted a big title—something similar to Tom Parker's title as the "Colonel." So Merle reached out to his friends in the state legislature for help. They convinced the Tennessee Senate to bestow Merle with the honorary title of "Senator." Merle milked that title for all it was worth, even putting it on his license plate. The name Senator suited him just fine. After all, he made big decisions and he represented a Country Music giant.

For that reason, they called him first.

Driving back to Paris from Nashville, Merle received a call on his cell phone; the people with ABC's Monday Night Football wanted to talk. Someone in Hollywood had a big idea for the show: Why not open with Hank Williams, Jr.? The country star seemed like a perfect fit.

This was big news—so big that Merle was forced to pull off the road. "Brother, they want to try you on Monday Night Football," he later told Hank.

The offer was for one year, but the gig lasted for more than two decades, and it introduced Hank to sports fans across America, making him a national icon. Additionally, "All My Rowdy Friends Are Here on Monday Night" won the Emmy for best composed theme song in 1991. It was the first of four.

"Something like that puts you out there in a whole different realm," Hank Jr. said during an interview in November of 2004 with *Billboard*

Magazine. "Millions of viewers. CEOs, or somebody slinging hot dogs in New Jersey, or some grandma in a nursing home—they all see it. Three Emmys and a one-year deal turned into fourteen, fifteen years . . . It's brought unbelievable attention to the touring, the shows. What a vehicle of publicity you don't even go after; it just happens. That's one of the big moments for me."

I think it was for Merle, too. He helped put the deal together, and I don't think it's any coincidence that CMA awarded him the very first SRO (Standing Room Only) Manager of the Year Award that same year.

Merle stayed onboard as manager with Hank Jr. for more than twenty years. They made a great team and shared a unique artist/manager partnership. They shared history, and they stayed best of friends, which made all the difference. The two always shared a laugh; they knew each other's stories. Hank had plenty of Merle Kilgore stories about the gags he played on him, like the time he arranged for someone to steal the tires from Merle's Lincoln and how even the town cops were in on it. Or about their bear hunting trips to Maine, or how Merle once got stuck in a tree and all the hunters heard his booming radio voice echo throughout the forest: "Attention, hunters! I am stuck in a tree and cannot get down." Hank Jr. later had steps built leading up to the deer stand.

Likewise, Merle told stories about Hank Jr. Most of his TV and radio interviews from the Eighties on ended with a plug for Hank Jr. *Nashville Now, Crook and Chase, WSM*—Merle never failed to plug Bocephus. It was all in the name of good PR work; he never missed an opportunity. "Brother, listen to me now. I've got the scoop. Hank's new album's a homerun. I'm sure of it, brother," he'd tell. "This one will make him millions!"

Merle was Hank's biggest promoter and his biggest fan.

What I want to leave you with is this: They shared an incredible story, spanning their entire lifetimes, and if you consider the big picture, you end up with more coincidences than you can explain, and maybe a glimpse of the handiwork of an unseen architect.

Merle stayed Hank's manager until his dying day, but Hank didn't get all his time. In many ways, Merle also became a representative of Country Music. It started in 1989, during the July meeting for the CMA Board of Directors. Jack McFadden, who managed such greats as Buck Owens and Billy Ray Cyrus, nominated Merle to be a member of the board. This came as a shock to a lot of the board members, and more than a few were amused. Joe Talbot, a song publisher and record manufacturer, was most vocal about it.

"Merle Kilgore?" he shouted. "*Merle Kilgore?* Jack, have you lost your goddamned mind?"

This was no sign of disrespect; Joe liked Merle just fine. But he didn't think Merle would take the job seriously or that Merle was a serious person. He made several incorrect assumptions: that Merle had no cares for the CMA or for the music industry and that Merle would likely contribute nothing to the board. The members listened, but they disagreed. Soon after, the CMA Board of Directors voted Merle in. Merle knew plenty about the Country Music Association—from its establishment in the late Fifties to its prime directive to promote, lobby, and safeguard the Country Music industry. The board aligned with Merle's personal convictions as a lifelong advocate of Country Music.

Merle gave his complete devotion to the job and stayed a member for sixteen years. He had plenty to offer; the other members learned to draw from his knowledge. His grasp of the industry spanned every aspect of the business. He knew movers and shakers of the industry; he enjoyed meeting new people. He brought enthusiasm wherever he went. Perhaps most importantly, he connected with the artists, the most important facet of the business. This came naturally to him; after all, he was one of their ranks. It also helped that they knew his name. Merle's reputation preceded him. Even Joe Talbot changed his mind about Merle.

In the following years, Merle served on the board, and sometimes as president, for numerous music associations. For a while, he headed the Nashville Songwriters Association International and served on the board for the International Entertainment Buyers Association (IEBA). He attended CMA board of directors all over the world, from Dublin to Holland, Seattle to Miami, traveling with stars like Clint Black, Garth Brooks, Kris Kristofferson, Martina McBride, Trisha Yearwood, and Emmylou Harris. There was the Leadership Music Songwriting/Publishing Conference. He even sat for televised interviews and documentaries. Later on, he became president of ROPE (Reunion of Professional Entertainers). In many ways, Merle became the official historian of Country Music.

These last decades also brought him endless accolades and honorable recognitions. ROPE honored him with a lifetime achievement award. He was inducted into several Hall of Fame organizations, including the North American Country Music Association, the Texas Hall of Fame, Louisiana Hall of Fame, and Alabama Hall of Fame. Just before he died, he was inducted into the Oklahoma Hall of Fame, where he put on his final performance.

The 1998 Nashville Songwriters Association International (NSAI) Awards proved a momentous occasion for Merle. Judy Kilgore recalled the entire night during a 2010 interview with me. The banquet welcomed a few hundred industry executives, songwriters, and recording artists for a night of top-notch entertainment and the coveted Songwriter of the Year Award. Judy had invited Merle's immediate family to surprise him. But Merle was nervous; he didn't dare believe he'd take home such a great honor. To win would far exceed his expectations.

But I wonder if he picked up on the clues scattered throughout the night's entertainment. For instance, John Anderson made a surprise stage appearance, and he'd only recently made a big hit with Merle's "When You Get on the Whiskey (Let Somebody Else Drive)," co-written with Mack Vickery (a song that received a letter of appreciation from the Reagan Administration, signed by President Reagan himself, for its message against drinking and driving, a message that aligned nicely with Nancy Reagan's *Just Say No* campaign). There were other clues, too, like some of the guests, friends of Merle's. As I said, there were clues.

Then it came time to announce the night's winner of the Hall of Fame Pre-1968 category. Country Music Hall of Famer Don Wayne, songwriter of the country standard "Saginaw, Michigan," took the podium. A pregnant pause fell over the conference room, with its dinner tables glowing with ambient candlelight, as everyone waited for the big reveal. But Don took his time, moseying his way through his speech, teasing his audience with a few clues.

Then, at the mention of the Louisiana Hayride, the tension at Kilgore's table snapped like an overstressed rubber band. There were gasps and a few sniffles, and Merle drew his heavy brows together, panged, no doubt, by a sharp sting of great pride—a stab in the heart. It was a significant recognition by one of the most prestigious Nashville associations, an affirmation of Merle's achievement as a master songwriter.

It was an important night and perhaps significant that his children shared it with him. In some ways, that award belonged to them, too; after all, Merle had sacrificed a great deal to achieve that award—they were part of that sacrifice. But tonight, they all shared in that award, the joys of success, and all the pain that went along with it.

Don Wayne went on to say that Merle's was the story of "One man's journey into the world of Country Music."

Daddy Merle

A lot of people knew Merle Kilgore, but his grandkids, and even family friends, all knew him as Daddy Merle. My childhood was in some ways built on memories of my grandfather; and you can bet they're good ones.

Those memories begin in the early Eighties, when Merle made rare but significant visits to our home. Back then, my family lived close together. My mother, Pam, and her siblings, Kim and Steve, all lived in Nashville within a few miles of each other. When Merle came, he swooped in with a lot of noise, impressing us all with his stories of the Country Music business. He took us out for dinner at fancy restaurants, and on our birthdays, he took us kids—cousins, brothers, the whole family—to Toys "R" Us to celebrate. We always felt special in his presence.

My earliest memories are of those summers spent with my brothers in Cullman, Alabama, where Merle and Judy owned a big A-frame house sitting at the end of a quiet country road. Surrounded by soaring pines, that house had the feel of a mountain cabin, and the air always smelled like evergreens and lake water. There was a satellite dish in the backyard (back then a satellite dish meant big money) and a large trampoline in the front. The house sat on a hillside, and if you jumped high enough on that trampoline to clear the lower treetops, you'd catch a glimpse of a sprawling lake. Inside the house, the rooms all had shag carpets and lofted ceilings with naked wooden rafters and a few bare-brick interior walls. The family room—the biggest room in the house—was decorated with stuffed turkeys, bearskin rugs, and an impressive boar's head that snarled at you from high above the fireplace.

I didn't know it then, but that home had once belonged to Hank Williams, Jr. I discovered this recently after finding an article in *Comfortable Living Magazine*, circa 1978, featuring that very house, only younger. There's even a photograph showing a young Bocephus sitting on an interior balcony overlooking the family room, his arms crossed over his chest, his legs dangling over the ledge. Hank's wearing a beard and sunglasses to hide the scars of his recent accident; he's also wearing that defiant grin that made him famous. Hank looks right at home.

That house, it turns out, served Hank Jr. as a kind of sanctuary after his accident. He went there to lick his wounds, mend his broken bones, and quiet his restless spirit. That house, I suppose, said a great deal about Hank Jr., about his character, his style and taste.

This is strange to me, because I know that place only as Merle's home. Growing up, feeling that house like only a kid can do—to me, that house was an expression of Merle and his larger-than-life character, his love for the country and for Country Music. That place was so Merle; it buzzed with his character and his own sense of style. I always thought it suited him so well. But now I know better. That house was part of each man's personal history, a place that they both deeply identified with; a common denominator for both men.

I think Merle and I were closest during my undergraduate college years. I often dropped by his Nashville office just off Music Row, where he always welcomed me with a smile, anxious to tell me about his latest projects with Hank Jr. Oftentimes he gave me backstage passes to Hank's concerts, where I got to hang out with famous people. I'd feel like a million bucks. "Mark, my man!" he'd always call out. "Come over here. I want to introduce you to someone."

Those same years we spent many clear summer days on Merle's pontoon boat at the Boogie Shack, while he sat in the captain's chair, big and relaxed, wearing a ball cap and a polo shirt and white shorts, his eyes hidden behind "Blues Brothers" type sunglasses. He'd steer the boat along Kentucky Lake, giving big belly laughs and telling stories, and if things got quiet, he'd throw in a tape of his favorite country songs, something like "Heartbreak Hotel" or "Kaw-Liga," and he'd get really into it, snapping his fingers, tapping his foot, and shaking his head. His energy was contagious. That smile—man, it would make you feel alive.

In my early twenties, I joined the Army Reserve, and Merle especially liked this. We kept in touch via email when my unit deployed to Baghdad just shortly after the United States invaded Iraq. During that long year, Merle wrote me often, always sharing news from Nashville, always promising to pray for me, and sometimes passing along a message from Bocephus: "Hank says 'Hello and keep your head down!'" Merle even kept a photo of me in my Army uniform in his briefcase. (One of my letters to Daddy Merle got selected for *Behind the Lines: Powerful and Revealing American and Foreign War Letters—and One Man's Search to Find Them* by Andrew Carroll. As a favor, Hank Jr. read my letter for an audio recording, and while the recording ended up on the Gilder Lehrman Institute of American History website, it seemed to me like a great way to reach out to Merle, even if he never got to hear it.) When my Army unit returned to Nashville, Merle joined a welcoming party at the airport. A local news team was there also, and a guy with a camera got a quick interview with me and Merle. It was a fine homecoming.

Time eventually caught up to Merle. Just a few months after I returned from Iraq, he hurt his back while pitching his briefcase into the backseat of his Cadillac Escalade. The doctors discovered one of his lower vertebrae had ground to dust. But the problems hadn't stopped there. The doctors were more concerned about his heart. He'd failed a chemical stress test. So they took him in that morning, injected glue into his vertebra, then the next morning, on May 19, hurried him into the operating room to perform a Quintuple-bypass heart surgery and stitched him shut.

On August 28, at Memphis Baptist Hospital, the doctors cut him open again and mounted steel rods along the length of his spine to secure eight levels of the lower thorax. But the rods didn't hold for long. While working on Merle, two technicians were sitting him up, when Merle startled them with his booming voice, "Get me up now!" The technicians jerked too hard, and the bolts snapped free of the bone. Instead of going home, it was back to the operating table for more extensive surgery.

This time I drove to Memphis to visit him. The surgery went fine, and I stayed that night at the hospital, letting Judy go back to the hotel and rest. I'd expected an easy gig; Merle would likely sleep through the night, given all the morphine flowing through his veins. I had only one instruction: *Don't let him get out of bed.*

We had the room to ourselves. I got Merle comfortable in his bed and watched a classic John Wayne Western on television. Then Merle asked me to put his headphones on; he liked to doze to Johnny Cash's reading of the Bible. I got him all settled, and then I curled up on the room's uncomfortable sofa with a novel. I'd read only a few pages when Merle stirred awake and started thrashing his feet.

I jumped up and turned on a nearby lamp in time to see Merle attempting to sit up. I hurried over and placed my hands on his shoulder. "Daddy Merle, you okay?"

He snatched the headphones off and tossed them aside, shaking his head, muttering, "That scared the hell out of me!"

"Just a bad dream," I assured him, looking at the headphones, wondering if maybe Johnny Cash had gotten to Revelation.

Merle's eyes went to the far wall, and I looked over my shoulder, following his gaze to the big window, moving with our reflections.

"Hey, Mark," he said. "Who's that man sitting over there by the window?"

I frowned, looked at my grandfather, and decided he was still dazed and half-asleep, clouded in a drugged stupor. Still, I felt a slight chill; if I were to believe Merle, we were no longer alone.

"I don't see him, Daddy Merle," I said, egging him on ever so slightly, interested in hearing more about his delusion.

Merle panted. "He's sitting there with his legs crossed. He's got three heads."

This time, I shivered. "I don't see him."

Suddenly he tried to get up. I panicked, worried he might injure himself should he try to stand. I moved around to block him, placing my hands on his shoulders and holding him down. "Hang on, Daddy Merle," I almost shouted. "You can't get up. You're gonna hurt yourself."

He wouldn't listen to me. He tried sitting up, and I pressed him down again.

"Let me up!" he shouted, and then bellowing like Moses to the Red Sea, "I *command* you!"

I kept my hold on his shoulders, uncertain with myself; I'd never dreamed of using force on my grandfather. But I couldn't let him up. He'd hurt himself. So I held him down.

"Daddy Merle," I insisted. "It's me—it's Mark. I love you, man. I wouldn't do anything to hurt you."

This seemed to get through to him. He lay back on his bed, panting and mumbling about a tall, skinny man with blue jeans and cowboy boots, and after a moment he calmed down. I patted his hand lovingly and let out a breath. He relaxed again.

I got the earphones and held them up. "Daddy Merle, you want to listen to more of the Bible?"

His eyes flew open and he looked at me as if I'd taken some of his morphine drip. "Hell no!"

He went back to sleep, and I returned to the sofa, but I didn't fall back to sleep for another hour or so. My eyes kept drifting back to the dark window pane, while I pictured the tall, skinny man in blue jeans and cowboy boots. And three heads.

I also couldn't stop thinking of Daddy Merle. Just a few days earlier during the pre-op exam, the doctors had made an alarming discovery: x-rays showed one blossom of cancer on one of his lungs.

The last time I saw Daddy Merle was on a night in late January 2005. My mother urged me to go see him, telling me, "You better go. It could be the last time you see him," although, I don't think anyone really believed that. Still, Judy and Merle had a flight to Mexico the following day, and I wanted to see him before he left.

I drove to his home in Paris, and when I arrived, Judy ushered me inside with a sad smile. I found Merle in the living room, watching television with Hank Jr. A football game was on. They hadn't seen me yet, and judging by the sounds of Hank's howling at the screen, the game was really cooking. Merle was parked in his La-Z-Boy recliner, dressed in a polo shirt and a ball cap and shouting things like, "All right!" and "Man, what a play!"

I brightened after hearing Merle's voice; it was business as usual at the Kilgore household. But then my grandfather turned and looked at me, and I realized my error. Merle looked bad. He looked *beaten*. He sat with an unnatural slump, elbows resting on his knees, face looking somehow puffy and sallow at the same time, a rubber mask made to look like my grandfather's face.

I grinned, hiding my alarm, and gave him a hug. It had all escalated so quickly; his body seemed insistent on shutting itself down. To make matters worse, the doctors had thrown in the towel, sending him home with just a few months to live; thus the trip to Mexico, Judy and Merle's last hope. They'd found an alternative cancer treatment center in Tijuana, and we were all praying for a miracle.

Only, now I wasn't so sure. Now, for the first time, the reality came crashing down on me. The Angel of Death had found Daddy Merle. I wondered if he had three heads.

"Hey, Mark! You came!" Daddy Merle spoke in his same deep, theatrical voice. "Sit down, my man. We're watching the game."

I sat down, and Daddy Merle and Hank Jr. brought me up to speed on the ballgame. I was indifferent, but I cheered anyway, and during commercial breaks we talked about the war in the Middle East, and they wanted to hear my stories about living with an Army unit in Baghdad. The hour grew late, and Hank Jr. said goodbye. I helped Merle back to his bedroom and told him goodnight. I started to leave, and I remember wanting to say more, to tell him how much he meant to me, to ask him about his life, and if he was afraid to die. But I kept these questions to myself, hoping to ask them at a later time.

That was ten years ago, and as I put these final words down, I can't help but return to that night and wonder if there was something more there. It was a quiet night, just the three of us watching football, nothing spectacular. It was my last time with Merle, and I shared it with Hank Jr.; without knowing it, we were both saying goodbye to him. Neither of us ever saw him again.

Merle died of heart failure only a week later in Tijuana, Mexico, on February 6, in a small hospital near the Pacific Ocean.

The morning following Merle's death, Channel 5 News ran B-roll footage from that airport interview. There we were, just the two of us, me in Army desert fatigues and Daddy Merle dressed in black, grinning and patting my shoulder, knuckles encrusted with diamond and gold.

I thought Merle would live forever. I really did.

"Ladies and gentlemen, for the first time at the Carousel Club—the first time ever in its *history*—not a single ugly woman is in the audience!"

This is one of my favorite thoughts of him. It's 1986. A live performance at the Carousel Club. Merle stands on stage, basking in the lights, his guitar cradled in his arms. He's probably the biggest man in the bar; he's got a Burt Reynolds look about him, a thick mustache, sparkling eyes, and a heavy brow. He wears a snakeskin cowboy hat. The band's got his back with drum rolls and guitar riffs.

"News from Hollywood," he tells the crowd. "My friend Bob Smith tells me, 'You missed *Playgirl Magazine* by that much.'" He holds up one hand and mimes a few inches with his fingers. "That much, ladies and gentlemen." A pause and then: "I told them, 'I ain't *cutting* that much off for nobody!'"

The audience erupts with peals of laughter and whistles and a smattering of applause.

Flashing a grin, Merle barks, "I won't take that kind of abuse!"

Merle has an amazing knack for catching the audience off guard. He never demands the audience's full attention; he sings and lets them go about their business. His songs become background noise. But then he tells a joke, and he reels them back in. They can never resist him for long. He tells jokes like he tells stories, and stories like he tells jokes, always with snappy punch lines and clever insights.

He's tonight's entertainment. A one-man show, he can carry

it all by himself into the late-night hours. He'll keep it going with country songs, from Eddie Arnold to Faron Young (and a few he's written himself), and stories about the past. His show is, in a sense, a Country Music review, and throughout this evening, he'll delve into music history, all while taking his audience on a ride through the past, exploring the roots of the industry—something undeniably important to him. The true country fans in the audience will get a kick out of seeing a genuine *Merle Kilgore Show*. Where else can you learn Country Music history and at the same time laugh until it hurts? Where else can you meet a living relic of Country Music?

He'll give shout-outs to the *Nashville Now Network* or Ralph Emery's televised show (which, he promises, will feature him next week). He'll name drop, and talk about his heroes, most of them rooted in the Louisiana Hayride show. There's a class on Elvis Presley, the man who changed Country Music by doing it *his* way, and Merle sings, "That's Alright Mama."

He'll talk about Hank Williams, Sr., who reigns supreme in his telling of history. It's obvious Merle idolizes Hank, portraying him as a kind of honkytonking mystical figure, a poet and visionary who brought Country Music into the modern era. Merle the disciple, like Peter, spreading the word about the greatest of all Country Music artists.

Merle tells them: "Hank wrote 115 hits. Some say Hank Williams wrote the best Country Music song ever written, 'Your Cheatin' Heart.'" Then he sings it himself, just to prove he's right.

He'll sing songs by Jerry Lee Lewis, and keep up a boogie-woogie tempo. He'll do his fidgeting Cash impression and cough into his fist and talk in his pitch-perfect lilt. He'll sing "Ring of Fire" and then tell how he wrote it during a hemorrhoid flare up.

Eventually, he'll segue into a discussion of Bocephus (something he never forgets to do). "I've spent the last twenty years with Bocephus," Merle says. "I know his daddy's proud of him. And guess what?

Bocephus is proud of him." Then he jams out with "I aint gonna call Hank Jr., junior anymore."

This is the *Merle Kilgore Show*, and tonight he'll tell all his stories, and sing all his songs, and eventually you'll get the gist. It's all right here, his entire career, played out as moments in his show. Country Music was his life, and by the end of the show, you'll understand why. He lived the music, on *and* off the stage. His was no normal career, no forty-hour-a-week job holed up in an office and surrounded by the same people every day. Merle did his work in dark, gritty barrooms and smoke-filled showrooms, noisy with clinking glasses and music so loud that people had to shout if they wanted to talk. Where Merle worked, there was always a honkytonk band in full swing, and the beer always flowed.

Maybe you understand now why rock stars and country singers all came to the Ryman to send Merle off. As I've mentioned, most people today don't know the name "Merle Kilgore," but those who knew him understood the enormity of his passing. They gave him an impressive memorial service; he finished big. I think Hank Jr. said it all when he stood on stage, tears hidden behind his sunglasses, and read from a crumpled piece of paper a poem he'd written for Merle.

> *Brother:*
> *I went to the office today,*
> *But found out you weren't there.*
> *And yet the more I searched,*
> *I realized that you were everywhere.*
> *'64, '79, '80s, '90s, Millennium, too.*
> *There were so many pictures,*
> *So many memories,*

Together, me and you.
You carried Dad's guitar in Shreveport.
You were my link to him.
Like a brother, like a father,
And always, always no matter what . . . my friend!
I had a dream so beautiful and serene.
Do not grieve, for from Heaven He's called.
"Brother, you won't believe . . . I've made the biggest deal of all!"

After a parade of famous people sang him farewell and adieu, Merle's longtime friend Greg Oswald took the podium with note cards in hand, cleared his throat, and reminded guests to join the party at the Hendersonville Memorial Gardens, where Merle would be laid to rest. He ended the Merle Kilgore Show with a final announcement.

"On our trip to the graveside, there will be no carpooling. Any of you who do try to carpool will be removed, given a car, and moved to the back of the line."

Everyone laughed, knowing how Merle would have approved. It was just *so* Merle. He would have wanted for all of Nashville to know of his passing; he would've wanted the traffic from the memorial service to the funeral home to choke the streets of Music City, U.S.A. He got his wish, too. The city closed down several major roadways for his funeral escort.

That afternoon, six of Merle's grandchildren—me included—carried his coffin to his final resting place. I remember that coffin weighing a ton and I worried we might drop it.

Oh, and get this: Merle and Johnny Cash are eternal neighbors at the Hendersonville Memorial Gardens. June's right there, too. All three have plots just a few feet from one another. This was Merle's doing. He had sentimental reasons, I'm sure (these were his *people*, after all, and of course, he'd served in their wedding as best man in addition to sharing a mega-hit song with them). But I think Merle was equally concerned about appearance. He wanted to ensure visits to his gravesite *long* after his death. "If I buy this plot," he told Judy just before making the purchase, "I'll know, at least, that my great-great-grandkids will come see me, even if it's only to see Johnny Cash."

His chances of future visits doubled when they put his grave marker in place. This was Judy's design, an unabashedly presumptuous six-foot slab of bronze, showing a cast of Merle's grinning face and outstretched hands as he presents his gold and diamond rings. If you stand over his grave and listen, you can almost hear him intoning: "Are you *shitting* me?" I suppose he'll be saying that forever.

"Merle got the star drop-off," Robyn Young later told me, recalling the days back in the early 1970s when he and Merle worked at The Possum Holler. Way back when, Merle and Robyn both lived at Faron's Old Hickory home, and they often rode together to the Holler. Many nights, especially if it rained, Merle insisted that Robyn give him the VIP treatment. "Nephew," he'd say, a term of endearment, "give me the star drop-off, please."

The star drop-off required Robyn to chauffer Merle to the nightclub, with Merle sitting in the backseat like a royal debutant, and dropping him off at the front door, thus sparing his hair from the elements. It'd been completely narcissistic of Merle (he was unabashedly vain about his hair), but always in good humor.

The star drop-off; in the end, Merle got his final wish. His star drop-off included proximity to a major American icon and his famous June, and a cemetery marker that outshines nearly every headstone there. But people talk. Some mentioned that Merle's marker overshadowed Cash's modest resting place, and that seemed somehow wrong. So the Cash Family did the only sensible thing and bought bigger plaques to match Merle's; now they all three have billboard-sized markers.

About a year after Merle's death, Kirt Webster, publicist for Hank Jr., invited me to a party at the William Morris building on Music Row. This was a private event, and Kirt refused to give too many details, saying only that it was a big surprise and it related to Merle.

The third-floor office party had a big turnout, with music industry folks and even a few celebrities, including Hank Jr., Big & Rich, and Wynonna Judd. We were all corralled into a corner office with windows offering a view of the controversial Musica statue on Music Row. A big oval wooden table took up most of the room. There was something in the far corner, standing maybe five feet tall, with a sheet of black velvet draped over it.

The room went quiet when Greg Oswald, vice president of the William Morris Agency's Nashville Branch, called for everyone's attention. "Folks," he said, "I know you're all wondering why we've asked you here today, and in just a moment, I'm going to show you. But before I do, I want to explain the significance of this room, especially to those of you who haven't been here before."

As it turned out, the agency makes its biggest business decisions here: this is the room where they sign on all their artists and talent. This room is the center of big business for them and a place where dreams come true for many songwriters, musicians, and performers.

Greg stepped over to the cloaked object and stripped away the cloth, revealing a bronze bust of Merle Kilgore.

"From now on," said Greg, "Merle Kilgore will be watching over all the business that happens at this table. Merle stood for good business. He stood by strong values, and he remembered the old ways of doing business, when the Country Music industry worked as a family. And so before any agent signs on an artist, I want him or her to see that bust of Merle Kilgore and remember what he stood for."

Everyone applauded, and Wynonna Judd said to the room, "Folks, we're losing our legends."

The bust still sits in that corner, overlooking the round table, and if you try hard enough, you can see its silhouette in the third-floor window from the roundabout on Music Row. Merle Kilgore had become an ideal. He'd become an icon.

Hank Jr. recently became the center of controversy. He did a guest appearance on the morning news show *Fox & Friends*. They were talking politics, which is par for the course on this particular show, when the conversation turned to a golf summit with President Obama and Speaker of the House John Boehner. The hosts were smearing the parties involved, calling it absurd, when Hank likened the match to Hitler playing a match with Israeli Prime Minister Benjamin Netanyahu. I think in some ways the comment was taken out of context. But the backlash was quick and severe. *Fox & Friends* quickly disavowed themselves from Hank's comment, leaving him hanging on his own, and ESPN dropped him from his twenty-year stint with *Monday Night Football*. In the aftermath, Hank retaliated with a few harsh words toward *Fox News* and even released a song telling Fox, more or less, to kiss his ass. Things got messy.

I'm sure he would've welcomed Merle's help at this time. Merle had helped him out of plenty of jams in the past. There'd been times when Hank told crowds to go to hell and pulled a no-show, or got completely "shit-faced" on stage. He'd always had Merle to bail him out.

But not this time. This time, Hank was all on his own.

A few weeks later, Pam, my mother, visited Merle's grave like she always does to straighten up the flowers and think about her father. This time she found a fresh arrangement along with a note, just a few scratchy words without a signature:

Well, Brother. Looks like we did it again.

She knew right away who wrote it, and why.

Oddly enough, Merle has made one final appearance since his death. This seems a suiting conclusion to his story, and so I will end it here.

It ends with Hilary Williams, daughter of Hank Williams, Jr., as she and her sister Holly rode together to attend the funeral of their grandfather on their mother's side. Hilary had decided to drive, and she and her sister were talking, and the tunes ended. Hilary had just reached for her iPod when she swerved and lost control of her vehicle.

Her SUV flipped, rolled several times, kicking up dirt and rock while the engine roared and the women went thrashing about inside.

Hilary suffered the worst, suffering from internal bleeding and shattered pelvic and leg bones and ribs. She was broken all over. By the time the EMT arrived and loaded her into an ambulance, she'd lost a lot of blood. Then her heart stopped beating. But there was more than darkness.

"My spirit came out, and I just felt so peaceful, and I remember an angel came and took my hand, and the angel was faceless. And I remember being torn, kind of wanting to stay, not wanting to leave my family, but then once I got to heaven, there was so much joy, and I just felt God, and the music, and it was amazing, and I heard all these angels, and I saw Merle Kilgore, my dad's manager and best friend, and Johnny and June. And Johnny was playing guitar, and June was playing the harpsichord, and there were other people sitting there that I didn't know, and they were all smiling, and singing, and having a good time. And then I saw my grandparents, Hank Williams and Audrey, and they were young and ageless, and they gave me a big hug, and I saw this big gold mansion that looked like diamonds glistening. Then I came back to Earth.

It's the inclusion of Merle Kilgore in her vision that rattles me, that leaves me wondering. After all, it seems almost logical; Merle spent most his life tending to the Williams Family. He carried the guitar for Hank Sr., and managed Hank Jr.'s career, and it makes sense to me that he'd be there, waiting to comfort Hilary. Helping out the Williams Family was always Merle's job. After all, he was there when she was born—he was there for the birth of all of Hank Jr.'s kids—and he would have been there when she died.

So that's my story of Merle Kilgore. I set out on this journey with several goals in mind. I loved the guy; he was sort of my hero, and I wanted to capture his funny anecdotes, to recognize his achievements, and to highlight his role in the unfolding narrative of Country Music. But during the years of putting all this down on paper, I discovered something that I'd missed at first. There was a bigger tale here. Merle's life wasn't just a collection of anecdotes, but a well-rounded story arc—a story spanning time and touching the lives of many unique people.

When I was a kid, I had a big vision of my grandfather. I suppose it's still with me. I hope his name lives on, that someday they remember him in the Country Music Hall of Fame, and that fans will always visit his grave (even if only in passing on their way to see Johnny Cash). Most of all, I hope Hilary really did see him in the afterlife in some special corner of Heaven, a celestial honkytonk where Country Music legends are playing on stage 'round the clock and God and His angels hoot and holler from the front rows. I hope there's such a place, and I hope Daddy Merle made it there.

If so, then he really did make the biggest deal of all. *Yes, Amen.*

---

[1] Richard Cromelin, "Merle Kilgore, 70; Co-Wrote 'Ring of Fire,' Managed Hank

About the Author

Mark Rickert grew up in a country music household, just a few miles from the Opryland USA Theme Park and the Grand Ole Opry, and only a block from the home of Colonel Tom Parker, Elvis Presley's manager. Mark's father even worked as a Nashville tour guide. But it was his grandfather Merle Kilgore who showed him backstage to the business.

Before publishing his first novel, *The Tone Poet*, Mark served eight years as a photo-journalist for the US Army Reserve, spending a year of that service in Baghdad, Iraq, writing for military publications. In 2008, he earned a Master's in English Literature from Middle Tennessee State University. Today, he works as chief of public affairs for an Army recruiting battalion.

Mark lives in Annapolis, Maryland. *These Are My People* is his second book.

Williams Jr.," *Los Angeles Times*, February 8, 2005.

[2] "500 Greatest Songs of All Time," *Rolling Stone*, December 9, 2004, 93.

[3] Horace Logan and Bill Sloan, *Louisiana Hayride Years* (St. Martin's Griffin, 1999), 10.

[4] Michael Kosser, *How Nashville Became Music City USA: 50 Years of Music Row* (Hal Leonard, 2006), 21.

[5] Ibid., 14.

[6] V1 Horace Logan and Bill Sloan, *Louisiana Hayride Years* (St. Martin's Griffin, 1999), 14.

[7] Jim Tharpe, "Hank Williams' last ride: Driver recalls lonesome end," AJC.com, July 2, 2013, http://www.accessatlanta.com/news/entertainment/hank-williams-last-ride-driver-recalls-lonesome-en/nYbpz/. (Originally printed in *The Atlanta Journal-Constitution*, December 30, 2002.)

[8] Horace Logan and Bill Sloan, *Louisiana Hayride Years* (St. Martin's Griffin, 1999), 100.

[9] "Webb Pierce," Country Music Hall of Fame and Museum: Online, http://countrymusichalloffame.org/Inductees/InducteeDetail/webb-pierce.

[10] Horace Logan and Bill Sloan, *Louisiana Hayride Years* (St. Martin's Griffin, 1999), 105.

[11] Diane Diekman, *Live Fast, Love Hard: The Faron Young Story* (University of Illinois Press, 2007), 127.

[12] Ibid., 129.

[13] Horace Logan and Bill Sloan, *Louisiana Hayride Years* (St. Martin's Griffin, 1999).

[14] Ralph Emery and Patsi Bale Cox, *The View from Nashville* (William Morrow, 1998), 209.

[15] Ibid.

[16] *Country's Family Reunion*, DVD Collection 2008.

[17] "Career Highlights," Hank Williams, Jr. Official Website, http://www.hankjr.com/career-highlights/.

[18] Hank Williams, Jr. and Michael Bane, *Living Proof: The Hank Williams Jr. Story* (New York: G.P. Putnam's Sons, 1979), 89.

[19] Ibid., 88.

[20] Ibid., 88.

bibliography

"500 Greatest Songs of All Time." *Rolling Stone*. December 9, 2004. 93.

"About Hank Williams." *CMT Artists*. http://www.cmt.com/artists/hank-williams/biography/.

"Career Highlights." Hank Williams, Jr. Official Website. http://www.hankjr.com/career-highlights/.

Carlin, Richard. *Country Music: A Biographical Dictionary*. London and New York: Routledge Taylor & Francis Group, 2013. 228.

Carroll, Andrew, editor. *Behind the Lines: Powerful and Revealing American and Foreign War Letters—and One Man's Search to Find Them*. New York: Scribner, 2005.

Cash, Vivian and Ann Sharpsteen. *I Walked the Line: My Life with Johnny*. Scribner, 2007.

Country's Family Reunion. DVD Collection 2008.

Cromelin, Richard. "Merle Kilgore, 70; Co-Wrote 'Ring of Fire,' Managed Hank Williams Jr." *Los Angeles Times*. Obituaries. February 8, 2005.

"Death of Hank Williams, The." Hank Williams: The Complete Website. http://www.angelfire.com/country/hanksr/death.htm.

Eder, Bruce. "Merle Kilgore: Artist Biography." Allmusic.com. http://www.allmusic.com/artist/merle-kilgore-mn0000413210/biography.

Emery, Ralph and Patsi Bale Cox. *The View from Nashville*. William Morrow, 1998.

Emery, Ralph and Tom Carter. *More Memories*. G.P. Putnam's Sons, 1993.

Erlewine, Stephen Thomas. "Johnny Cash." Allmusic.com. http://www.allmusic.com/artist/johnny-cash-mn0000816890/biography.

Franks, Tillman and Robert Gentry. *Tillman Franks: "I was there when it Happened."* Sweet Dreams Publishing Company, 2000. 118.

"Hank Williams Biography." Rock and Roll Hall of Fame online. https://rockhall.com/inductees/hank-williams/bio/.

"Hank Williams: Honky Tonk Blues." BBC Four, Arena. July 17, 2010.

"Hank Williams: Singer, Songwriter (1923–1953)." Bio.com. http://www.biography.com/people/hank-williams-9532414.

"Haunted Places in Tennessee: The Ryman Auditorium." *Haunted Places to Go.Com.* http://www.haunted-places-to-go.com/haunted-places-in-tennessee.html.

Heatley, Michael. *Johnny Cash: In Words, Pictures, and Music*. Chartwell Books, 2014.

Kosser, Michael. *How Nashville Became Music City USA: 50 Years of Music Row*. Hal Leonard Publishing Corporation, 21.

Laird, Tracey E.W. *Louisiana Hayride: Radio & Roots Music along the Red River*. Oxford University Press, 2005.

LeVine, Michael. *Johnny Horton—Your Singing Fisherman*. Vantage Press, Inc., 1982.

Logan, Horace and Bill Sloan. *Louisiana Hayride Years: Making Musical History in Country's Golden Age*. St. Martin's Press, 1999. 10.

Malone, Bill and Judith McCulloh, editors. *Stars of Country Music: Uncle Dave Macon to Johnny Rodriguez*. Chicago: University of Illinois Press, 1975.

Nash, Alanna. *Behind Closed Doors: Talking with the Legends of Country Music*. Alfred A. Knopf, 1988.

"No Cash for Johnny Cash Daughters over 'Ring of Fire'" *Daily News*. October 29, 2007. http://www.nydailynews.com/entertainment/gossip/no-cash-johnny-cash-daughters-ring-fire-article-1.226001.

Rickert, Mark. "Discovering a mass grave in Iraq, 2003." *Gilder Lehrman Institute of American History Online*. 2009–2016. http://www.gilderlehrman.org/history-by-era/facing-new-millennium/resources/discovering-mass-grave-iraq-2003.

Tharpe, Jim. "Hank Williams' last ride: Driver recalls lonesome end." AJC.com. July 2, 2013. http://www.accessatlanta.com/news/entertainment/hank-williams-last-ride-driver-recalls-lonesome-en/nYbpz/. (Originally printed in *The Atlanta Journal-Constitution*, December 30, 2002.)

"This Day in History: The Louisiana Hayride Radio Program Premieres on KWKH-AM Shreveport." History.com. http://www.history.com/this-day-in-history/the-louisiana-hayride-radio-program-premieres-on-kwkh-am-shreveport.

Waddell, Ray. "Bocephus! Superstar's Son to Young Gun To Country Icon." *Billboard Spotlight*. Nov 15, 2004.

Waters, Robert A. *Kidnapping, Murder and Mayhem: The Murder of Hank Williams (blog)*. November 12, 2011. http://kidnappingmurderandmayhem.blogspot.com/2011/11/murder-of-hank-williams.html

Williams, Hank Jr. and Michael Bane. *Living Proof: The Hank Williams Jr. Story*. New York: G.P. Putnam's Sons, 1979.

Williams, Hilary and M.B. Roberts. *Signs of Life; A Story of Family, Tragedy, Music, and Healing*. Da Capo Press, 2010.